TEN STEPS
TO A NEW YOU

TEN STEPS
TO A NEW YOU

A complete guide to
revitalizing yourself

LESLIE KENTON

EBURY PRESS . LONDON

1 3 5 7 9 10 8 6 4 2

Text copyright © Leslie Kenton 1998

First published in the United Kingdom in 1998
by Ebury Press
an imprint of Random House
20 Vauxhall Bridge Road
London SW1V 2SA

Random House Australia (Pty) Limited
20 Alfred Street, Milsons Point, Sydney,
New South Wales 2061, Australia

Random House New Zealand Limited
18 Poland Road, Glenfield,
Auckland 10, New Zealand

Random House South Africa (Pty) Limited
PO BOX 337, Bergvlei, South Africa

Random House Canada
1265 Aerowood Drive, Mississauga
Ontario L4W 1B9, Canada

Random House UK Limited Reg. No. 954009

A CIP catalogue record for this book is available from the British
Library

ISBN: 0 09 186487 9

Printed and bound in Great Britain by Butler and Tanner Ltd,
Frome and London

Acknowledgments

The publishers thank the following photographers and organizations for their kind permission to reproduce photographs in this book:

11 Comstock; 13 Images; 17 Camera Press; 29 Images; 31 Tony Stone Images; 33 Images; 36 Tony Stone Images; 37 Images;
41 Tony Stone Images; 44 Tony Stone Worldwide; 49 Images; 51 Tony Stone Worldwide; 52 Tony Stone Images; 53 Tony Stone Images;
56 Tony Stone Images; 59 Tony Stone Images; 63 Comstock; 65 Tony Stone Images; 73 Camerapress; 75 Comstock; 78 Tony Stone Images;
82 Tony Stone Images; 89 Tony Stone Worldwide; 90 Images; 94 Images; 99 Comstock; 107 Robert Harding; 109 Tony Stone Images;
110 Comstock; 114 Comstock; 116 Tony Stone Images; 119 Tony Stone Images; 120 Tony Stone Images; 131 Tony Stone Worldwide;
132 Tony Stone Images; 136 Camerapress; 140 Images; 141 Camerapress; 146 Images;147 Tony Stone Images; 149 Images; 151 Images;
155 Images; 160 Comstock; 164 Tony Stone Images; 169 Tony Stone Images; 172 Tony Stone Images; 174 Robert Harding; 175 Comstock;
179 Comstock; 181 Robert Harding; 189 Camerapress; 192 Tony Stone Images; 194 Camerapress; 195 Robert Harding; 199 Robert Harding;
200 Robert Harding; 204 Images; 205 Robert Harding; 206 Images; 210 Images; 216 Camerapress; 221 Tony Stone Images;
223 Camerapress; 231 Tony Stone Images; 234 Comstock; 236 Images; 238 Images; 241 Tony Stone Images; 242 Tony Stone Images;
243 Tony Stone Images; 244 Robert Harding.

Introduction   6

REVEAL YOURSELF

Step 1: Take stock   10

Step 2 : Spring clean   24

Step 3 : Eat well   48

Step 4 : Move on up   72

RESPECT YOURSELF

Step 5 : Look inside   106

Step 6 : Stop check   130

Step 7 : Heal yourself   152

REVIVE YOURSELF

Step 8 : Self indulge   178

Step 9 : Look great   202

Step 10 : Beat the clock   236

Resources   253
Index   255

INTRODUCTION

Step Into Transformation

Transformation is not an empty dream. The ability to transform ourselves has been deeply encoded in our genes. It is a though every part of us knows how to bring it about.

This book is designed to help you trigger your own powers of transformation in order to enhance your good looks, regenerate your energy, rejuvenate your body, and help you to come closer to living from the core of your being – with authenticity. The ten steps you will find here – from different ways of altering your lifestyle, detoxifying your body and eliminating the burden of physical, emotional and spiritual waste to shifting your attitude towards yourself – are merely the nuts and bolts of transformation. These are time-tested techniques that work because in one way or another they trigger your own genetic programming for deep change and renewal. The magic of transformation comes from you alone.

And magic it is. A programme to detoxify your body using a high level of raw food or juices will not only remove fine lines from a face beginning to show the wear and tear of life. It will also shift your perceptions of reality so that you wake up in the morning feeling more like a child does, with a sense of excitement about the day ahead instead of having to ply yourself with coffee and sweet things to keep you going.

As you become more closely in touch with your body you will find it easier to hear its needs. This, in turn, carries you towards a way of living in which exercise becomes a natural part of your day-to-day life – not something you have to force yourself to do because somebody has told you that it is good for you. It can also help you to recognize some of the beauty that is intrinsic to your soul. This is something that happens not in any superficial, narcissistic way, but quite naturally and honourably as you learn to care for yourself in simple ways. And one good life change attracts others. Altering your diet, for instance, or learning a technique for deep relaxation brings such benefits in terms of health and beauty – over time – that you are likely to find yourself interested in making other changes, too. You may find yourself taking three steps forwards and two back. But that is great. For that is how real transformation happens – not by slavishly following some programme. It will lead you down a path that transforms the way you look and feel, and enables you to bring more to life while life brings more to you.

Beauty and health are so completely wrapped up in each other that they cannot be separated. Many years ago, I became aware that health and beauty are not states. They are processes of unfolding, processes by which each of us become more fully who we are. Real beauty is the expression of the individual nature of a man or woman. Real health is the full expression of your unique nature in day-to-day life. It brings the greatest joy to you and, at the same time, enables you to share with others the greatest gifts you bring to life – enhancing the quality of your relationships with your family and friends, your community and even the planet as a whole.

From the time we are born to the moment of our death, each of us is involved either consciously or unconsciously with our own health process. When the involvement is conscious, we are aware when the way in which we are living needs adjusting. Our bodies warn us when we need to eat different foods – for example, if we are to prevent getting a cold. They give us signals that maybe we need to have 15 minutes to ourselves to rest, recuperate or meditate in the late afternoon if we are to be able to connect fully with our children or friends in the evening.

When we are unconscious of our health process, we tend to get sick, whether it be temporarily – such as a cold, 'flu or back pain – or more long-term, when we develop chronic fatigue syndrome or depression or anxiety. Illness, fatigue, depression, anxiety and lack of self-esteem are not things to be feared. They are merely a call from the core of our being – one might say the soul – to let us know that something in the way we are living needs to be altered if we are to come fully into our own beauty, joy, energy and creativity. They are a call for transformation.

What you will find within this book are some of the tools, techniques, facts and exercises that can aid your own transformational processes. They have been carefully broken down into ten steps just to make them easier for you to use. They are not difficult; in fact, most of them can be a lot of fun and – most important of all – they work.

They work because, like all the tools that have developed out of the long tradition of natural health and beauty, they are formulated specifically to work with the body's own self-healing, renewing, rejuvenating powers. All transformation comes from the power of life within you. They are only useful ways of helping you tap into that power.

The health process is one of the major ways in which such beauty opens and unfolds to radiate its unique glory. **Ten Steps to a New You** is a simple-to-follow way to help the transformation processes within you get on with the job of your own unfolding. The benefits are obvious: more energy, clearer, fresher skin, a firmer body, a better attitude towards yourself and your life, and coming into your own more fully so you are freer to express your own brand of joy.

Transformation is a process that has always fascinated me. It is one of the great mysteries of life. It is by no means always easy, but it is so exciting and so rewarding that who cares if you have to experience a headache while your body is detoxifying or shed tears over the loss of a relationship. Such events are milestones along the road each one of us walks towards wholeness, authenticity and freedom. They are momentary experiences firmly anchored in space and time, like sights we see looking through the windows of a train on the most exciting journey any of us will ever take – the journey of our own unfolding within the magnificent web of life to which we belong. May your own transformative experiences be rich and rewarding. Life needs the unique beauty and energy you have to bring to the rest of us.

Leslie Kenton
January 1998

REVEAL
YOURSELF

STEP ONE: TAKE STOCK

Starting out

Each human being is utterly unique. Like the seed of a plant which has encoded within its genetic material the characteristics that will in time produce the full-grown flower, each of us comes into this world carrying a package of as yet unrealized but incredibly rich potential. Like the individual brushstroke the zen painter uses to represent one leaf on a shaft of bamboo, the leaf he paints is totally singular – like no leaf which has ever existed. And yet within its uniqueness is encompassed universal beauty and life energy of the highest order. So it is with each human being. Within the individual genetic package which is you is nestled your very own brand of uniqueness that encompasses far greater physical, creative and spiritual potential than any of us could hope to realize in only one lifetime.

The remarkable thing about a seed is that very little is needed for it to develop into a plant: some good earth rich in organic matter, some rain (not too much or the seed will rot), the sun (not too much or the young leaves will burn). These three simple things can provide the environment in which the tiny plant grows into a full-blown flower.

People are very much like plants. All we need is a good healthy environment which allows this unfolding to take place. The only problem is, more often than not, the environment – physical, emotional, spiritual, social – in which we grow does not support our full unfolding. And so, like a plant trying to develop in depleted soil with too little rain and too little sun, or a seedling trying to grow around a stone, we develop our own brand of *distortions*. These distortions can be physical – a sunken chest, poor posture, or an excess of fat created to cushion us against a harsh external world. They can be emotional – a sense

that we cannot trust ourselves, intense shyness, lack of confidence, or a feeling of being unworthy or guilty. They can even be spiritual – a sense of meaninglessness which leads to addiction, a greed for material things, a lust for power. Gradually such distortions become so much a part of our lives that we come to feel they are part of who we actually are.

Of course, distortions are by no means all bad. Some help define our values. For instance, a woman who has grown up in a family where she was continually treated as the scapegoat may develop a passion for helping the oppressed and make a fine career for herself as a social worker or political reformer. Someone raised on bad food who grew up constantly ill, like myself, may develop a fascination with finding out what kind of lifestyle promotes good health, and then spend much of her life helping to create it for herself and others. A woman growing up in a bourgeois family where

social hypocrisy is the rule, in her rejection of it, may be driven to creating a life for herself of breathtaking authenticity. Perhaps this woman will become an artist who wrestles with the deepest of human questions, in an attempt to bring her own truth into material form.

But there are also negative aspects to the distortions that develop when individuality is thwarted. In some way each of us has been pushed too hard in an attempt to negotiate obstacles in our path. We've had too much responsibility, perhaps, inadequate nutrition, or hypercritical parents and teachers. Sometimes we have been born into a family with which, no matter how benign, we have little in common. As a result we can spend a lot of our lives feeling like a toad among ducks.

This situation can produce artificial behaviour, like phoney personalities or false images, psychic prisons into which we try to squeeze ourselves. A lot of energy which should be available for creativity, high level health and joy, instead gets bound up trying to maintain these artificial creations. What is worse this can result in a sense of feeling separate from yourself, not trusting yourself, and never being able fully to enter into what you are doing with joy. We can feel as though we are not comfortable in our own skin, feel bad about our bodies and bad about ourselves. We can feel that being who we are is not enough – that in order to be acceptable we have to change... get thinner... drink a particular brand of coffee... wear certain perfumes... buy expensive clothes... give successful dinner parties.

Journey to the centre

The 'new you' – the one you are looking for – is not going to come from the outside. It is within you waiting to be discovered. The new you is, in fact, who you really are.

The process of becoming who you are means going to the core. It means rediscovering what you are all about beneath any distorted habit patterns you may have developed. It means reasserting your trust in yourself. It means, too, posing some interesting questions which can help make your own journey conscious. 'Who am I?' for instance, and 'Where do I want to go?'. It also means making use of simple, but health-enhancing, techniques – from making use of exercise to eating well – all designed with one end in mind: to bring you back to who you are.

Most importantly, it means making time to take care of yourself. This may seem like a total impossibility, but ask yourself, 'Am I really so disorganised that I can't find the time to look after myself properly? Or is it that I don't like what it suggests – am I selfish, grasping, demanding?' Or do you just think that you are not worth it? If so, stop right here. There is no point in reading any further. You can do nothing so selfless as looking after yourself, for it is only then that you can be of benefit or worth to others. Believe you are worth it and reap the rewards.

For most of us, such a journey demands that somewhere along the way we detoxify our bodies of the rubbish that may have accumulated over the years from poor eating, a sluggish lifestyle and a build-up of internal toxicity from the stress of living in a polluted environment. Even a simple spring-clean diet can help to remind you of what it feels like to live in your own body. But detoxification needs to take place on a psychological and spiritual level as well. Most of us carry around a burden of false ideas, notions and habit patterns which have nothing to do with who we are. They are false – they have not grown out of our own selves but have been imposed upon us by our families, our religion, the cultural norms of our society. This rubbish needs to be cleared away.

In the following chapters, you will find all sorts of tips, tricks and techniques to guide you on your travels through the maze of distractions, compromises and temptations that conspire to divert you from your task. The information, tools and techniques in this book are here for one purpose only – to serve *you*. *You* are not here to serve *them*. Only *within* will you find the real expert on what is right and wrong for you, both in terms of high-level health and in how your individual nature needs to unfold. What works for you will have done its job. What doesn't work, discard. Following anything slavishly never creates freedom. And individual freedom of the highest order is the real key to the new you.

But before you can make the best use of the information contained in this book you need to take the most important step of all: to find out where you are now.

Depth sounding

You have probably had the experience of waking up with the sense that the whole world is against you, and the events of the day confirm your opinion. The opposite is also true. When you feel good about yourself it can seem as though you are living a charmed life where everything (or just about everything) falls into place with ease. You find a parking space, the bank stops losing your deposits, everyone seems to remember your birthday.

Despite the way our culture tends to separate body and mind, your body is nothing less than your soul incarnate. Like opposite ends of the continuum, mind and body play an equal part in who you are. We need to address the outer and inner issues simultaneously. Take a look at the next set of questions and answer them honestly. In fact, get a pen and write down your answers. Come back to these questions and your answers to them periodically as you work through this book, and use them as depth-sounders at times in the future when you feel you have given in to compromise or distraction.

Analysing your answers

Really pour out how you feel in response to these questions. There are no right or wrong answers – just your answers. Nobody is ever going to read this except you. If some of your answers seem negative, great. At least you know where your starting point is. It is virtually impossible to bring about real transformation in your life (and this is what this book is all about) without being very honest about what is happening

right now. Only when we establish this kind of base awareness do we open the door to real change.

Self-check list

Answer the following questions honestly. I have given you some examples as a guide, but write whatever comes to mind first. Just let rip.

1 What are your first thoughts on waking?
I am confused.
I just want to go back to sleep.
I am excited about the day ahead.
I am anxious/depressed.
Other?

2 When you look in the mirror what do you feel?
I fret over my wrinkles/grey hair/blemishes and feel down about myself.
I feel happy with the way I look – imperfections and all.
I don't think I matter much.
Other?

3 When confronted with a difficult task at home or at work what do you think?
What a pain, maybe if I avoid it someone else will do it.
Here's a challenge, something to really get my teeth into.
I feel overwhelmed but determined.
Other?

4 When looking forward to a romantic evening what do you do?
I create a scenario of doom in case

things don't work out – that way I won't be disappointed.

I enjoy imagining how wonderful the evening is going to be.

I live in the moment and just let the chips fall as they may.

Other?

5 When you have an argument with your partner what do you think?

This is typical, he/she doesn't understand me.

There must be something wrong with me.

How do we build a bridge back to each other?

Other?

6 When you get a cold what do you think?

Just my luck. I always catch a cold at the worst possible times.

I must be run down. What can I do to improve my overall health?

I'll take a lot of cold remedies and aspirin and just forget it.

Other?

7 When you are paid a compliment what do you do?

I dismiss it and try to work out what they want out of me.

I accept graciously and thank them for their kindness.

Feel embarrassed and that they don't mean it.

Other?

8 What do you think about your job?

I hate it. I'm overworked and underpaid but I have to do it, there's so much unemployment

and where am I going to find another one?

I enjoy my work. It gives me a chance to do something I'm good at, and get financially rewarded for doing it.

It isn't what I want ultimately but I am moving towards changing it.

Other?

9 When you look back on your past what do you think?

I feel resentful about the opportunities I missed and regret many of the things I have and haven't done.

I am happy that the decisions I have made – good and bad – have brought me to this point. If I went back I wouldn't change anything.

I don't think much about the past, I am more concerned with now.

Other?

10 On what do you feel your happiness depends?

Finding the right relationship, the right job, earning lots of money, winning the lottery, and hoping not too much goes wrong.

Me living the way I want to live without compromise and letting my life unfold in optimistic anticipation.

Luck.

Other?

Secrets of truth telling

When it comes to living out who you are, the big secret is simple: TELL THE TRUTH. This may sound trivial or even

15

beside the point. Yet being able to *be* whoever you are means *saying* whatever you think and *feeling* without guilt, recrimination or justification whatever you feel. This can bring back the sense of freedom we have as children but lose when we take on the trappings of adulthood.

As we grow up we learn to change ourselves or mask what we really want or think, because we fear we are not acceptable. Yet pretence of any kind – either to yourself or to others – denies your full potential. There is a way of learning to live in relative peace and harmony with people around you and still be who you really are. It asks that you affirm not only that you matter but also that each and every other being on the planet matters and has an equal right to be what they are and live true to themselves.

Energy from the source

At the core of each of us sleeps our soul – that part that makes us utterly unique and has encoded within it our goals, characteristics and potential – both physical and spiritual – all these traits and powers we are ultimately on the earth in order to realize. The more we are aware of the nature of our *soul energy*, of its real intentions and of what brings us joy at the deepest levels, the easier it becomes to live out who we are – to tell our truth. Once truth begins to be told, it becomes easier to clear out our unfulfilling behaviour patterns, relationships, and ways of living, which drain our life energies and do not feed our soul. As we are able to identify and

lift off these things, we release the most enormous surge of creative energy. Think of how you feel when you are doing something you love – the energy just seems to pour forth. Compare this to the way you feel when you lie, compromise, and do your duty. Which would you rather experience?

Believe it or not, it is possible with each passing month – regardless of the situation, relationship, job, or physical condition you find yourself in – to move closer and closer to living from your core, feeding your soul, expanding your creativity and empowering others to do the same. As you do this, those parts of your life that are not now working as well as you would like them to, begin to change for the better. The road to a new you requires that each of us learns to listen to what I call the whispers of the soul – and then slowly but surely to start putting what they tell us into practice.

Soul secrets

Most of us have never learned to do this. Instead we have been taught not to listen to our inner voice. We have been filled with all sorts of stuff by our parents, our educational system, our bosses, our spouses, and the media which teaches us not to trust ourselves but rather to live our lives according to external 'rules'. These rules may be homilies like 'always think of others first', 'you must not succeed or somebody might be jealous', 'you must not do that – so and so wouldn't like it'. Or they may come from advertisements that would have us believe that what we are is not good enough and that we need a new car, job, image, body, home, just so that we will be OK.

very dangerous to me – the kind of things a gypsy might wear to dance on the table – something not allowed (I felt) in the life of a 'responsible' woman like me. Well, one day I decided to go out and buy a pair.

A passion for red shoes

It was great. This simple, trivial act made me feel freer and lighter. Whenever I wore the shoes I found myself having a lot of fun. They seemed to release a hidden side to my character which had been lurking beneath my rather conventional, 'proper' personality. With it came lots of creative, playful, energy.

What I discovered from heeding the call to own a pair of red shoes was something far more important than the shoes themselves. I found out that when you begin to listen to inner whispers about relatively trivial things, your inner voice gradually, yet inexorably, gets louder. Before long you are hearing the answers to much more important questions and getting much more vital information about your health, your values, your goals, and your life. And as soul whispers grow louder and clearer, your experience of meaning in your life grows with them.

To live out who we really are asks that we build a bridge between the inner and outer parts of our life so that less of our potential gets blocked, suppressed, or dissipated. This depends on listening to the whispers, becoming more aware of how you want to live, eat, exercise and live your life, and putting into practice what you hear, bit by bit, to see what works for you and what doesn't.

The kind of internal dialogue that goes through our minds as we are continually bombarded in this way drains our sense of who we are. It also creates a lot of 'static' which obscures the softer voice from our core – soul whispers about what we really value, what we want or what we are.

It takes a little practice to develop the skill of listening to your inner voice. Strangely, the first whispers you hear may make no sense at all. For instance, for many years I longed for a pair of red shoes but I never bought them. I guess it seemed selfish and trivial to me when I was earning a living to support four children. But also (and I didn't realize this until much later) red shoes seemed

Four keys to yourself

This powerful process is an ongoing one. Ask yourself the questions below one at a time. Then, letting your mind roam free, write down whatever comes to you. You may feel that the answer to one demands reams of words while the answer to another is very short. Explore each question fully before going on to the next.

1 Who am I?
This does not mean your name and where you come from but rather what comes to your mind when the question is asked. How do you see yourself? What do you like?

2 What do I want?
This should include everything you feel you want or anything you secretly dream of, from the tiniest thing such as 'I want to take up tapestry', or 'I have always wanted to ride a motorbike', to huge desires you may never have dared to voice: 'I want to go off to Africa to help people dig wells', 'I want to look and feel 15 years younger', or 'I want to write a novel'. It doesn't matter, just write it down.

3 What do I think is stopping me?
Make a note of any circumstance, person, place, thing, thought or feeling that you feel stands in your way.

4 Where am I right now in relation to what I want?
To create what you want in your life – from greater self-esteem to your

dream home – you need two things. First, you need as clear a vision as possible of what it is you are seeking, and secondly, you need to be certain of where you are right now in relation to that vision. The greater your desire to achieve a goal and the clearer you can be about where you are in relation to that goal, the easier the achievement of that goal becomes.

By the way, these four questions are not the kind of things that there are pat answers to. The answers to your questions are going to change as you change. Look back at them and revise your answers as you work through this book.

Dare to be you

The core of a human being – that source of virtually boundless creative power as well as physical and psychic energy – will never be found by dissecting the human body. Nor can it be arrived at by analysing the human mind. Yet a sense of what I call living from the core or the soul, an experience of living – living truthfully to your own values – is something each of us experiences at certain times in our lives.

Although most of us only happen upon this experience accidentally, it can also be cultivated by pursuing actions which we enjoy or which make us feel good about ourselves and our lives. It can happen when we fall in love, when we feel happy because everything seems in harmony around us, or when we feel pleased with ourselves, our children, or some accomplishment. In such moments, everything seems to fit together, or feel right, and life has meaning. Such a sense is central to living out who you really are.

Helping yourself

The techniques for helping you to be the person you believe you should be are only of lasting value if you value yourself and live your life on that assumption.

Tuning into core energy

Psychologist Abraham Maslow, who spent his life studying not human pathology but rather human beings who lived their lives with great energy, creativity and joy – he called them self-actualizers – referred to the special moments in our lives as 'peak experiences'. After examining the experiences of thousands of creative and happy people he came to the conclusion that these self-actualizers have certain things in common. They tend, for instance, to be the healthiest people in society, both mentally and physically. They tend to have a lot of values in common too, such as prizing simplicity, wholeness, effortlessness, truth, honesty, uniqueness, completeness and perfection – in fact, the same values you might expect mystics to possess. They are, in effect, people who tend frequently to have peak experiences – moments of great happiness, rapture, ecstasy – in which life's conflicts are at least temporarily transcended or resolved. Other

psychologists, anthropologists and philosophers have also described Maslow's self-actualizing person. Carl Rogers – perhaps most appropriately of all – refers to Maslow's self-actualizer as a 'fully functioning' person.

Out of this work there has emerged a whole new picture of what it is to be human. No longer do we see a human being the way Freud did – as a collection of repressed destructive urges, only barely restrained by learned moral constructs from destroying ourselves and others. Now we realize that people are as potentially autonomous human beings. We recognize that the destructive and self-defeating tendencies that we all have are far less indicative of the hidden truth of a person than they are the results of a frustration in the expression of what Maslow called the Self – or soul – of life itself. You can achieve happiness and freedom from this frustration and from negative thought patterns and the behaviour they engender simply by letting your natural self-actualizing tendencies (which in most of us are still weak or dormant) develop. Until they grow, we all regress into fear and frustration or laziness. Once they become stronger, your life becomes an ongoing process of growth, and unfolding of potential as well as, quite simply, much happier.

What are your peak experiences?

On a nice clean sheet of paper describe a moment or moments in your life where you felt a sense of 'living from your core' – a time when everything seemed to work for you, where you felt fulfilled and good about yourself. If you are not sure you understand the idea, simply describe a moment when you felt particularly happy. Remember the scene as vividly as possible and use as much detail as you can to recall your impressions. Use this description as a reference point from now on for how good you can feel and how wonderfully life can fit together. As you become more and more self-actualizing and come to live more and more from your soul, peak experiences become more frequent.

Create new visions of you and your life

Start to dream of what it will be like for you to be living your life as you. Begin to play with a number of clear images of yourself as fit, well and looking great. But don't just consider the physical changes you would like to make. Get to know the person you aim to be and see yourself in this image. Remember what you see, hold that clear picture and the way it feels, and call it up when you feel unsure of your goals and direction. Here are some of the characteristics of a self-actualizer to use as inspiration:

An exceptional ability to cope with change and to learn from it

Most people have trouble with change. It is unsettling and frightening. It needn't be. It all depends on how you look at it. We all face fear with changes but the more you come to live from your core – to manifest your soul energy – the more you will tend to view change not as threatening but as a challenge to learn from and grow from, whether any particular change at face value appears to be 'good' or 'bad'. As far as failure is concerned, instead of being a source of fear, it can be viewed as something that shows us how to deal with a similar situation in the future. After all, human beings do fail sometimes.

No great worry about saying 'No'

Assertiveness, not aggression, plays a central role in being who you are. It implies a strong sense of your individual right to your values and opinions and a tendency to respect the rights of other people. You need to be able to say no to a food or drink you don't really want, a request from a lover or spouse, a demand from a child or a colleague. The best way to develop healthy assertiveness is simply to practise it. It feels a bit strange at first but the more you do it, the easier it becomes. Paradoxically, only when you are positively assertive can you discover what real unselfishness is, because then what you give is what you choose to give, not what you feel obliged to give.

A well-conditioned body

This brings you energy, helps you cope with stress better, look better and younger, and strengthens your sense of self-reliance. It also shifts hormonal balance and brain chemistry making you highly resistant to depression and anxiety, and highly prone to feeling good about yourself and your life. Top-level fitness leads to a freedom to achieve excellence in other non-physical areas of your life as well. It increases stamina, strength and flexibility, not only physically but emotionally as well.

A marked absence of common minor ailments and troubles
Most people believe that the Monday morning blues or the aches and pains in joints after the age of forty are a normal part of living. But they take up little space when you are living from your core. 'Normal' means moving with ease, and feeling pretty good about things day after day – sometimes feeling very good indeed – not because something stupendous has just happened but because when you are really fit and well that is the normal way to feel.

Laughter comes easily
An ability to laugh at the absurd (including at yourself when appropriate) and a sense of fun are perhaps the most important of all the high-energy characteristics. Joy is health-giving. The most delightful sense of humour often parallels a strong sense of purpose in a person – another high-energy characteristic.

Integrity
The more you become a self-actualizer, the more you set your own standards and live up to them. Your values become a source of strength and energy for you. You don't have to compromise them to achieve some temporary advantage. You can feel the truth, be who you really are and make your life work. Hard to believe? It's time to act.

Now individualize your vision
Not all of these characteristics will appeal to everyone although they do tend to be pretty universal amongst the healthy people whose lives 'work' – Maslow's self-actualizing or Carl Rogers' fully-functioning people. Any of them which don't seem relevant to you, forget – for the moment. Take a closer look at those that do seem to have meaning. Keep them in mind and identify with them as much as possible. In addition to the characteristics listed, add your own. Then, when you are relaxing, let your mind play upon some of these things. As you travel on your journey to a new you, keep track of the changes in your body, your vitality, in how you look, and in your feelings as you go along. Are your goals changing or are they simply becoming clearer and more focused?

Plan your way

The best way to make a commitment to living out your true self and to stick to it is to make a plan. The better organized and more definite a plan you make for yourself, the more you will benefit from the material in this book. Such a plan should set out your commitments and clarify your intentions. A definite plan helps you to take seriously what you are doing. It can also be a source of considerable personal insight. It must also be flexible; it will change as you change. That is part of the excitement of self-actualization.

What do you want?
Go back to your answer to the question 'What do I want?' Start with a desire you believe is within your reach and set yourself the goal of achieving it. When you are well on the way to achieving that goal, choose another and do the same again or, if you like, do as I do, making several related goals all at once and working with them. Doing this over and over will gradually allow you to come to

know and trust your own power to make the life you want. Learning to set goals is really helpful. It is easier to achieve anything if you have a goal to reach. Achieving a goal is also the biggest incentive to achieving the next one and the best reinforcement for a sense of personal development and power. But be realistic; even big goals are made up of lots of little ones, so concentrate on achieving the achievable in a sensible time.

Achieving your goals

When it comes to more specific commitments, pick your goals and write them down in clear positive terms and in the present tense. For instance, do not say 'I will never eat chocolate again', say 'I am eating wonderful fresh foods today – a taste sensation of a salad for lunch made from beautiful vegetables'. Stick it on the fridge. Be very specific about what you want to gain from doing this. Exactly how do you want to feel? Why are you doing it?

Be as specific as possible

The more specific your plan, the better. Pick one of your goals. Often a very practical one is best to start with – say, becoming more physically fit, or learning better methods of stress control, or losing weight. Having written it down, plan how to go about it. Ask yourself what techniques you might use to reach your goal. Here is an example: you might write 'Tomorrow morning I will go through my cupboards and throw out all the junk foods. I can then make a list of

the types of foods I want to look for when I go to the supermarket at the end of the week.' Or, 'I will find out about local suppliers of organic vegetables,' or 'I will get up fifteen minutes early to practice a breathing technique.' It usually works best to identify both the practical goals you want to work towards and at the same time to define the more spiritual ones and record them too. In this way they will reinforce each other. Such a preliminary plan helps establish a good sense of direction and enables you to work out just what you have to do and what you have to learn in specific terms to reach your goals.

Recording progress

Record your progress as well as any setbacks. This continues the process of refining and focusing your goals and identifying values.

When in doubt, act as if

There is a lot of power in this suggestion. Pretence, which many people look askance at and demean, is often the mother of genuine improvement. The dilettante, whose main interest in painting comes from a desire to impress at parties, can find one day, wandering through the National Gallery that, caught unawares between silly statements about the pictures before him, he has been stung by the bee of real aesthetic experience. Many a genuine passion has begun with such pretence and turned into something life-transforming for the pretender in the end. By 'pretending' to be as strong, healthy, energetic and self-aware as you would like to be, you both raise your expectations and put yourself in the frame of mind that can help to bring these things about. In the last step of this book (see pages 236-52) we look at what a powerful tool the mind can be. You can programme your subconscious to change your conscious life for the better. If you tell your subconscious that you have an abundance of energy, it will get on the grapevine and tell your conscious mind that you do, indeed, have an abundance of energy.

Ask questions

How many times in the past have you asked yourself 'Why is this happening to me?' or 'Why am I always so thick?' Did you get answers to these questions? Did they make you feel good about yourself? Try a positive alternative – it works far better to empower you. Try 'What can I do to make the situation I am in better?' For instance, instead of asking yourself why you always look a mess, ask yourself what you can do to improve your appearance and make yourself feel better about yourself. You can alter just about anything. For example, 'What do I need to do to be happier?'

The daily practice

Try this practice for two weeks. It can help you make the great shift from negative to positive. Each morning ask yourself the following questions and put down your answers.

1 What am I *happy* about this morning?

2 What am I *excited* about this morning?
3 What am I *grateful* for this morning?
4 What can I *do today* to help me achieve my goals?

Then, each evening, take another look at these questions and your answers, then answer the following questions:

1 What have I *learned* today?
2 What have I *done* to be proud of today?
3 What did I do towards *reaching my goal*? OR Now that I have achieved this goal, what is my *next one*?

All of these simple questions and answers can constitute a tremendously powerful support for your journey to the real you. Play with them and see for yourself how helpful they can be.

The journey you have undertaken to live out who you really are is enormously dynamic. Sometimes it is a lot of fun and sometimes it can be very demanding. The individual journey each of us takes along the road is unique. No matter where you are now in relation to where you want to be, remember that the journey which will take you there begins with small, single steps. Be patient and just keep working (and playing) with it.

STEP TWO: SPRING CLEAN

Spring-cleaning your body

Having taken the decision to work towards living out who you really are, the next step on your journey is to clear out some of the junk you have been carrying around. Are you sluggish, dull-eyed and overfed? No! You are bright, clear-headed and vital. Start your journey with a refreshed body and a spring in your step.

Detoxify your body to bring it a new sense of vitality and to regenerate all its systems for maximum good looks and energy. You can spend hundreds of hours and thousands of pounds on lotions, potions and treatments to improve the look of your skin, to firm your flesh and to renew your body. But none of these things is likely to bring you the same benefits as simple natural methods for periodic internal spring-cleaning.

Health and good looks from within
Beautiful skin, a firm and healthy body and a clear mind are strongly dependent on your system being able efficiently and effectively to get rid of toxic materials and the waste products of your bodily metabolism before they have the chance to do damage to cells and tissues, organs and systems. This principle forms the foundation of the long European tradition of natural medicine and is what keeps health farms and beauty spas all over the world earning money hand over fist. Remove whatever obstructs rapid and near-complete elimination in the body. Thanks to the natural laws of self-healing when you eliminate foreign substances from your blood, organs, glands and tissues, bodily functions will

tend to return to normal. The implications of this natural law for good looks, in terms of restoring troubled or ageing skin to its natural beautiful state, firming flesh, eliminating cellulite, and even improving the health and appearance of your hair and nails, are enormous – so enormous in fact that, in our age of pill-popping and quick fix solutions, many people find it hard to believe. That is, until they try it for themselves.

Clearing the cobwebs
In fact, the human body is magnificently designed to cleanse itself automatically without any thought ever needing to be given to the process. The trouble is that the kind of food and drink most people in the West put into their bodies, the tendency we have to lead stressful but sedentary lives, and the increasing number of pollutants to which we are exposed through the air we breathe and the water we drink have created a situation in which often far more toxins are taken into the body, and far more metabolic wastes produced by it, than we can effectively get rid of. They are stored in the tissues where they lower vitality, encourage the development of degenerative diseases and early ageing,

and rob your system of nutrients necessary to keep your skin and hair – indeed, your whole body – looking their best.

A growing number of doctors who are using natural methods for the treatment of cancer and other degenerative illnesses believe that our cells are literally chock-full of metabolic and environmental wastes gathered over a lifetime. To live at a high level of health and vitality and to make the most of our potential for good looks we need to get rid of them.

The 10 Day Spring Clean is an excellent way to begin and an excellent stepping-stone to a whole new you – one which will last.

Remarkably raw

The 10 Day Spring Clean is a regime based on wholesome fresh foods, most of which are eaten in their natural state – raw. This is because raw foods have remarkable properties. Famous European clinics such as the Bircher-Benner in Zurich have traditionally used high-raw diets to heal both chronic and acute illnesses. Research at the University of Vienna has shown that uncooked foods improve cellular functioning and so lead to increased overall energy and stamina. This is why raw foods form a basis of regenerative and rejuvenating diets at the world's most exclusive and expensive spas, from the Golden Door in California to Mexico's celebrated Rancho La Puerta.

Subtle magic

For someone who has never experienced it before there can seem something magical about the high-raw 10 Day Spring Clean. A way of eating in which most of your foods are taken raw increases your vitality, makes you look and feel great, and even helps protect your body from both degenerative illnesses and premature ageing. Uncooked foods such as fresh crisp vegetables, luscious fruits and natural unprocessed seeds, grains and nuts have a quality of energy which is light yet strong and extraordinarily health-giving. They seem to impart the same sort of lightness and energy to the person eating them. Such foods are the richest natural sources of vitamins and minerals and enzymes – all of which are important for high-level health, as well as fine-quality protein, easily assimilated natural carbohydrates and essential fatty acids. They are also an excellent source of unadulterated natural fibre.

Following the 10 Day Spring Clean can bring you many of the benefits of a well designed spa programme. The alternative to it is spending a week at a health farm. Great if you can afford it. But you can do it yourself a lot more easily (not to mention more cheaply) at home.

Slender secrets

The 10 Day Spring Clean works for shedding excess pounds too – in several ways. First, it supplies your body with the highest complement of nutritional support it can get anywhere in the form of vitamins, minerals, easily assimilated proteins and essential fatty acids, so that you don't suffer the fatigue often linked with a calorie-restricted diet. Neither do you end up with those dangerous subclinical vitamin-deficiency conditions associated with off-again/on-again crash diets. Second, the natural fresh foods used in the meals and recipes are rich in fibre. This is particularly important for weight loss since a high-fibre way of eating not only makes you feel full and satisfied but will also help your body stabilize blood-sugar levels and thereby reduce feelings of hunger. Some kinds of fibre, such as pectin, which is found in good quantities in apples and some other fruits, even help detoxify your body of poisonous wastes such as heavy metals like lead and aluminium.

Eliminate the negative

Shedding fat on conventional diets tends to render your blood more acidic because the by-products of fat-burning tend to be acid. This can make you feel nervous and irritable. The high potassium content of fresh raw vegetables and some fruits and the ability these foods have to alkalize the body help eliminate those unpleasant feelings of strain and nervousness dieters know so well, leaving you feeling well and calm as the pounds melt away.

An end to cravings

The 10 Day Spring Clean also helps wipe out the cravings for foods which can defeat the most determined dieters.

Such cravings, and the kind of uncontrollable eating which they spur,

are often the result of a food intolerance – sometimes called a food allergy. As experts in food allergies will tell you, you tend – for complex biochemical reasons – to crave those foods to which you are intolerant or allergic, so that they become a kind of addiction. You simply can't stop eating them once you take a bite or two. This is a common problem – particularly among those who have experienced off-again/on-again yo-yo dieting. The most frequently occurring intolerances are of milk and milk products and wheat. Many people who find losing weight difficult discover that eliminating milk and wheat products from their diet makes all the difference for success. But more of this in Step 3.

Staying lean and vital

The 10 Day Spring Clean is helpful in yet another way. The experience of it leads many people quite naturally to increase the number of fibre-rich fresh raw foods in their menus at other times. And the vast majority of people find that when they continue to eat this way they are able quite easily to keep their vitality up and their weight down without ever having to count calories or restrict the quantities they eat of energy-rich foods such as seeds, grains and oils. To anybody who has conscientiously fought (and frequently lost) the battle of the bulge, this can seem almost a miracle. It is not. It is simply a physiological result of the kind of rebalancing which takes place in the body on a high-raw diet.

In my experience, about 80 per cent of people fall into this category. The other 20 per cent (to which, incidentally, I belong) are only slightly less fortunate. To keep excess weight off naturally all we must do is cut back on the fattier foods such as the seeds and cheeses and avoid rich dressings and sauces, while eating as much as we like of the rest. Then our weight steadily reduces again.

Brush your skin

One of the best helpers for encouraging lymphatic drainage and naturally spring-cleaning your body is known as skin-brushing. It stimulates the movement of interstitial fluids and breaks down congestion in areas where the lymph-flow has become sluggish and toxins have collected. An extraordinarily gentle yet powerful technique, it can with skill be used to relieve puffiness, to smooth the look of your skin, and to stimulate skin vitality.

It can also be used to great advantage in the elimination of cellulite in women – a condition in which a stasis of lymph-flow has concentrated excess proteins, fats and waste materials in certain areas of the body. This eventually results in puckered skin, alterations to connective tissue and distortions of the natural body-shape.

I first learned the technique of skin-brushing from a British medical doctor who specialized in the treatment of chronic illnesses by natural means. It consists of spending five minutes a day, before your bath, brushing your skin all over with a natural-fibre brush. You begin at the tips of your shoulders and cover your whole body (except the head) with long smooth strokes over the shoulders, arms and trunk in a downwards motion, then upwards over the feet, legs and hips.

You need only go over your skin once for it to work. How firmly you press depends on how toned your skin and body are now. Go easy at first. Your skin will soon become fitter and then you will be able to work far more vigorously over it.

This kind of skin-brushing, if done daily, is one of the simplest and most effective treatments for lumpy thighs and hips that you will find anywhere. It does two things: it eliminates toxic wastes through the surface of the skin – not only in the specific cellulite areas but all over the body; and it stimulates lymphatic drainage.

Test for yourself

You can check for yourself just how dramatic is the skin's elimination of wastes by performing a practical experiment with the help of a flannel: Every day before your bath, brush your skin all over for three to five minutes. Then take a damp flannel and rub it all over your freshly brushed body. Hang the flannel up and repeat the process with the same flannel the next day. After a few days, the smell of the flannel will be quite revolting because of the quantity of waste products that have come through the skin's surface.

Let's get started

A diet always begins tomorrow. And tomorrow it begins the day after ... It is so hard to find a diet that will fit into your daily routine that you can put it off forever. The 10 Day Spring Clean is different. It is designed to begin on a Friday with a pre-diet day and to spread over two weekends and the intervening week. It is also made as convenient as possible so that even if you have a nine-to-five job, or you have to eat at least one of your meals in a restaurant, you can follow it with relative ease.

And remember that the 10 Day Spring Clean doesn't affect just your body but your mind and spirit too. It is important for the entire you.

How and why it works

The diet is divided into four parts:

- *A pre-diet day: to prepare your body for the elimination process.*
- *Days 2 and 3: fruit-fast days which spur rapid elimination.*
- *Days 4 to 8: replenishing fruit and vegetable days.*
- *Days 9 and 10: reorientation days to lead you to practise a better way of eating permanently.*

Pre-diet day: Day 1 (Friday)

To prepare your body for the change involved in eating a raw diet, begin on Day 1 by eliminating all stimulants, such as coffee and tea, and all depressants, such as alcohol. Also avoid bread and cooked carbohydrates such as pasta

and cereals, and make your last meal of the day a large raw salad of vegetables and fruits. This is a good time to start preparing your home-grown sprouts if you are going to use them; you may be able to buy them in a health-food shop or supermarket if you prefer.

Preparing your sprouts

Sprouts form an important part of the 10 Day Spring Clean. As they take a few days to germinate, you will need to begin preparing them on Day 1 of the diet, or even before. If they become ready too quickly you can always refrigerate them. (See pages 40-1 for how to grow them.)

Day 1: What to Do

Follow the guidelines outlined above. Have your raw salad early in the evening, say about 6.00 pm, and then don't have anything else except a cup of herb tea before you go to bed. This gives your system a good 12 hours to start eliminating.

The fruit-fast: days 2 and 3 (Saturday and Sunday)

The fruit-fast is one of the best ways of clearing your system quickly. Because the effect is so dramatic you may find that you experience some mild elimination reactions such as a headache, irritability or tiredness at some point within the first three days. For this reason Days 2 and 3 are done at the weekend so that you can rest as you feel necessary.

The fruit-fast is effective in several ways. In a purely physical sense, fruit is mildly laxative and a wonderful intestinal 'broom' to sweep your alimentary canal

clean. Also, fruit is alkaline-forming; most stored wastes which are responsible for aches and disease in general are acidic. When your body is given the chance to throw off these wastes, they first enter the bloodstream. The alkalinity of the fruit helps to neutralize them so that they are not harmful and can be quickly expelled. In this way you minimize the possibility of any cleansing-reactions.

Fruit also has a high potassium content. This is helpful in ridding the system of excess water and oedema in the tissues, increasing oxygenation in the cells and raising cell vitality.

Cleansing-reactions
Because the effect of eating all-raw foods is so dramatic, it is possible that you may experience one or more cleansing-reactions (although many

people don't). If you do, there is no need to worry. It is all part of the elimination process. But it is important to acknowledge them. Such reactions can include headaches, muscle or joint pains, sensitivity, tiredness and unsettled emotions. They are due to the rapid mobilization and release of stored toxins and wastes. Should they occur it is best to retire to a quiet, dark room and rest for a while. Also try to get plenty of fresh air – breathing deeply is another way of ridding your body of wastes. During the first two days especially, beware of overtaxing your body by strenuous exercise: it is working very hard to clean and renew itself and therefore just now it doesn't need added strain.

For Days 2 and 3 it is up to you to choose the single fruit which you intend to eat throughout the day. Each fruit has its own specific health-benefiting properties. I have found that apples, grapes, pineapple, papaya, mango and watermelon are particularly successful.

Choosing your fruit

Apples: excellent for detoxification – the pectin in apples helps remove impurities from the system. Pectin also helps prevent protein matter in the intestines from putrefying. The high fibre content of apples also makes them great 'brooms'. Apples are good for strengthening the liver and digestive system and for stimulating body secretions. They are rich in vitamins and minerals.

Grapes: very effective cleansers for the skin, liver, intestines and kidneys due to their potent properties which counter excessive mucus. Grapes provide a quick source of energy which is easily assimilated and, being rich in minerals, they make good blood- and cell-builders.

Pineapple: has a high concentration of bromelin, an enzyme which supports the action of hydrochloric acid in your stomach and helps to break down protein wastes in the system. Eating pineapple is also believed to soothe internal inflammation, accelerate tissue repair, regulate the glandular system and clear mucus.

Papaya and mango: these tropical fruits (mango to a lesser degree) contain an enzyme called papain which resembles the enzyme pepsin in the stomach and, like bromelin, helps to break down protein waste in the tissues. Papaya and mango are good for cleansing the alimentary canal and helping digestive disorders. Mangoes are also believed to relieve depression.

Watermelon: a wonderful diuretic and great for washing your system clean. It is used to ease stomach ulcers and high blood-pressure and to soothe the intestinal tract. Juice the rind with the seeds and a little flesh and drink it about half an hour before a melon meal to get all the benefit of the chlorophyll-rich skin and vitamin-packed seeds.

First thing in the morning: Skin-brushing (see page 27).

Eat several fruit meals throughout the day. Choose one of the following for Day 2 and a different one for Day 3:

apple	**papaya**
grape	**pineapple**
mango	**watermelon**

You don't have to eat the fruit 'straight' – try grating, slicing or dicing and pouring a little of the juice over the fruit in a bowl. Or make a frappé by putting the chilled or partly frozen fruit in a blender, perhaps adding a little water to make it more liquid, plus some crushed ice, and spicing it lightly with cinnamon, allspice, nutmeg or ginger. You can also juice the fruits, although you lose the valuable 'bulk' this way, so it is best to drink the juice only once or twice a day and have the whole fruit the rest of the time.

One fruit only is eaten throughout the day because this is least taxing for the digestive system. (It is also, incidentally, the best way to lose weight.) If, however, the amount of a certain fruit available is limited you can change fruit mid-day as long as you leave a gap of at least two hours before starting the new fruit. How much fruit you choose to eat is up to you. Eating fruit by itself will not make you gain weight. You will find that you need to eat more frequently than usual as fruit is digested very quickly and does not remain in the stomach for more than an hour. You might want to take about four to five fruit meals spread throughout the day (eating continually is tiring for the digestive system), but should you feel hungry at any point have a fruit snack.

Days 2 and 3: what to do
On rising: An orange and half a lemon juiced and topped up with spring water in a tall glass, or a cup of herb tea with a squeeze of lemon added. Lemon verbena or peppermint are also very good 'wake-up' teas.

Replenishing: days 4 to 8 (Monday to Friday)
This part of the diet is designed to allow the elimination process to continue while nourishing your newly cleansed cells with all the nutrients needed to fortify and rebalance your system. The vitamins, minerals and enzymes in the raw vegetables and sprouts will boost sluggish cells into action and vitalize your whole being. It begins with a fruit breakfast (as the entire diet does); this is very important for it encourages the liver (most active early in the day) to continue the rapid elimination of stored wastes. Lunch is basically a large raw salad (or crudités) and sprouts with some seeds

or blanched almonds. Dinner is a dish of steamed or stir-fried vegetables with a blended raw topping. (Lunch and dinner are interchangeable depending upon which is more convenient if, say, you eat lunch at work; and even if you have to eat at a restaurant there should be no problem.)

Days 4 to 8: what to do
Have your wake-up drink and skin-brushing as for Days 2 and 3. Then follow the menu suggestions below. During the day – throughout the spring clean – you can drink any variety of herb tea (sweetened, if you like, with honey) as well as fresh fruit and vegetable juices. I find that a drink of vegetable juice can quite easily sustain me when I feel like a snack between meals.

Breakfast: Fruit. Either one fruit or a combination (not bananas). You can make a simple fruit salad dressed with fruit juice, a little honey and spices, or a delicious fruit shake made in the blender – such as a Mango Smoothie, made by combining the flesh of a mango with some freshly squeezed orange juice.

Lunch: A large salad made from raw vegetables. Invent new combinations each day from what you can find at your greengrocer. For instance select from the following:

beetroot	*red peppers*
celery	*sliced mushrooms*
chicory	*tomatoes*
cos lettuce	*white/red cabbage*
grated carrots	*watercress.*
radicchio	

The possibilities are endless. Top the salad with generous helpings of sprouted seeds, pulses and grains and dress with an olive oil and lemon or cider-vinegar dressing or an avocado or mayonnaise dressing. Complete it with lots of fresh herbs such as basil and parsley. An avocado is an excellent addition to such a salad, which can also be sprinkled with sunflower, pumpkin and sesame seeds – either whole or ground – or a few blanched almonds.

Dinner: Steamed or wok-fried vegetables prepared in a tiny amount of olive oil and cooked for just a few minutes, then seasoned with fresh or dried herbs and perhaps a little soy sauce. Use three or four different vegetables together, such as broccoli, cauliflower, courgettes, spinach, green beans, mangetout, Chinese cabbage and sprouts. Toss a few sunflower, pumpkin or sesame seeds or a few almonds or pine-nuts into the wok with the vegetables and spike with spring onions. Make a delicious sauce such as Avocado Dip-Dressing (see page 43) to pour over the top.

You can exchange lunch for dinner, dinner for lunch, if it is more convenient. If you work in an office and take your lunch, prepare a large bag of raw vegetables (carrots, celery, chicory, etc.) and take them with your sprouts to the office aloge with some seeds and perhaps a jar of avocado sauce or other dressing to dip your vegetables into.

At a restaurant: When you have to eat in a restaurant, ask them to prepare for you an all-raw mixed vegetable salad or simply order steamed vegetables without any butter.

Reorientation: days 9 and 10 (Saturday and Sunday)

The final two days are designed to adjust your system to a diet containing more cooked food and to set you on the pathway to enjoying a high-raw way of eating afterwards. The focus of each meal is still fresh uncooked foods, but one meal a day (lunch or dinner) will contain a cooked dish such as a thick peasant soup, some pulses and/or grains, or a piece of game, poultry or fish. I have given some tips and ideas for recipes on pages 46-7.

Days 9 and 10: what to do

Wake-up drink as before, and don't forget the skin-brushing!

Breakfast: Birchermuesli with or without yoghurt, or a fruit breakfast as on Days 4 to 8.

Lunch: A sprout and vegetable salad as on Days 4 to 8.

Dinner: Crudités or fresh vegetable juice. Then four ounces of poached or grilled fish, or four ounces of chicken roasted without the skin, or a country soup made from beans/grains/lentils and vegetables. Steamed vegetables, brown rice or millet if desired. A green salad. A piece of fresh fruit for dessert (optional).

As with Days 4 to 8, lunch and dinner are interchangeable

And that, believe it or not, is all there is to it!

Recipes

Breakfasts and drinks

Birchermuesli – Swiss magic

Fruit muesli was the invention of the renowned Swiss physician Max Bircher-Benner, who made it famous as part of his effective system of healing based on a high-raw diet. When making muesli you can either use a food processor and so enough for a whole family at once or, with a simple hand grater, make one bowlful. But be sure to experiment with all the many variations depending on what kinds of fruits are in season. Each has its own delicious character.

BIRCHERMUESLI (FOR ONE)

- **2 tbsp oatflakes (or a combination of oat, rye, wheat, etc.) soaked overnight in a little water or fruit juice (e.g. pineapple)**
- **1 apple or firm pear grated**
- **a handful of soaked raisins**
- **1/2 lemon**
- **2 tbsp plain yoghurt**
- **1 tbsp minced nuts (e.g. almonds and brazils)**
- **1 tsp honey, cinnamon or powdered ginger**

Soak the flakes with the raisins overnight in a little water or fruit juice. Combine with this mixture a grated apple or pear with a squeeze of lemon juice and one or two tablespoonfuls of natural plain yoghurt. Drizzle with honey if desired (the dish is beautifully sweet even without it) and sprinkle with chopped nuts and cinnamon or ginger.
The above recipe calls for an apple or pear, but you can use almost any other fruit instead, or add extra fruit in season.

Muesli variations

Banana: add a banana sliced in quarters lengthwise and then chopped crosswise into small pieces. Or mash a banana with a little yoghurt or fruit juice and use as a topping.

Summer: add a handful of raspberries, strawberries, blackcurrants or pitted cherries to the basic muesli, or substitute a finely diced peach or nectarine in place of the apple or pear.

Winter: soak overnight in water a selection of dried fruits such as apricots, sultanas, figs, dates and pears. Dice into small pieces or cut up with a pair of scissors, and add to the other muesli ingredients. Spice with a pinch of nutmeg.

Dairy-free: in place of the yoghurt use some fresh fruit juice such as apple, orange or grape. To thicken the juice, blend with a little fresh fruit such as banana, pear or apple.

Shakes

FRUIT SHAKE
1 cup plain yoghurt
1 ripe banana
few drops vanilla essence
1 tsp honey
1 tsp coconut (optional)

Combine the ingredients in a blender. As a variation, try replacing the banana with a handful of berries, half a papaya, or a few chunks of fresh pineapple.

NUT-MILK SHAKE
The dairy-free alternative to the fruit shake. For the basic recipe use:

1/3 cup almonds (blanched)
2/3 cup water
5 pitted dates
few drops vanilla essence
1 tsp honey

Blend the water and the almonds really well until the mixture is smooth. If you have used unblanched almonds, strain the mixture at this stage to remove the ground up husks. Add the other ingredients and process well. Serve immediately.

APRICOT SHAKE
Use apricots, fresh or dried, instead of the dates, and add a handful of sunflower seeds to the nuts before you blend.

GRAPE SHAKE
Use fruit juice such as grape or apple instead of the water, and raisins instead of the dates. Omit the honey and vanilla if desired.

For extra goodness add a teaspoonful of brewer's yeast (the de-bittered kind is the most bearable), a tablespoonful of wheatgerm, or the yolk of an egg. Blend.

Instant low-fat yoghurt

If you are using yoghurt, why not try making your own? It's very simple and doesn't require a lot of expensive equipment. The easiest way to make it is in a wide-mouthed flask, but an earthenware crock or dish kept in a warm place will do just as well.

One of the very simplest methods of making yoghurt is to use low-fat skimmed milk powder. Mix up two pints of milk using one and a half times the amount of powdered milk suggested on the packet. If you use boiling water from a kettle and add cold water to it you can get just the temperature of milk you need (blood heat) and don't have to bother heating your milk in a saucepan. Add two tablespoonfuls of plain yoghurt as a 'starter' and leave in a suitable container which will retain the heat (such as a thermos flask) for about eight hours.

Herb teas

A simple tisane or herb tea is light and refreshing and can either be drunk hot with a little honey for sweetening or made double-strength, chilled and served with mint and a slice of lemon in a tall iced glass.

Herb teas make seductive but healthy alternatives to tea and coffee. They come in two varieties: those which you drink for medicinal purposes – such as sage for a sore throat, dandelion to eliminate excess water from the body, lemon grass for indigestion, and St John's Wort for skin problems – and those which you drink for pure pleasure. Some herb teas, such as camomile and vervain which are natural sedatives and peppermint which calms the digestive system, belong in both categories. Some of my favourites include lemon grass, lemon verbena, orange blossom, hibiscus and linden blossom.

You can make your own from dried herbs, or you can buy herb teas ready packaged in bags which you use as you would ordinary tea-bags – allowing them a little longer to steep. There are some wonderful herbal combinations on the market in these little bags – cinnamon-and-rose flavour, for instance, or apple-and-cinnamon. Or you can drink single-herb teas.

To make herb teas

Take about a tablespoonful of the dried herbs (either a single herb or a mixture) to make two cups. Pour boiling water over the herbs and let them steep in a pot for 5-10 minutes, stirring every now and then to extract the aroma. Now strain and serve with a slice of lemon and/or a little honey for sweetening.

Other drinks

Aside from the herb teas, the only other drinks you should think of taking while on the 10 Day Spring Clean are water and fruit and vegetable juices.

The water which you drink should be either filtered or spring water, and certainly not just tap water, which contains all sorts of chemical additives your body can well do without.

Similarly, don't just drink any fruit or vegetable juice: a lot of the ones you find in the shops have additives, are reconstituted from concentrated or frozen juices – or aren't really juices at all but flavoured drinks! You can make your own with a juice extractor, or you can look out for commercial ones where the processing has been done at low temperatures.

Sprouts

There are so many delicious ways of using raw vegetables that it would be hard to list them all. Let's start by looking at how to sprout and then at some salad suggestions (see page 41).

Sprouting

When a seed is sprouted its vitamin content increases by up to 700 per cent – sprouts even contain vitamin B12 (very few vegetables have this one). During the sprouting process starch begins to be broken down into simple sugars, fats into fatty acids, and proteins into amino acids (the ratio of essential amino acids to non-essential ones even increases). Because of this the seed is already, as it were, partially digested and therefore very easily assimilated. Remarkably, a grain even loses its mucus-inducing properties when sprouted.

Sprouts are the finest rejuvenating foods available. They are simple to grow, taste delicious and, what's more, they're cheap. All you need to start your own indoor germinating 'factory' are a few old jars, some pure water, fresh seeds/beans/grains and a warm spot in the kitchen.

Sprouters

A home-made sprouter can be anything from a bucket to a polythene bag, but the best ones are wide-mouthed glass jars. Some people like to make a neat sprouter by covering the jar with cheesecloth, nylon or wire mesh and securing it with a rubber band, or using a mason jar with a screw-on rim to hold the cheesecloth in place. The easiest and least fussy way is simply to use open jars and cover a row of them with a tea towel to prevent dust and insects from getting in.

Growing your own sprouts

SMALL SEEDS Soak 6-8 hrs except as stated				
Seed	Dry amount to yield 1 litre (1 3/4 pints)	Ready to eat in	Length of shoot (approx.)	Growing tips and notes
Alfalfa	3-4 tbsp	5-6 days	3.5 cm (1 1/2 in)	Rich in organic vitamins and minerals, the roots of the mature plant penetrate the earth to a depth of 10-30 m (30-100 ft).
Fenugreek	1/2 cup	3-4 days	1 cm (1/2 in)	Have quite a strong 'curry' taste. Best mixed with other sprouts. Good for ridding the body of toxins
Mustard no soaking needed	1/4 cup	4-5 days	2.5 cm (1 in)	Can be grown on damp paper towels for a week or more. The green tops are then cut off with scissors and used in salads.
Radish no soaking needed	1/4 cup	4-5 days	2.5 cm (1 in)	The red hot flavour is great for dressings, or mixed with other sprouts. Good for clearing mucus and healing mucous membranes.
Sesame	1/2 cup	1-2 days	Same length as seed	If grown for longer than about two days sesame sprouts become very bitter.

LARGER SEEDS Soak 10-15 hrs				
Seed	To yield 2 litres (3 1/2 pints)	Ready to eat in	Length of shoot (approx.)	Growing tips and notes
Aduki (adzuki) beans	1 1/2 cups	3-5 days	2.5-3.5 cm (1-1 1/2 in)	Have a nutty 'legume' flavour. Especially good for the kidneys
Chick peas	2 cups	3-4 days	2.5 cm (1 in)	May need to soak for about 18 hours to swell to their full size. The water should be renewed twice during this time
Lentils	1 cup	3-5 days	0.5-2.5 cm (1/4-1 in)	Try all different kinds of lentils – red, Chinese, green, brown. They are good eaten young or up to about 6 days old.
Mung beans	1 cup	3-5 days	1-5 cm (1/2-2 1/2 in)	Soak at least 15 hours. Keep in the dark for a sweet sprout
Soya beans	1 cup	3-5 days	3.5 cm (1 1/2 in)	Need to soak for up to 24 hours with frequent changes of water to prevent fermentation. Remove any damaged beans which fail to germinate.
Sunflower	4 cups	1-2 days	Same length as seed	Can be grown for their greens. When using sunflower seeds soak them and sprout for just a day. They bruise easily so handle with care.

GRAINS Soak 12-15 hrs except as stated				
Seed	**To yield 1 litre (1 3/4 pints)**	**Ready to eat in**	**Length of shoot (approx.)**	**Growing tips and notes**
Wheat	2 cups	2-3 days	Same length as grain	An excellent source of the B vitamins. The soak water can be drunk straight, added to soups and vegetable juices or fermented to make rejuvelac
Rye	2 cups	2-3 days	Same length as grain	Has a delicious distinctive flavour. Good for the glandular system
Barley	2 cups	2-3 days	Same length as grain	As with most sprouts, barley becomes quite sweet when germinated. Particularly good for people who are weak or underweight
Oats soak 5-8 hrs only	2 cups	3-4 days	Same length as grain	You need whole oats or 'oat groats'. Oats lose much of their mucus-forming activity when sprouted
Millet soak 5-8 hrs only	2 cups	3-4 days	Same length as grain	Must be unhulled millet. The only grain that is alkaline

Growing your own sprouts

Good sprouts to start with are from:

alfalfa seeds   fenugreek seeds
brown lentils   mung beans.
chickpeas

Put the seeds/beans/grains of your choice (for example, mung) in a large sieve. (For the amount to use see the charts on previous pages and above – remember most sprouts give a volume about eight times that of the dry beans.) Remove any small stones, broken seeds or loose husks and rinse the sprouts well.

Put the seeds/beans/grains in a jar and cover with a few inches of pure water. (Rinsing can be done in tap-water, but the initial soak, when the seeds absorb a lot of water to set their enzymes in action, is best done in spring, filtered or boiled water, as the chlorine in tap-water can sometimes inhibit germination.

Leave the sprouts in a warm place to soak overnight or as long as is needed (see charts on previous pages and opposite).

Pour off the soak-water. If none remains then you still have thirsty seeds/beans/grains on your hands, so give them more water to absorb.

Rinse the seeds/beans/grains, either by pouring water through the cheesecloth top, swilling it around and pouring it off several times, or by tipping them from the open-topped jars into a large sieve and rinsing them well under the tap before replacing them. Whichever way you do it, be sure that they are well drained, as too much water may cause them to rot. The cheesecloth-covered jars can be left tilted in a dish-drainer to allow all the water to run out. Repeat this every morning and night.

After about 3-5 days the sprouts are ready to eat. Rinse them and pop them into polythene bags and then store them in the fridge for use in your salads. Most sprouts will keep fresh in a refrigerator for from 5 to 7 days this way.

Salads

Here are some salad suggestions – salads which you can make in one dish for one person and which are meals in themselves. But do experiment using different combinations of root, leaf and bulb vegetables – whatever is available in the shops – to make up your own recipes as well.

The appearance of any salad is important. Fortunately the brilliant colours of fresh vegetables and fruits are quite stunning. It is nice to experiment with different decorative ways of chopping fruits and vegetables to make attractive garnishes.

41

RED DEVIL SALAD

Make a base of radicchio (or any other lettuce) leaves to line the dish. On this arrange in segments:

- **grated carrot placed inside a ring of red pepper and topped with a few fresh garden peas**
- **a small bunch of watercress inside a ring of sweet yellow pepper**
- **half an avocado (brush with lemon juice or olive oil to prevent it going brown) filled with radish slices**
- **a handful of Chinese (mung) bean sprouts**
- **a few diagonal slices of cucumber**
- **a few cauliflower and broccoli florets**
- **some grated raw beetroot**
- **some grated white radish**
- **mustard and cress**
- **a tomato sliced into segments but not all the way through, so that it looks like a flower with its petals open.**

SPROUT MAGIC SALAD

Make a base with alfalfa sprouts, and around the dish arrange:

- **beetroot**
- **grated carrot**
- **red cabbage**
- **white cabbage.**

Add:

- **black olives**
- **sliced mushrooms**
- **spring onions.**

Sprinkle raisins over the grated vegetables and add a spoonful of seed or nut cheese.

SPINACH WITH A DIFFERENCE

Make a base by shredding tender spinach leaves finely (remove the stalks), and on it arrange:

- **a handful of baby button mushrooms with their stems trimmed**
- **half an avocado diced (simply slice the flesh in its shell several times first vertically and then horizontally, and then scoop out the flesh with a spoon)**
- **some diced red pepper**
- **apple rings (remove the core from the apple and slice crosswise)**
- **thin slices of Jerusalem artichoke, kohlrabi or new potatoes (raw)**
- **toasted pumpkin seeds.**

Dressings

You can make a simple dressing by mixing herbs and mustard with a little yoghurt (the thicker the yoghurt the better) or you can explore some of the beauty of classic oil-based dressings instead. Oil dressings are especially good for leafy salads such as those in which lettuce and spinach predominate. With the right seasonings, such as a tasty mustard and/or various herbs, they can be very flavourful and not at all the plain 'oil-and-vinegar-dressing' most people know.

Basic French dressing

3/4 cup oil
1/4 cup lemon juice or cider vinegar
1 tsp whole-grain mustard (French Meaux mustard is my favourite) or mustard powder
2 tsp honey
a little vegetable bouillon powder and pepper to season
a small clove of crushed garlic (optional)

Combine all the ingredients in a blender or simply place in a screw-top jar and shake well to mix. Some people like to thin the dressing and make it a little lighter by adding a couple of tablespoonfuls of water.

Rich French dressing

To the basic French dressing recipe add:

1 tbsp tamari
1 finely chopped scallion
dash of cayenne

Wine dressing

To the basic French dressing recipe add 1 tablespoonful of red or white wine – white is good for salads containing fruit, red for cabbage salads.

Herb dressing

My favourite combination of herbs for the basic French dressing recipe is:

basil
dill or lovage
marjoram
mint
thyme

You need about 3-4 tablespoonfuls in all of fresh, finely chopped herbs, or 2 teaspoonfuls of dried.

Spicy Italian dressing

Follow the basic French dressing recipe but using cider vinegar and adding:

dash of red wine or tamari
2 ripe peeled tomatoes
1 tbsp finely chopped onion or garlic
1/2 tsp oregano and basil powdered bay leaf

Blend all the ingredients well.

Avocado dip or dressing

This is my favourite of all salad dressings. You can make it thick as a dip for crudites or thin to pour over a salad.

1-2 avocados
1 cup fresh orange juice (use more or less to give the desired consistency)
1 tsp curry powder
2 tsp vegetable bouillon powder
fresh herbs (e.g. lovage and French parsley)
1 small clove garlic (optional)

Peel and stone the avocado(s). Blend all the ingredients together in a food processor until smooth.

Grains and pulses

Grains and pulses are wonderful natural staples. Grains such as brown rice, wheat, barley, oats, millet, bulgar wheat and buckwheat are superb staple foods – high in fibre, a good source of protein when eaten with vegetables, and very filling. They are exceptionally useful for athletes or people who want to have sustained energy.

There are many delicious ways to serve grains. On their own with a few herbs tossed in, with a few vegetables such as onions and mushrooms, and in thick nourishing country soups. Cold leftover grains can be mixed into salads.

Cooking grains

The basic rule is that you need about half a cup of dry whole grains to serve each person.

Wash the grains in cool water, using a strainer to gently loosen the dust and small bits of dirt. Check to see there are no little bits of rock left. When the water rinses through the strainer clean the grains are ready to cook.

There are two basic ways of cooking whole or cracked grains. The first uses cold water mixed with the grain; in the second you add boiling water to the grain.

I usually prefer the boiling-water method. Sauté the grain either in a heavy dry pan or with the smallest possible amount of olive oil to brown it a little; this is not necessary with rice or barley, but the others benefit greatly from it. Now add boiling water (for guides to quantity see below), a handful of herbs and some vegetable bouillon powder to the pot and cover immediately. Bring to the boil and continue to cook at simmer on the hob or (I prefer this) pop it all into a moderate oven to finish (see notes on times below). Do not stir the grains as this breaks them up and makes them stick in clumps.

Grain guidelines

Every grain needs a slightly different length of cooking time; the amount of water needed varies too.

Barley: use twice as much water as grain and cook for 90 minutes.

Brown rice: use twice as much water as rice and cook for 45 minutes. Usually I cook rice by simply adding cold water to the grain, bringing to the boil, and then simmering.

Bulgar wheat: this is wheat which has been cracked, toasted and steamed before you buy it. Use one part bulgar wheat to one and a half parts water. Cook for 20 minutes.

Millet and buckwheat groats: use one part grain to two parts water and cook for 20-25 minutes. Millet can be cooked using the cold-water method.

The humble pulses

One cup of beans, lentils or peas measured dry makes about four average servings. Like the grains, these inexpensive foods are rich in fibre and have good sustaining power. And they come in such wonderful varieties – black beans, lima beans, kidney beans, soya beans, lentils of all sorts and colours, aduki (adzuki) beans and chickpeas. I use them as the base for delicious soups and casserole dishes lavished with fresh herbs; I also mix them with salads sometimes.

Cooking pulses

Unless they are very dirty they need only one rinse under running water before cooking. I usually soak pulses for several hours – or overnight – in a cool place before cooking them. This softens them and cuts the cooking time considerably. It also helps break down some of the starches they contain and renders them more digestible. After soaking, put them in a pot, add three times as much water as pulses, bring to the boil and simmer until done; remember that kidney beans must be boiled for at least 10 minutes, as otherwise they're poisonous. Like grains, pulses can be cooked in the oven instead of on the hob. I prefer oven-cooking because you don't have to be so accurate about when you take them out and because they are less likely to stick to the pot. Beans and lentils love carrots, onions and celery, which I often add – as well as herbs and seasoning. (Vegetable bouillon powder works its magic here as well.)

A brief guide to timings

Red lentils: 20 minutes (don't need soaking either)
Split peas and other lentils: one hour
Others (except soya beans): one and a half hours
Soya beans: two and a half hours
Chickpeas: one and a half hours.

Soups and woks

These winter soups are hearty and full-bodied. I make them from whatever vegetables I happen to have, adding some millet, lentils, peas, rice, barley or whatever is handy for thickening, lots of fresh herbs from the garden or a few dried herbs, and perhaps some bouillon powder for seasoning.

THICK VEGETABLE SOUP
1 large onion
2 leeks
1 head of celery
4 carrots
2 turnips
1 parsnip
any other vegetables you happen
   to have or want to substitute
2 tbsp olive oil
3 pints stock or water (boiling)
1 tbsp bouillon powder
2 bay leaves
3/4 cup brown rice or millet
2 cups garden peas
1 cup runner beans
fresh parsley

Wash and peel the vegetables and peel the onion. Cut root vegetables into small cubes – the leeks first lengthwise 4 to 6 times and then across so that you get tiny pieces. Add oil to the pot and sauté the leeks and onions. Then add chopped celery, carrots, turnips and parsnip; put the lid on and allow them to sweat for five minutes. Now add your boiling stock or water, the vegetable bouillon, the bay leaves and the rice or millet and allow to cook for 30 minutes. Now add peas and beans and cook for another 15 minutes. Sprinkle with chopped parsley and serve.

This makes enough for a large family; 4 to 6 good size servings.

BORSCHT
3 raw beetroots (with their green
   tops, if possible)
3 carrots
1 medium onion
1/2 small cabbage
2 tbsp olive oil
2 pints stock or water (boiling)
1 tbsp vegetable bouillon powder
juice of one lemon
3 tbsp honey
dash of nutmeg
1 cup thick yoghurt or sour cream

Wash vegetables – do not peel – and cut them into small strips. Retain half of one beetroot which you will add grated to the soup later. Heat oil in pot and sweat beetroot and onions for five minutes, then add the rest of the vegetables, including the sliced beet greens (if you have them) and stew for another 5-10 minutes stirring occasionally. Add stock or water – boiling – together with bouillon powder, and cook vegetables until tender. Now add lemon juice, grated beetroot and honey and cook for another 5 minutes. Serve topped with the thick yoghurt or sour cream and sprinkle with nutmeg.

Serves 4 to 6 people well.

POTATO SOUP

6 medium potatoes
2 1/2 pints water or stock
1 tbsp vegetable bouillon powder
1 cup sliced, chunked or diced
vegetables (e.g. leeks, celery,
carrot, swede, green beans,
peas)
herbs (e.g. marjoram, winter
savory, basil, garlic)
garnishes (e.g. sliced spring
onions, chopped hard-boiled
egg, chives, watercress, grated
hard cheese)

Wash vegetables and scrub potatoes, cutting them into medium-sized chunks. Cover the potatoes in the water or stock to which the bouillon has been added and boil until tender. Remove from heat and blend in a food processor until smooth. Now sauté the vegetables and cut into small pieces, add them along with your seasonings to the potato mixture, and cook for five minutes. Sprinkle with your garnishes and serve.

Serves 4 to 6 people.

Wok frying

The most delicious way of all to cook vegetables is to stir-fry – in a wok or simple frying pan. It is quick, simple and a lot of fun to do. Here's how.

Take whatever vegetables you happen to have. A good combination would be:

2 tbsp vegetable oil
handful of cashew nuts
onions cut in rings
cauliflower broken into florets
spiked spring onions (their green parts slit lengthwise)
mangetout – topped and tailed
diced red pepper
sliced mushrooms
tamari soy sauce

Put the oil into your pan and heat. Add cashews on their own and brown, then add those vegetables which take the longest to cook such as onions and cauliflower. Sauté for 2 to 3 minutes turning constantly. Now add the rest of the vegetables and continue to toss them in the pan for another 3 to 5 minutes. Add a little tamari soy sauce and serve.

STEP THREE: EAT WELL

Changing your habits

The chances are that having treated yourself to a good spring clean, the processed, packaged foods that looked so great before, simply won't appeal to you. It is at this point you need to ask yourself why you eat. Most of us have probably never even thought about it. Here are some common answers to the question, it may interest you to think about them for a few moments.

1 *I eat to stay alive, but have no real interest either in the taste or the health effects of foods.*

2 *I eat-to-stay-thin/worry about what I eat making me fat.*

3 *I am constantly changing my diet to fit in with the latest research on diseases such as cancer or heart disease.*

4 *I choose foods that titillate my palate without much thought to anything but the way they taste.*

We are all, to some extent, motivated by some of these considerations at some time. But to support your quest to live out who you really are, you need to be eating to feel as healthy and full of vitality as you possibly can. Incidentally, this will help you look great, too.

For most people, this means making a few changes. And changing your eating habits is almost always a slow process, taking three steps forward and two back. But this kind of slow change tends to be far more permanent than throwing over everything you are used to in favour of a whole new regime. Your goal here is to eventually come to like, want, and delight in the foods which will do you the most good, not because someone tells you they do, but because you find they work best for your body and mind, help energise you, and keep you calm in the face of stress. After a while this will become second nature.

Here are a few pointers to help you on your way, things to look out for in your foods both good and bad – but remember, these are merely pointers and suggestions. It is up to you to find out what works the best for you and to throw out the rest.

Fat chance for freedom

We all know about fat. It prevents your body from making efficient use of carbohydrates and can encourage the development of diabetes. It raises fat and cholesterol levels in your blood as well as uric acid which contribute to the development of gout, arthritis and arteriosclerosis. A high-fat diet plays an important part in premature ageing and degenerative illnesses as well.

There are two kinds of fats, both of which you need to watch carefully: saturated and unsaturated. Saturated fats in milk products and meat are pretty useless except as a way of laying down more fat on your belly and hips. Eat a lot of saturated fats and you undermine health and leanness. The rest – unsaturated fats – are found in the processed oils you find on supermarket shelves gleaming all golden, or in margarines and convenience foods. Most have been chemically altered so your body cannot make use of the essential fatty acids they once contained. This can lead to fatty-acid deficiencies. Such deficiencies have now become widespread in the West despite our taking in almost half of the calories we eat in the form of fats. Avoid them. Use only cold-pressed, good quality oils for stir-frying or for salads. Their composition has not been altered so your body can use the excellent essential fatty acids they contain.

Don't sugar your blood

It is common knowledge that the consumption of refined sugar has been linked with the development of degenerative illnesses. Sugar, the end of a complex refining process which takes away every vitamin, mineral and trace of natural fibre from the beets or cane from which it is made, is a food virtually empty of nutritional benefit – except for calories. Eating sugar tends to raise your blood-sugar level and puts stress on your pancreas, challenging it to maintain normal blood-sugar levels. Sugar can also contribute to the development of arteriosclerosis. Yet most of us eat one kilogram or about two pounds a week of the stuff. In fact, about 20 to 25 per cent of our daily calories in the West come from it. Unless sugar is eaten naturally – that is, the way you find it in a piece of fresh fruit – it is very hard on your body. It can make you tired, depressed and emotionally unstable due to the insulin resistance and raised blood-sugar level triggered in your body. It also leads to deficiencies in the B-complex vitamins and to an imbalance in important trace minerals. (See also step 6.)

Junk the coffee

One of the best things you can give up to improve your health is coffee. Just a few cups a day can both undermine your wellbeing and encourage you to age long before your time. Coffee contains caffeine and caffeine is a drug. One of the xanthine group of chemicals, it stimulates the central nervous system, pancreas and heart as well as the cerebral cortex – which is why, when you drink it, you feel temporarily more alert. Studies show, however, that while coffee drinking makes you think you are being more efficient, in reality it impedes your mental performance. Every time you drink a cup of coffee you are getting between 90 and 120 mg of caffeine. A cup of ordinary tea yields 40 to 100 mg, cocoa or cola drinks 20 to 50 mg. If you drink two to eight cups of coffee a day, you are getting a dose of the drug which any pharmacologist would reckon considerable. Day after day, such a dose can be dangerous. It will burn you out.

Caffeine addiction

Caffeine can affect the heart, causing it to beat rapidly and irregularly. It increases the level of free fatty acids in your blood, stimulates the secretion of excess acid in the stomach and raises blood pressure. This raised blood-fat level is one of the suspected factors in arteriosclerosis, while secretion of excess acid in the stomach makes people more susceptible to gastric ulcers. Recent studies have also linked habitual coffee drinking to many stress disorders and certain mental illnesses – from quite simple depression and anxiety neurosis to overt psychosis. Coffee, if you are a steady 'user', is addictive. Its removal can cause powerful withdrawal symptoms. These usually appear as nausea or a headache, but they are short-lived and worth going through to be rid of caffeine once and for all.

Go light on protein

The idea that you need to eat meat to stay healthy is also untrue. Studies show that a mixed diet of roots, grains, vegetables and fruits is a much better source of high-quality protein than are the traditional meat, fish and dairy products which are high in fat and too concentrated in protein. Eat meat, fish and game by all means if you want but in small quantities, say 85-112 grams or three or four ounces a day, instead of as the main food in a meal. Or eat them only occasionally. Try to make sure it is really lean meat too, like venison for instance or wild boar. And remember that the vegetables you eat contain a good quantity of protein, as do pulses. Eat them together with your grains for high-grade protection. A bowl of chilli beans eaten with a piece of corn bread will give you the full complement of all the essential amino-acids without the excess of fat. You don't need to eat flesh foods at all if you prefer.

Carbs are king

Another common assumption is that you mustn't eat too many carbohydrates because 'starches are not really good for you'. Carbohydrates are the best thing you can eat for physical and emotional balance, provided, of course, they are complex carbohydrates – unrefined grains, pulses, vegetables and fruits eaten in as natural a state as possible. Starches such as brown rice or wheat which have not been milled to death and deprived of most of their natural vitamins, minerals and fibre, when taken together with fresh vegetables, provide a steady stream of energy. What's so special about vegetables? Plenty. They have powerful health-enhancing

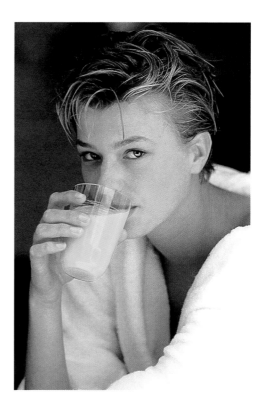

properties which is why diets high in fresh vegetables are recommended as protection against degenerative diseases such as cancer, arthritis and arteriosclerosis. Important, too, is making sure that a good proportion of your vegetables is eaten raw. This can increase the micro-electric potential of your body's tissues, making cells function better, improving intra- and extra-cellular exchange and imparting high levels of mental and physical vitality. Fresh vegetables are also a rich source of natural fibre, vitamins and minerals and they can heighten your resistance to illness. Meanwhile, eating grains affects the chemistry of the brain by enhancing the production of serotonin, which helps you keep your cool when all around you people are losing theirs.

The question of alcohol

Alcohol, like caffeine and nicotine, is a drug. As such, it is capable of bringing about serious damage to your mind and body when taken over a long period of time. And it affects the brain, adversely affecting the specific centres that govern self-control, judgment and personal inhibitions.

Alcohol is a depressant. The transient feeling of wellbeing that goes with a couple of glasses of whisky or a dry martini – the 'lift' – is followed by a series of miseries to which your body is subjected, not the least of which is the effect drinking alcohol has on the liver. And the insidious thing about the detrimental effects which alcohol has on health and good looks is that they occur even to the average social drinker, not just to the serious drinker and the alcoholic.

Researchers have found that liver-cell damage and the increase in fat in the liver can be reversible if the drinker abstains from alcohol for long enough. But long-term damage to the liver resulting from daily consumption of alcohol over the years can be irreversible. Persistent drinking can also be a precursor not only to specific diseases of the liver such as cirrhosis, but also to other toxic conditions in the body.

Forget the extra salt

Recent studies indicate that the daily sodium requirement for a human being is probably not more than 200 mg a day, perhaps slightly higher in someone who performs great physical exertion or in nursing mothers. This small quantity is available naturally in foods alone – vegetables, meats and fish, fruits, and grains for instance – without our ever having to add salt to our foods. Where we do add it, not only when cooking but also at the table, the average sodium intake is thought to be more than twenty-five times that amount.

Excess salt intake can severely upset the body's water balance and create high blood pressure in someone who has inherited a tendency to it. Along with potassium, which also occurs naturally in fresh foods, the sodium in foods and in salt itself (which is sodium chloride) plays an important part in the movement of electrons through the body's water-based proto-plasm. Too much sodium, which most of us get from eating salt, forces the body to hold on to extra

amounts of water to dilute the extra salt you have eaten. Tissues become waterlogged, and this salt-caused oedema can interfere with the blood's oxygen transfer to cells as well as creating extra pressure against the blood vessel walls themselves.

Water: take a look at what you drink

After oxygen water is the most important thing you consume – more important, even, than your foods, although they contain some of the most beneficial water you will ever take into your body. Besides helping to regulate body temperature, it is the best solvent for nutrients and wastes stored in your tissues which it can help eliminate quickly and easily.

Tap water vs mineral water

Natural spring water, laboratory-tested for quality as it is in France and uncontaminated by chemical additives, is one thing; the water that flows from your taps is quite another. Far from promoting your good health, it may actually be damaging it, due to the chemical pollutants it contains.

Most mineral waters contain a good proportion of the natural minerals necessary for good health such as potassium, calcium and magnesium as well as trace elements which we need only in very small quantities such as iodine, copper, and iron. And drinking these waters is one of the best ways of ensuring that your body gets the minerals it needs in an easily assimilable form. The fizzy waters are full of carbon dioxide, either because they come from the ground that way or because it is artificially added when the water is bottled. The bubbles do not affect the mineral content of the water. Fizzy waters are absorbed into your body faster and you can usually drink more of them without feeling unpleasantly bloated. Each water has its own special taste and qualities. Experiment with them and you will develop an awareness of flavour and selectivity that will rival any wine drinker's palate.

What price convenience?

Highly processed convenience foods have been stripped of their natural fibre, denuded of most of their vitamins and minerals, and reduced to easily regulated chemical substances. They also contain a vast quantity of food additives: into them are poured some 3,000 chemicals, the long-term effects of which no one is sure about. Some food additives are designed to prevent spoilage or to replace a few of the vitamins lost in the manufacturing process, but about half of them are used only for cosmetic effect. Only 7 per cent have any nutritional value whatever.

There are three main ways that food additives can be threats to health:

• Carcinogenic (tending to produce cancer)
• Teratogenic (tending to harm the unborn child in the womb)
• Mutagenic (tending to produce changes in the gene pattern which can be passed on to future generations).

One can add the danger of producing genetic changes in the cell material which promote early ageing in the body – of particular concern to anyone intent on preserving their youthfulness and good looks.

Only 60 per cent of the additives used in Britain have been tested at all and even then only for acute toxicity – that is, to determine whether or not they bring immediate adverse reactions to an organism ingesting them – not for teratogenicity nor for possible genetic effects.

Food additives

Food additives are not the only problems with convenience foods. Their simple nutritional worth is highly questionable. For in addition to their lack of fibre (natural fibre is largely removed in the manufacture of convenience foods), government surveys in Canada and the United States, where 80 per cent of food eaten is now factory-produced, show that in spite of the great wealth of these countries and the availability to the public of a vast variety of foods, in general people are not getting enough vitamins and minerals in their diet. This is in large part because so many of the nutrients are lost in processing.

Go green

The old adage 'Eat your greens if you want to stay healthy' is now scientific fact. Green foods fuel sustainable energy better than other kinds. And the fun of it all is that so far advanced nutritional scientists know that green works wonders but nobody is yet sure why. The chlorophyll? The enzymes? Mystery ingredients? Yes, probably, but maybe other reasons too. You will find that many of the leading-edge nutritional energy supplements have gone green – spirulina, chlorella, green barley, blue-green algae. Why? Because the nutrients they contain – from vitamins and minerals to trace elements, phytohormones, plant anti-oxidants, enzymes and as yet unidentified health-promoting factors – are not only richest in green foods but are found there in perfect balance and synergy as well as in a highly bioavailable form. Your system just laps them up. Meanwhile herbs and plant factors – facets of Nature's green world – have much to offer when it comes to energy enhancement.

Grass secrets

Some of the most useful green foods for energy are the cereal grasses. They are also some of the least known. In dried form, a teaspoon or more of dried juice of cereal grasses stirred into a glass of fresh vegetable juice can really spike it up. Taken in capsule form they can be used daily as nutritional supplements. In ancient times young cereal plants were treated with the respect they deserve. Tiny green tips of baby wheat plants were eaten as a delicacy in the Holy Land 2,000 years ago.

Young grasses are very different from the mature grains they eventually turn into and from which we make our breads and porridge. When rice, wheat, corn, oats, barley, rye, or millet are planted in good healthy soil, given plenty of rain, and then harvested at exactly the right moment, not only do they taste sweet but they are unbelievably rich in energy-giving vitamins and minerals, enzymes and growth hormones.

Chlorophyll

An energy-promoting ingredient in young cereal grasses and green foods which has been well established is chlorophyll – the stuff that makes plants green. The chlorophyll molecule is unique in the universe. It is the only substance which has the ability to convert the energy of the sun into chemical energy through the mysterious process of photosynthesis. It is thanks to the chlorophyll molecule that plants make carbohydrates out of carbon dioxide and water. All of life on earth draws its power to be from the sun's energy thanks to photosynthesis in plants. After more than 75 years of research most scientists have come to believe that it is probably the synergistic effect of the chlorophyll and the vital nutrients – both known and unknown – found together with it in the plants from which it comes that has such a positive impact on human health. These nutrients include iron, copper, calcium, magnesium, pyridoxine, folic acid and Vitamins C, B12, K and A. Wouldn't you like to tap into the sun's energy?

Pick your weeds

Some of the very best of the green foods are weeds – plants that grow wild in your garden or in fields and hedgerows in the

delicious and can be used in salads without ever imparting too heavy a green flavour to what you are making.

Replenish your minerals

Seaweeds are full of trace elements that are essential to the body – but in minute quantities. When boron, silver and sulphur (to mention only a few elements!) are not present, the body's metabolism can experience big problems. Unlike the chalk, which is added to bread to 'enrich' it with calcium, and most of the mineral supplements that you buy in pill form in stores, the minerals in green plants are organic, which means that your body can easily make use of them. Adding seaweeds such as nori, dulse, kombu, wakami and arame to your soups, salads, casseroles and other foods will gradually restore optimal levels of vital minerals and trace elements to your body.

countryside. Dandelion, nettles, ragweed and lamb's quarter are especially good sources of the minerals that our bodies lack as a result of chemical farming which has removed them from the subsoil. This is especially important when it comes to trace elements. Plants such as nettles only grow on mineral-rich soils. Weeds are deep feeders. They are capable of absorbing through their root systems all sorts of goodness that crops cultivated on depleted soils have no access to and they store up valuable nutrients in a wonderful, easily digestible balance. A handful of young nettles (they don't sting yet) is a great boon to a glass of carrot and apple juice. Lamb's quarter, a wayside spring and summer plant, is not only rich in minerals, thanks to being a particularly 'deep diver', it also tastes

Magic algae

Queen of all the green foods is spirulina. A near-microscopic form of blue-green fresh water algae, spirulina is one of the finest green foods that you will ever find. Spirulina is probably the single most important nutritional supplement you can use to support energy at the very highest level. It has a superior amino acid profile, and is unusual in that its protein is alkaline-forming in the body rather than acid-forming. This can be very important for detoxifying the system and also for helping you deal with high levels of stress, for the by-products of prolonged stress tend to be acid in character. Spirulina is also rich in vitamins E, B12, C, B1, B5 and B6 as well as beta-carotene and the minerals zinc, copper, manganese and selenium. It also contains good levels of the anti-ageing, anti-oxidant sulphur amino acid methionine and phycocyanin – a blue pigment structurally similar to beta-carotene which experiments have shown to enhance immune functions. Finally it is rich in important essential fatty acids, although very low in fat. Add from a teaspoon to a tablespoon to a glass of fresh juice or broth.

Adaptogens are ace

When it comes to long-term nutritional support and enhancement there is nothing like using the adaptogens. Adaptogens are very special plants which began to be identified 40 years ago by Russian scientists looking for ways of preventing illness and increasing people's abilities to handle stress without doing damage to the body. Their effect on the body is non-specific, enabling them to increase a person's resistance to illness, help protect from damaging elements such as chemicals and internally-manufactured wastes as well as from lifestyle pressures such as overwork or too little sleep. Adaptogens, unlike any drugs, also tend to have an ability to normalize bodily functions. In other words, they can help lower blood pressure that is too high, yet raise blood pressure in people where it is too low. Finally, adaptogens are non-toxic and they cause minimal disruptions in a body's biochemical and physiological functioning.

Since the early Russian studies of adaptogenic plants, primarily Oriental and Siberian ginseng, many more have been identified, a good number of which have long played an important role in Chinese medicine. The best way to use any adaptogen is to take it for a period of a month, then stop for two weeks and begin again. (This is one of the principles of natural medicine: since the body tends to become accustomed to whatever it is given over a long period of time, its beneficial effect can be decreased. By opting for regular periods of 'rest' one can prevent this from happening and reap an adaptogen's greatest benefits as a result.)

Stress buster

Oriental ginseng, grown in China, Korea and Japan, is probably the most studied plant of modern times. It has been praised for centuries for its rejuvenating properties, its ability to protect against illness, to enhance the body's ability to handle stress – even to prolong life. There are a couple of things to note about ginseng, however: that a lot of ginseng on the market is not very good; and that many of its effects will be lost if you take more than 2 grammes of vitamin C a day, whereas taking vitamin E will enhance its actions.

Ginseng helps to heighten immunity, improve the functions of heart and lungs, counter fatigue and balance female hormones. Always buy the best quality you can afford and take it either as a fresh root tincture (5-20 drops 1-3 times a day), as an infusion, or as a tea in which 25g (1oz) of the dried root is taken in a cup of water each day, or by chewing on a piece of the root the size of the tip of your little finger every day. Ginseng's effects are cumulative so you will need to take it for at least six to eight weeks to feel its full benefits. (See Resources on pages 253-4, for a good source.)

Get to know the super foods

Some of the best supplements you can take for maintaining sleek, shining hair, youthful skin, a well-shaped body, and the unmistakable energy that comes with vitality, are not pills at all but foods, such as liver and blackstrap molasses, that are packed full of nutritional value in beautifully balanced forms that make them easy to assimilate. They are special foods – not exactly 'wonder foods', but then not far from it either. Many of them are rich sources of the 'protectors' – such nutrients as the important anti-oxidants vitamins C and E, the B complex with all its important value to nerves, hair and skin, selenium to improve the action of vitamin E and perhaps preserve cellular youth, and the sulphur amino acids. Get to know each of the super foods and make them an everyday part of your diet, week after week, year after year. Twenty years from now, you will be glad you did.

Supplements and what they do for you

- *Blackstrap molasses: a tablespoon of blackstrap molasses supplies as much calcium as a glass of milk, as much iron as nine eggs, more potassium than any other food, and the B-complex vitamins in good balance.*
- *Eggs: the richest source of choline known, and they contain good quantities of biotin and also vitamins A, B, D, and E.*

- *Garlic: a powerful detoxicant, garlic, like onions, helps to clear fat accumulations from the blood vessels, lower cholesterol, and protect against bacterial and viral infections.*
- *Kelp and seaweed: a combination of all minerals essential for life and health in an easily assimilable form.*
- *Lecithin: high in phosphorus; lecithin works with iodine, iron, and calcium in the body to give energy to the brain, and helps in the digestion and absorption of fat.*
- *Live sprouts (see Sprouts on pages 37-41): sprouted grains and seeds are without equal anywhere as powerhouses of live food nourishment.*
- *Liver: a powerhouse of anti-stress vitamins and protein, liver from organically raised animals also contains good amounts of trace elements and minerals such as potassium, sodium, and magnesium. Liver from any other animals is to be avoided as it is likely to contain antibiotics and hormones.*
- *Pumpkin, sesame and sunflower seeds: ground in a blender or coffee grinder in equal proportions make a wonderful complete protein to sprinkle on yoghurt, salads, or fruits. They are exceptionally rich in vitamins.*
- *Wheat germ: the richest known source of vitamin E. It is also rich in magnesium, copper, manganese, calcium and phosphorus.*

- *Yoghurt: provides the B-complex vitamins, and it is richer in vitamins A and D than the milk from which it comes.*

Putting it into practice

For lasting health, you need the very best complement of nutrients you can get with foods left in as natural a state as possible. This is the basic principle of eating to support you in the best way possible. Seems complicated? Here is a rough guide to the kinds of foods to go for and those to avoid.

FOODS TO ENJOY	FOODS TO AVOID
Very lean meat, wild fish, game, poultry (preferably without the skin as this is very fatty)	Ham, sausages, bacon, smoked meats, farmed salmon, any processed meat or fish
All wholegrains such as brown rice, rye, millet, wholewheat, rolled oats, wholegrain breads, wholewheat pasta	White bread or pastry products made with sugar or bleached flour, packets of biscuits, cakes, etc
All beans and pulses	Refined sugars and sweeteners and products made from them, packaged breakfast cereals
Fruits and vegetables, unlimited amounts, eaten raw, steamed, or lightly stir-fried	Fats and oils: you will get plenty from what occurs naturally in grains, seeds and nuts, vegetables and fruits. Add a little cold-pressed extra-virgin olive oil to salads and stir-frys
Fresh fruit and vegetable juices, mineral water	Soft drinks such as squashes, colas, diet sodas, fizzy drinks. Alcohol, coffee
Dairy products such as fresh cheese, natural unsweetened low-fat yoghurt – especially goat's milk yoghurt	Processed cheeses, margarines and yoghurts
Fermented foods – natural sauerkraut for instance, or Miso	Highly processed foods and ready-made meals
Green foods like spirulina, chlorella, green barley, alfalfa and seaweeds	Preservatives, additives, artificial flavouring, colouring, stabilizers, emulsifiers

Take a look in the kitchen

What do you see on your shelves that doesn't fit in with your new principles? Spaghetti made from white flour. Use it up, then next time you buy pasta, go to a supermarket or wholefood store for the wholewheat or buckwheat variety instead. Jams and spreads? Look for the variety that contains no sugar and no preservatives. It is delicious – far nicer than the sickly sweet ordinary variety.

Get rid of the chocolate and cocoa and substitute carob powder for recipes that call for chocolate. Look for the coffee substitutes made from grains or roots. They are delicious and can be drunk with powdered skimmed milk if you like. Also stock up on herb teas and keep a jar of country honey on hand to sweeten them.

Open your fridge

What in your refrigerator doesn't belong there? Let your family eat that rich cheese if they must, but you go for the low-fat cottage cheese instead, mixing it with fruit, herbs and spices for variety. For milk you can substitute soya milk – but be careful. Most soya milk is packed in aluminium-lined cartons. The soybean, being acid, leaches aluminium from the lining and you end up with an unwelcome toxic substance in your body. If in doubt, ask.

Free-range eggs are OK. So are the lean cuts of meat, poultry, and fish. But when buying fish, make it fresh fish or go for the simple frozen fish steak or fillet without all the breading and food additives.

For ordinary yoghurt complete with its undesirable butterfat, sugar and fruit flavourings, substitute your own homemade variety (see recipe page 36). If you want it flavoured, add a teaspoonful of honey or a few raisins, a little cinnamon and a grated apple or any other kind of fresh fruit. Instead of butter to spread on bread, create your own spreads with cottage cheese and fresh or frozen fruits or herbs and vegetables. A little mustard, tomato and green pepper combined in a blender with half a cup of cottage cheese and then sprinkled with fresh chives makes a super spread you can refrigerate and use for days.

To sweeten

Instead of sugar, try honey. You can make another sweetener of dates puréed in a blender with a little water, mashed bananas and other fruits, or of raisins plumped up in water overnight and then puréed in a blender. Another useful sweetener is concentrated frozen orange juice straight from the container.

Get rid of your white flour too. Recipes calling for it should be altered to use wholewheat varieties instead. For thickening sauces you can call on wholewheat flour or cornflour. For thickening a vegetable stew try simply putting a cupful or so of the stew through a blender and then pouring it back into the pot. Seldom is any other thickener necessary. Perhaps the best way to thicken a sauce or gravy is simply to let its water slowly evaporate as it cooks.

When you head for the stove

Forget about frying things in oil. Instead, buy yourself a good non-stick frying pan and use it without fat to cook meat, scrambled eggs, pancakes and anything else that has to be fried. When you prepare chicken, stew it or braise it, removing the skin first because skin is particularly high in fat, or simply bake it and then take off the skin from your piece before you eat it.

Some of the most nourishing main dishes you can make are based on grains and such legumes as:

- beans
- black-eyed peas
- broad beans
- chick-peas
- dried peas
- lentils
- lima beans
- red, black and brown lentils
- red beans.

You can make excellent stews or casseroles using these legumes by boiling them and then adding chopped onions, carrots, celery, or other vegetables, and herbs such as:

- basil
- marjoram
- oregano
- thyme.

They add such wonderful flavour to dishes – each has its own character and own personality imprint, quite different from all the others. Buy yourself a little book on herbs (there are many on the market) and experiment to find out which herbs you particularly like.

Wholegrains, too, make delicious main dishes. Groats, or hulled whole wheat, soaked and then boiled for an hour or so, can be served hot as you would serve rice, perhaps with some onions or chopped vegetables added, or you can chill it after cooking to make a delicious salad. Brown rice can make an excellent main dish – a pilaf – when it is cooked with mushrooms.

Learn to substitute

Don't throw out all your old cookbooks, keep them and experiment by substituting other ingredients for the usual old favourites. Also look around for new cookbooks that offer low-fat recipes or wholefood cookery and adapt their recipes to suit, leaving out such ingredients as sugar and white flour where necessary. The process can be fun and you will discover a whole new world of tastes – hardly a deprivation.

What happens when you are stuck in a restaurant?

There is no great problem, particularly if the restaurant is a good one. They can easily adapt their fare to suit your wishes. I ask restaurants to do it all the time, since I eat at least a third of all my meals in them one way or another. Vegetarian restaurants are often good, as are health food restaurants. They have a lot of wholegrain products (although you sometimes have to question them about the fat added) and an excellent selection of salads, casseroles and soups. Just avoid the cheesy dishes and desserts and you're pretty safe.

What if you cheat?

Everybody cheats sometimes. So what? Provided you are following your basic principles, you can eat the occasional extra piece of meat or dish of ice cream or tablespoonful of mayonnaise with your poached salmon without doing damage. But when you do cheat, do it openly and enjoy it. Remember that the good effects of a long-term way of eating for optimum health only come by eating that way long-term. There is no way you can continue to eat pieces of processed cheese, slices of chocolate cake, or bars of chocolate without affecting your body and your psyche.

Don't worry too much at first about slip-ups; just concentrate on getting the principles right in the way you cook and eat and the kinds of food you buy. And remember that you alone are responsible for what you do – no one else. You must choose to cheat when you do, not pretend it is some kind of unavoidable compulsion. Chances are that the urge to take something which is not going to support you will fade pretty quickly when you are tolerant of yourself about slip-ups and when you get to experience how much better you look and feel by following this kind of diet.

How to keep fats out of your life

- *Choose only the leanest meats and trim all fat from them before cooking.*
- *Make your own yoghurt with non-fat dried milk.*
- *Chill all soups so that the oils float to the top and solidify. Then lift off*

the solid fat and discard it before reheating the soup to serve.
- *When you cook vegetables, steam or boil them in a very small amount of water which you can reserve for soup stock.*
- *For frying, use a non-stick pan and a very small amount of cold-pressed, extra-virgin olive oil. (You can make delicious sautéed vegetables in a few tablespoons of broth which quickly boils away, browning the vegetables and giving them a super flavour.)*
- *Make a bag of raw vegetables such as carrot sticks, green pepper slices, tomatoes, celery and cucumbers, and keep them in the refrigerator all scrubbed so you can just reach in and take some whenever you are hungry.*

Crash course menus

Here are a few more recipe suggestions to add to those in Step 2. Mix and match to increase your repertoire.

Fruit or vegetable breakfasts

Eating just fruit or raw vegetables for breakfast is a wonderful kick start to the day. They are best eaten on an empty stomach as their vitamins and minerals are absorbed into the bloodstream almost immediately.

- Eat as much as you like – up to 1 lb at a time – but make sure you chew very thoroughly.
- If you get hungry mid-morning have another piece or two of fruit.

- Steer clear of dried fruit if you are wanting to shed fat.
- Eat bananas only if they are very ripe and you feel that you need a heavier food. If eaten mid-morning, leave 45 minutes before you have your lunch.
- Forget fruit and eat only vegetables if you have a blood sugar or candida problem.
- Never over-eat – but likewise never under-eat. Have just as much as you need to feel satisfied.

You could try one of these fruit recipes (below and overleaf), which can also be eaten as a light supper or energizing lunch.

PEAR SUPREME
Slice four unpeeled pears and lay slices out in a dish. Mix together 2 tbsp runny honey, the juice of two lemons and three drops of oil of peppermint in a glass and pour over the pear. Chill in a refrigerator for 30 minutes and garnish with half a cup of fresh blackcurrants just before serving.

LIVE APPLE SAUCE
Core and chop four apples and liquidize with enough apple juice to make a medium thick sauce. Add a dash of cinnamon or nutmeg and a little honey to sweeten. Serve immediately. (Add 100g [4oz] chopped pecans for a nutritious all-fruit meal later in the day.)

TROPICAL DELIGHT
Peel, slice and deseed a papaya. Place in a bowl with two chopped, ripe bananas and a peeled and diced mango. Pour a quarter of a cup of apple juice over the fruit and serve immediately, garnished with nutmeg. (Add 2 tbsp coconut to make this Tropical delight an all-fruit lunch or supper.)

APPLE RASPBERRY FRAPPÉ

Core and chop (but don't peel) two sweet apples. Place in a blender with half a teaspoon of finely chopped lemon balm or mint, quarter of a cup of fresh raspberries, a little spring water (and a small handful of ice cubes if you want a chilled drink). Blend thoroughly.

The vegetable choice

I personally prefer fresh pressed vegetable juices for breakfast. I especially like carrot with beetroot and some green leaves of dandelion, lettuce, or spinach from the garden. More often, however, my breakfast consists of a glass of spring water into which I have stirred a heaped tablespoon of Pure Synergy which I find gives me greater support for sustained energy than anything I have ever eaten (see Resources, pages 253-4). To this I add a handful of green leaves.

If you have been used to a diet of convenience foods, however, you will probably want to begin slowly to introduce yourself to the green foods – whether this be by adding a handful of dandelion leaves, lettuce, or spinach to your breakfast drink or spooning in some powdered spirulina, green barley, or Pure Synergy. Green foods are about as far away from convenience foods as you can get and for some people they take a little getting used to. The first green drink you make you may only add a leaf or two of a green vegetable or as little as half a teaspoon of powdered green superfoods to a glass of fresh fruit or vegetable juice. Give yourself time to get used to the green flavours. As your body detoxifies you will not only find the greens easier to take – you are likely to

end up loving them. When this happens you can use as much as 100g (4oz) of green leaf herbs and vegetables in a big glass of fresh fruit or vegetable juice or a heaped tablespoon of powdered green superfoods.

Salads – lunch, dinner, anytime!

To most people a salad is a pleasant side dish used to set off a main course, but all the salads here can be used as the mainstay of an individual meal. Always choose only the freshest vegetables. Cucumbers, celery and sweet peppers should be firm to the touch. Ingredients such as carrots and broccoli should be snappy and crisp. Cut all the ingredients into bite-size pieces, except for lettuces and greens which should be left as leaves or torn into smaller shreds.

DEVIL'S DELIGHT

Put 2 tbsp olive oil, 1 tbsp lemon juice, 1 tbsp Meaux mustard, 3 tbsp chopped parsley, 4 chopped spring onions, finely ground black pepper to taste and 1 tbsp vegetable bouillon in a screw-top jar and shake. Pour dressing over salad and toss all the ingredients together.

ROOT-IS-BEST SALAD

Mix together 2 finely grated turnips, 3 finely grated parsnips, 2 grated carrots, 3 chopped spring onions, half a green pepper and half a red pepper (chopped) and 1 tbsp chopped savory or lovage. Pour the juice of 1 lemon over the salad. Toss and serve on a bed of grated Chinese leaves or lettuce. Finally, serve with grated hard-boiled egg or a good quality mayonnaise, or add some toasted rye bread.

WATERCRESS SALAD
Mix together 3 handfuls of Cos lettuce, a bunch of chopped watercress, 4 chopped spring onions, 3 large courgettes that have been grated, 2 grated carrots and 4 quartered tomatoes. Then make a light vinaigrette by blending 2 tbsp cider vinegar with 4 tbsp olive oil, half a teaspoon Meaux mustard, half a teaspoon tarragon, half a teaspoon chervil and half a teaspoon sea salt. As a finishing touch, add a small tin of tuna in brine or sprinkle over 3-4 tbsp of sunflower seeds, or serve the salad with some buckwheat or steamed brown rice.

Most of the salad recipes above are quite elaborate, but you can always make up your own to suit your individual taste, mixing salad vegetables with either tuna fish, egg, cold chicken, or red kidney beans or baked potato, toasted rye bread, rice or buckwheat cooked with spicy vegetable stock.

However, you can try a deliciously quick and simple alternative by using this classic salad formula:

take a grated root vegetable such as a carrot, parsnip or turnip and combine it with an equal amount of a leafy vegetable such as watercress, lamb's lettuce or Chinese leaf and a bulb vegetable such as red or green pepper.

Use the salad dressing of your choice taken from any of the recipes above to flavour the salad and add a protein or starch element (which you can also pick at random from any of the recipes) as you require.

Tasty toppings

The following dressings can be poured over salad or steamed vegetables to make a delicious lunch or dinner or used as a dip with crudités.

PINK TOFU DRESSING

Mix together 1 teacup of tofu, 4 tbsp tomato purée, 1 tsp Meaux mustard, half a clove finely chopped garlic and half a teaspoon vegetable bouillon powder. Add 1 tbsp chopped shallots and mix again. Serve chilled. (Will keep for five days in the fridge.)

RAW HUMMUS

Put 2 big teacups of sprouted chickpeas (sprouted for 2 or 3 days), a chopped clove of garlic, 3 tbsp tahini (sesame seed paste), the juice of three lemons, 2 tbsp tamari and enough water to thin the mixture, into a blender or food processor. Blend thoroughly, then mix in 3 tsp chopped spring onions or chives and chill. (Will keep for 2 or 3 days in the fridge.)

Souper soups

YUMMY AVOCADO AND TOMATO

Blend 6 ripe tomatoes, a ripe avocado, 2 finely chopped spring onions, quarter of a teaspoon dill seed, a pinch of cayenne,

300ml (1/2 pint) spring water, 2 tsp vegetable bouillon powder and 1 tsp kelp (optional). Add 2 finely chopped tomatoes and a raw, finely chopped green pepper. Serve hot or cold, with wholemeal bread or topped with chopped, grilled bacon.

CORN SOUP

Wash 2 fresh corn cobs and cut the kernels off the cob. Mix the corn with 300ml (1/2 pint) warm spring water, 2 chopped spring onions, 1 tsp olive oil and 1 tsp vegetable bouillon powder or sea salt. Season with tahini (sesame seed paste) if desired, and blend until creamy.

Lunch or dinner recipes

Leave at least four to five hours between lunch and dinner for efficient digestion. Do not snack unless you really can't manage without, or a meal is going to be delayed and it is more than four or five hours since you have eaten, in which case you can have a little fruit or a few raw vegetables. Eat as much as you need, depending on how hungry you are. Take your time, chew thoroughly and stop as soon as you feel you have had enough. Do not overeat.

Most of the recipes given will feed four, but you can actually eat as much as you like, as long as you listen to your appetite. All you have to remember is to chew your food slowly and thoroughly and stop eating as soon as your appetite signals that you have had enough.

Super stir-fries

These attractive and marvellously quick meals are based on the Chinese principle of frying foods very quickly in a minute quantity of light oil to preserve texture and vitamins. They are easy to prepare with whatever is to hand. Simply chop all your ingredients finely so they cook in around three minutes.

GREEN SALMON STIR-FRY

Heat 1 tbsp soya oil or extra virgin olive oil in a wok or large frying pan. Stir-fry 125g (4oz) fresh salmon cut into strips with 2 cloves of finely chopped garlic for 2 minutes. Add 225g (8oz) Chinese leaves, 225g (8oz) broccoli florets and 225g (8oz) green beans, all finely chopped, and stir-fry for a further 4 minutes. Add 1 tbsp vegetable or fish stock to the juice of 1 lemon, pour over the ingredients, stir in well and serve immediately with a watercress salad.

ULTRA-HIGH STIR-FRY

Heat 2 tsp of soya oil or olive oil in a wok or large frying pan. Stir-fry 225g (8oz) bean sprouts and a large, thinly sliced red pepper for 2 minutes. Add soy sauce to taste, season with black pepper and serve. Add thin strips of pork or chicken to create a satisfying meal, or serve with fine noodles.

MANGETOUT AND ALMOND STIR-FRY

(Replace almonds with finely sliced chicken or prawns if desired.) Top and tail 225g (8oz) of mangetout. Heat 2 tsp soya oil in a wok or large frying pan. When hot, add 50g (2oz) blanched almonds and stir-fry for three minutes. Add the mangetout, 125g (4oz) button mushrooms and soy sauce to taste. Serve immediately.

SPICY SHISH KEBAB

This is a delicious, marinated vegetable dish that you can grill or barbecue. You can serve it on a bed of brown rice, buckwheat or quinoa, that has been cooked in bouillon powder with a little chilli or tamari to make a satisfying meal. Alternatively you can cut down on the vegetables and add 450g (1lb) of lamb or chicken chunks to the marinade and cook on the skewers for a delicious protein option.

Make a marinade in a large bowl by mixing together 1 1/4 teacups of olive oil, the juice of 3 lemons, 2 tbsp finely chopped parsley, half a teaspoon ground nutmeg, 1 tbsp chopped fresh basil and 1 tsp dried oregano. Add 1 large aubergine cut into 3cm (1 1/4in) chunks, 10 halved fresh tomatoes, 24 large mushrooms, 1 red pepper, 1 green pepper, and 2 large red onions, all cut into chunks. Let it stand for three hours. Skewer the ingredients alternately and use the remaining marinade to baste them as they are grilled or barbecued.

POLENTA

This peasant dish made from corn-meal is delicious with a salad dressed in a spicy sauce.

Heat 450 ml (3/4 pint) water in a kettle. Pour the boiling water into the saucepan over a teacupful of polenta corn-meal seasoned with a little sea salt. Stir until smooth and then cook very gently until all the liquid has been absorbed. Cool and drop by the spoonful onto a lightly oiled baking sheet. Grill until brown, turning once.

The special foods

To make eating more exciting make the most of some of the more unusual ingredients available from larger supermarket branches and healthfood shops.

Sea Vegetables: available in oriental food shops and healthfood stores, sea vegetables impart a wonderful spicy flavour to soups and salads. They are also the richest natural source of organic mineral salts and are particularly beneficial for the proper functioning of the thyroid gland. You can use powdered kelp as a seasoning as you would salt and pepper. Nori – a seaweed that comes in long thin strips – is a delicious snack food, raw or toasted. The other sea vegetables such as dulse, arame and wakami need to be soaked for a few minutes in tepid water before being chopped and added to raw salads or soups.

Sprouts: bean and seed sprouts make tasty additions to just about anything. Sprouted foods supply unique combinations of enzymes, minerals and vitamins. Try alfalfa seeds, adzuki beans, mung beans, lentils, fenugreek seeds, radish seeds, buckwheat, flax, mint and red clover. You can buy them sprouted or sprout them yourself in jam jars in the kitchen.

Nuts and seeds: rich sources of body-building protein and essential fatty acids, nuts and seeds should be eaten regularly as part of your diet but never in great quantities. It's also a good idea not to combine them with any other concentrated food in the same meal. Try almonds, brazils, caraway seeds, cashews, coconut, hazelnuts, pecans, pine kernels, pumpkin seeds, sesame seeds, sunflower seeds or walnuts.

To supplement or not to supplement

Controversy rages over whether or not you need to take supplementary vitamins and minerals if you are following a good dietary lifestyle. If you do not live in a city and you eat most of your foods out of your own garden where they have been organically grown, you probably don't. If not, many experts in nutrition insist it is a wise thing to do. But how do you choose a formula? By carefully reading labels and by knowing what you are looking for. Basically there are two ways to go when it comes to food supplements – the conservative 'guard against any possible deficiencies' and the more avant-garde mega-nutrient approach which is based on the notion that nutritional supplements should be used to counter pollution, protect against ageing, and the belief that in larger quantities they may be able to increase energy levels and even promote a higher level of health. Your own requirements need to be worked out with the help of a physician knowledgeable about nutrition or a qualified nutritionist. If you decide to take supplements, you will probably find the ones you choose will lie somewhere between the two extremes.

VITAMINS AND MINERALS	CONSERVATIVE	AVANT-GARDE
Vitamin A	5000 IU	25,000 IU
Vitamin B1	25 mg	100 mg
Vitamin B2	25 mg	100 mg
Vitamin B3	50 mg	100 mg
Vitamin B5	40 mg	100 mg
Vitamin B6	40 mg	100 mg
Vitamin B12	40 mcg	100 mcg
Folic Acid	200 mcg	400 mcg
Biotin	100 mcg	500 mcg
Choline	100 mg	100 mg
Inositol	100 mg	100 mg
PABA	50 mg	100 mg
Vitamin C	500 mg	2000-10000 mg
Bioflavonoids	50 mg	00 mg
Vitamin D	300 IU	400 IU
Vitamin E	100 IU	200-1200 IU
Calcium	100 mg	500-1000 mg
Magnesium	50 mg	250-500 mg
Potassium	10 mg	50 mg
Iron	10 mg	25 mg
Copper	1 mg	1 mg
Zinc	10 mg	35 mg
Manganese	2 mg	10 mg
Molybdenum	50 mcg	75 mcg
Chromium	25 mcg	200 mcg
Selenium	25 mcg	200 mcg
Iodine	75 mcg	150 mcg
Boron	1 mcg	2 mcg

Vitamins and sources

Vitamin A
An important anti-stress vitamin, involved in all the body's repair and growth processes.
Sources: green and yellow vegetables (spinach, cabbage, carrots), eggs, fish-liver oils, liver.

B-complex vitamins
Essential for brain and nervous system health, they help keep skin healthy and hair lustrous.
Sources: raw fruits and vegetables, whole grains, liver, wheat germ, the three seeds, blackstrap molasses and brewer's yeast.

Vitamin B1 (thiamine)
Aids digestion, supports good muscle tone in the heart and alleviates fatigue.
Sources: wholegrain cereals, blackstrap molasses, liver, pork, fresh green vegetables, potatoes, brewer's yeast, beans.

Vitamin B2 (riboflavin)
Essential for healthy hair, skin, and nails, and to protect adrenal glands from stress damage.
Sources: milk, brewer's yeast, organ meats (liver and kidney), fish, nuts, green leafy vegetables and legumes, wheat germ.

Vitamin B3 (niacin)
Improves circulation, is essential to brain metabolism, and has been used in high doses to treat schizophrenia and other mental disorders.
Sources: nuts, fish, poultry, whole grain cereal, soybeans, brewer's yeast, organ meats (liver, kidney).

Vitamin B5 (pantothenic acid)
Increases the body's ability to withstand stress and decreases toxicity of many drugs, as well as protecting against radiation damage to cells.
Sources: wholegrain cereals, legumes, organ meat (liver and kidneys), eggs, brewer's yeast.

Vitamin B6 (pyridoxine)
Important to the formation of collagen and elastin, as well as DNA and RNA in the cells.
Sources: liver, fish, lean muscle meats, whole grains, bananas, peas, brown rice, brewer's yeast, sunflower seeds, milk, peanuts, hazelnuts.

Vitamin B12 (cyanocobalamin)
Plays a primary role in the synthesis of nucleic acid.
Sources: yeast, wheat germ, organ meat (liver and kidneys), meat, milk, sardines, oysters, egg yolks, cheese, salmon, herring, clams.

Biotin, choline, inositol, folic acid, and PABA
Often neglected and even left out of inexpensive commercial vitamin supplements, all five are as important for health and beauty as the rest.

Vitamin C
A natural anti-oxidant, it helps prevent colds, coronary heart disease, swollen and painful joints, and counteracts the toxic effects of drugs.
Sources: citrus fruits, tomatoes, raw green vegetables, rosehips, strawberries, potatoes, broccoli, spinach.

Bioflavonoids
Occur naturally in foods containing vitamin C and enhance its actions.
Sources: fruits, vegetables (with vitamin C).

Vitamin D
Essential for health and growth of bones.
Sources: fish liver oils, tuna, salmon, egg yolks.

Vitamin E
A natural anti-oxidant which stimulates skin cell metabolism, and is a treatment of female complaints.
Sources: wheat germ, seeds, vegetable-based fats, green leafy vegetables, whole grains.

EFAs (or vitamin F)
Helps reduce excessive cholesterol and prevent heart disease and arteriosclerosis.
Sources: grains and seeds, especially linseeds.

Vitamin K
Important for liver functions, needed for blood clotting and gives energy to cells.
Sources: yoghurt, eggs, blackstrap molasses, fish liver oil, milk.

STEP FOUR: MOVE ON UP

The joy of exercise

Exercise is good for you. We have had that message from the psychopath who taught us PT at school to the 'do it my way' fitness videos on the supermarket shelves. We know it is probably the single most important thing we can do to stay young, healthy, well toned, energetic. But do we do it?

Exercising out of guilt – facing a run, swim or cycle as a chore – is missing the point. For movement – exercise – whether running, dancing, swimming, cycling, playing sports, is far more than something you do because you are supposed to. It is the key to uncovering your true self, to linking the three aspects that make you who you are: the physical, the mental, and the spiritual.

The cultural roles imposed on us, almost from birth, too often limit our habitual assumptions about our bodies, our strengths and weaknesses, what we are capable of and what is simply impossible. We find ourselves having to fulfil others' expectations of us, or having to rely heavily on other people because we have not yet found our own strength and identity other than in the roles we dutifully fulfil. Our sense of our own bodies is often distorted or restricted, and so our sense of life and its possibilities becomes limited. Exercise can alter this dramatically.

Taken regularly over weeks and months, strenuous exercise can help you discover the truth that all things are possible. It is a discovery that can turn your life around. And if this sounds exaggerated or if this is not what some complex and tedious exercise programme has brought you in the past, then you have a whole new world of enjoyment and experience just waiting to be discovered.

Thrive on motion

The human body, which we often treat like a machine, is in reality nothing of the sort. For unlike a machine, which wears out with use, the more your body is used, the stronger, healthier and more expressive it becomes. Most people tend to ignore their body and its needs. Or they treat it in a narcissistic way – more like an object to be pushed and pummelled and pampered than a living thing. Many of the exercise programmes in books and magazines have been geared to this attitude – calisthenics designed for the self-obsessed woman who literally spends hours doing some boring movement in the hope that it will whittle away yet another inch from her right thigh (something which seems of prime importance to her although probably nobody else will ever notice). This kind of attitude to exercise really misses the point.

Body beautiful

In part, it comes as a result of our culture. A woman's body has traditionally been regarded as a passive sex symbol, beautiful in its quiescence, something separate from the woman herself. Seldom is it recognized as a simple physical expression of who you are – an inseparable part of you and, as such, a vehicle for you to communicate and respond to life, to experience pleasure and pain – a means of relating intimately with your environment. If your feelings about your body and your relationship with it are not as intimate and as at ease as this, it probably means that you are not experiencing your life fully. Neither are you using your mental and creative abilities as successfully as you could. Regular exercise can change all this. For in addition to all the well-known physical benefits, such as firm muscles and increased strength and stamina, it will also bring you a feeling of being intensely alive, along with greater self-confidence and a lively sense of play that comes from knowing you are able to meet each new challenge in your life spontaneously with openness and enthusiasm. For to be free, your body needs to move – it needs to be put through its paces, pushed near the limits of its heart and lungs, freed from the habitual day-to-day restrictions on muscles and joints that result from living the modern life, which is strongly mentally oriented.

Pleasure activities

Once you discover this for yourself, then far from being something you do quickly to get it over with – a chore you virtuously suffer through because you know it is doing you good – exercise will

become one of the most enjoyable parts of your life. American exercise enthusiast the late Dr. George Sheehan, who has done much to make people aware of the essential nature of exercise, said: 'Exercise that is not play accentuates rather than closes the split between body and spirit. Exercise that is drudgery, labour, something done only for the final result is a waste of time.' Moving freely down a country road at dawn, gliding through water, speeding down mountains covered with fine snow are things that you will do for their own sake, for the pleasure of it. The fact that these activities are good for you will become incidental to the lovely unexpected pleasure. Then you will have discovered for yourself what exercise is really all about. But let's begin at the beginning. What happens when you exercise regularly?

Heart power

A number of recent enquiries into the relationship between levels of physical activity and the incidence of coronary heart disease confirm what experts in sports medicine have been saying for years, that regular exercise significantly reduces the risk of heart attack. A ten-year study of 17,000 men between thirty-five and seventy-four, for instance, showed that those who spent less than 2,000 calories a week in exercise were 64 per cent more likely to suffer a heart attack than those who spent more (2,000 calories are burned off in two and a half hours of running a week, four hours of swimming, or three hours of squash or bicycling).

US/Irish study

In fact, there is a lot of evidence now to indicate that the benefits of regular exercise far outweigh those of dietary management in the prevention of heart diseases. A joint research project between Harvard University and Trinity Medical School in Dublin looked at 600 Irishmen between thirty and sixty who had lived in Boston for ten years or more and compared them to their brothers who still lived in Ireland. The Irishmen ate 500 more calories per day than the Americans, and they consumed double the eggs (Ah! the poor maligned egg). In fact, they averaged fourteen to eighteen eggs plus a pound of butter a week. Yet for all that, the Irish weighed on average 15 per cent less than the Americans, had lower cholesterol levels and only half the incidence of high blood pressure. The reason? They got far more exercise.

Your heart is fed by coronary arteries on its outside surface. Fats are deposited inside these arteries, they calcify and a kind of plaque forms on them which can impede the flow of blood. If the plaque builds up so much that the blood supply is cut off, then the area of the heart muscle that is nourished by that blood vessel dies. You suffer a heart attack. When this happens to a large portion of the heart muscle, it is no longer able to pump blood throughout the body and the body dies.

Heart benefits

* *Your heart is a muscle and, like any muscle, when it is put to work as it is during physical exertion and made to beat harder and faster it becomes stronger, larger, and more efficient. It is able to process more blood with each beat and doesn't have to work as hard as it did before it was strengthened.*

* *Exercise lowers the concentration of blood fats such as triglycerides so they do not form the heavy plaque in the coronary arteries which results in heart attacks.*

* *Exercise enlarges the coronary arteries which nourish your heart and increases the number of auxiliary capillaries that feed an area so that if the blood does become blocked in one coronary artery, blood from another can supply the area.*

* *Exercise lowers blood pressure.*

> • *Finally, exercise trains the heart to draw oxygen from the blood with greater efficiency; it simply works better.*

Other organs in your body, such as the liver and the lungs, are also pushed to greater efficiency with physical exertion so that the whole organism is able to maintain itself in optimum condition. When you exercise regularly and strenuously, the lungs become stronger. You also learn to breathe more deeply and soon are able to draw more oxygen from each breath you take. (While you are running, for instance, the oxygen the lungs process increases twelve-fold over the resting state.) Your nerve reflexes become brisker too. This has the effect of making your body muscles able to respond to commands more promptly and to resist stresses and strains.

Staying lean

The old injunction to eat less and exercise more is good not just for overall fitness but for weight loss itself – but probably not in the way you imagine. For burning calories is not the only way exercise helps you lose weight and stay thin, probably not even the most important way.

Many people neglect exercise because of the mistaken idea that physical activity increases the appetite. This is not true. On the contrary, studies show that people don't react to moderate physical activity with a blossoming appetite. Regular exercise, unless it is excessively strenuous, will decrease your appetite (see box, overleaf).

Exercise can also make you lose inches because it helps turn fat into energy while at the same time building muscle. Muscle tissue weighs more than fat which is why, when you begin to exercise, you find you are losing inches more rapidly than pounds. In fact, to lose weight successfully and keep it off you have to exercise. Researchers have shown that a large percentage of the weight lost by restricting calories alone is lost in muscle tissue. If you go on a slimming regimen without exercising, you will lose this muscle tissue and then later, if you regain any of the weight lost, you will regain it in fat, not in muscle. This means you will be even more flabby than you were to begin with.

Decreasing your appetite through exercise

1 You get hungry when your blood sugar level drops drastically. Regular exercise keeps blood sugar levels from fluctuating dramatically, because when muscles are regularly exercised the amount of fat they oxidize is increased and the amount of carbohydrate burned is reduced. Since your muscles are using more fat, they don't take as much sugar from the bloodstream.

2 When you exercise, peristaltic movement in the intestines increases. The transit time for foods to pass through the body and wastes to be excreted is diminished. As a result, your body actually absorbs fewer calories.

3 Exercise also raises your metabolic rate so that your cells burn oxygen more efficiently, make better use of nutrients from your diet, and more thoroughly eliminate waste products. This also probably contributes to the appetite-decreasing ability of exercise – because you are getting better nourishment value from your foods, you are inclined to eat less.

4 When you exercise, your temperature is raised. The elevation of body temperature brought about by physical activity also helps inhibit the feelings of hunger. Fat mobilized in the process supplies enough energy to inhibit the desire for food for up to forty-eight hours after strenuous physical activity, probably because your body is producing enough blood lactate to affect the metabolism of glucose in the satiety centre. And this beneficial, exercise-caused elevation of temperature, or 'thermogenesis', is not short-lived either. Your resting basal metabolic rate remains raised by as much as 10 per cent for up to forty-eight hours after strenuous activity.

Shape and weight

And just in case you have fears of exercising because you think you will develop big bulky muscles, forget it. This won't happen with the kind of rhythmic exercise such as running, swimming, bicycling, or dancing. These activities tend to form long muscles and beautiful bodies. So does most weight-bearing exercise, including good weight training, believe it or not. Only exaggerated gym training and special dietary practices such as those body builders use will bring bulk. This is unlikely for women as big muscles occur only in the presence of sufficient male hormones, and most women have far too few in their bodies to make it possible.

The body within

Each body has its own potential perfect shape. It is how your body was meant to be, regardless of how much until now it has been distorted by neglect, overweight, or habitual poor posture. I know people who have spent enormous amounts of money and undergone expensive medical treatments in an attempt to restore their bodies and their normal form. Exercise can do it better, more cheaply, and more rapidly than anything else. And this is something that occurs naturally as part of the process of the body's getting back into shape – the line of a thigh changes, an obscured waistline begins to reappear, a breast becomes firm and rounded again and loses its sag.

Cellulite

One of the things that worries women most is cellulite – the lumps and bumps that simply won't go away and are the result of toxic wastes, fat and water stored in the body. In a sedentary person these by-products of metabolism are often not fully oxidised. Instead, they get deposited in the tissues and there they stay as a kind of tissue sludge to make thighs pucker and bottoms sag. Later the flesh hardens and becomes lumpy like suet under the skin to mar the line of even the thinnest thigh. Exercise helps prevent this because it stimulates metabolism and the elimination of wastes, both from the individual cells and the body as a whole.

Energy boost

Many people don't function at anywhere near peak. They tire easily. They feel under strain and look for any escape from fatigue. When the body is under stress it produces large quantities of adrenalin, a powerful substance that is a chemical product of the sympathetic nervous system. Adrenalin is the emergency hormone that mobilizes the body for fight or flight, giving extra power when it is needed most. It increases your heartbeat, calls forth

sugar reserves, and causes your muscles to contract.

In modern life the adrenalin produced through emotional and physical stress is not all used up as often as it should be in physical movement. Instead, it is stored up in your heart and brain, and if the phenomenon known as the adrenalin build-up is great, as it often is in city dwellers, the efficiency of your heart decreases while excess adrenalin in your brain adversely affects your moods and emotions, making you feel tired, irritable, and at the end of your tether.

Exercise can call forth these stores of adrenalin, dispersing them into the system, burning the adrenalin up and so clearing away the build-up and resulting in a renewed feeling of vigour and freshness. This is why after a hard day when you feel completely exhausted or very irritable, if you can resist the temptation to collapse on the sofa and instead take exercise, you will be amazed to find that in about thirty minutes your energy returns.

Cell changes

But there are other reasons for the increase in energy that sedentary people experience when they take up regular exercise. When you exercise regularly, changes occur in the cells of your body. As muscle is built through exercise, there is an increase in the number of mitochondria, the microscopic factories in each cell where energy is produced. This creates more sites for the production of an energy-rich compound called adenosine tri-phosphate (ATP) so the quantities of this mitochondrial enzyme increase and it is produced

more rapidly than before. Recently, two researchers showed that as a result of the increase in this enzyme and others in the cells after an eight-week training programme, the cells' energy content had increased dramatically.

Mood maker

The positive effect exercise has on your mental and emotional state is well known to anyone who exercises regularly. Ask anyone who in the past couple of years has taken up running or other vigorous activity and they will tell you that it has brought enhanced mental energy and concentration plus a feeling

of heightened mental acuity. Some claim too that, as a result of taking up regular exercise, they discover a sense of willpower they didn't know they had. It seems to pervade their whole life, making it possible for them to carry through arduous tasks or bear with difficult situations without becoming discouraged even when they are fatigued.

A number of studies have also shown that vigorous exercise taken regularly every day or so alters one's mood for the better and is capable of bringing about a long-term sense of well-being. Professor Tom Curetin at the University of Illinois studied 2,500 sedentary people who took up exercise. He discovered that they quickly developed significantly greater energy and less tension than they had when the study began. Herbert de Vries at the University of Southern California looked at stress levels and muscle tension in subjects who had either been given tranquillizers or who engaged in physical exercise every day. He found that even as little activity as a fifteen-minute walk is more relaxing and efficient in dealing with stress than a course of tranquillizers. At the University of Arizona Medical School, psychologist William P. Morgan discovered that exercise significantly lowers anxiety levels.

Student studies

In an interesting study, psychiatrist John Greist experimented with depressed university students, treating some with conventional psychotherapy and others by asking them to run for a few minutes each day. After ten weeks he found that the runners felt significantly better, studied better, and did better in their exams than the conventionally treated group. Another psychiatrist, Dr. Thaddeus Kostrubala, has been treating a variety of emotional disorders successfully by getting his patients to run. He has even found it useful in severe cases of paranoid schizophrenia as well as in helping drug addicts and alcoholics to kick the habit.

Brain hormones
Scientists are not yet able to explain fully why these positive mental effects come

about from simply exercising regularly, but many believe that they are at least in part related to increased levels of noradrenalin in the brain. This is a hormone essential for the brain's messages to be transmitted along certain nerves in the body. People with high levels of noradrenalin in their blood tend to be cheerful and happy, while those who suffer from moodiness and chronic depression show low levels. Taking up regular exercise can turn the moody into the calm. Another possible contributor to the sense of well being and positive mental attitudes exercise imparts may be its ability to increase the blood supply to the brain so that brain and nerve tissue receive more oxygen, enabling the cells to function better.

Finally, exercise improves your ability to sleep deeply. Recent studies have shown that people relatively free of emotional conflicts and depression sleep deeply, while at least 85 per cent of those with psychological disturbances have long-term insomnia in one form or another.

Positive addiction

Many researchers into sports have commented on the ability regular strenuous exercise has of developing qualities of courage and character as well as greater physical stamina. Some even believe that this is because regular strenuous movement is a natural need of human beings, one for which we have been inherently programmed and one which, if denied over a period of time, leads to feelings of timidity, negativity, lack of creativity, and chronic fatigue as well as physical illness. Psychiatrist William Glasser, author of *Positive Addiction*, and others have noticed that once people become regularly involved in an exercise programme for several weeks and months, they develop a kind of addiction to it that replaces many of the negative habits they had before they started, whether it be the excessive use of alcohol, smoking, or self-deprecating thoughts and unproductive behaviour in relationships.

Elimination of negative addictions

It is certainly true that once you discover the joy of exercise, and the feelings of wellbeing and mental and physical freedom that come with it and carry over into the rest of your life, you don't want to give up. Meanwhile the negative addictions tend gradually to disappear, almost automatically. For instance, you almost never meet a swimmer or runner who smokes, although many did before they took up the sport. The whole process of eliminating negative addictions appears to be quite simple and to require no great effort of will. It is just that the pleasurable feedback you get from the habit of overeating or smoking in no way approaches the sense of exuberance and satisfaction that exercise brings. And since cigarettes interfere with running by making it harder for you to breathe, and overeating interferes by making you feel sluggish and creating more weight to carry about, you find (even subconsciously) that you no longer want to sustain your negative habits. They are just not as satisfying as the positive ones. That is something that large numbers of people have experienced,

and something that I know firsthand because it happened to me.

Fine tool for growth

We live in a culture that puts increasing emphasis on the use of human potential and individual growth. Exercise can contribute a great deal to both. In *The Complete Book of Exercise* by James Fixx, the author (himself a runner) comments on this when he says, 'Zen Buddhism, transcendental meditation, assertiveness training and similar movements are all directed at making us fulfilled human beings. Sometimes, however, they do not, and I suspect the reason in many cases is that they fail to mesh with the inescapable peculiarities and idiosyncrasies of individual character. In contrast, while running often alters a person profoundly, the changes all come from within and are, therefore, tightly integrated with the total personality'.

To some extent, of course, this is true of all athletics since they alter the mind by altering the body. Dr E.J. Kane of the University of London, who is well known for his investigation of the psychology of sport, has written, 'The way an individual characteristically perceives his body has long been held as an important factor in forming his image of himself and his general integration'.

Charisma
There is a certain charisma that surrounds some people. It is not altogether connected with the form of their body or the shape of their face (the conventional criteria for judging

someone beautiful) nor with the perfection of their skin and bone structure. It is a kind of vibrancy of personality that is reflected in their physical appearance. It is this difficult-to-describe quality that makes one woman a great beauty regardless of her age and another, with what would seem to be equal physical endowments, simply plain. Charisma has a great deal to do with body image, self-image, and overall energy level – all of which are significantly improved by frequent strenuous exercise.

Transcendental movement

In many ways the most interesting results of exercise lie in its ability to induce a state of stillness of mind and inner-peace which meditation aims at and which was, until recently, considered the exclusive province of religion and mysticism. In *The Psychic Side of Sports*, Michael Murphy and Rhea A. White record numerous phenomena that have been experienced by people during the self-imposed physical stress of exercise. Murphy and White draw strong parallels between the experiences of mystics and the descriptions athletes have given of altered states of consciousness that happened on the road or playing field. They say:

> The many reports collected show us that sport has enormous powers to sweep us beyond the ordinary sense of self, to evoke capacities that have generally been regarded as mystical, occult, or religious. This is not to say that athletes are yogis or mystics.

Very few of us approach games with a lifelong dedication and conscious aspiration for enlightenment that the mystical path requires. It is simply to recognise the similarities that exist between the two fields of activity, both in their methods and in the states of mind they both evoke.

The authors also point out that until now we have been but little aware of the parallels because athletes tend not to talk about this kind of experience, say:

> There are probably several good reasons for this, among them a wisdom about talking the spiritual side of athletics to death and a refusal to build up false expectations about it. The athletes' silence about these matters is not unlike the old Zen Buddhist attitude: if you experience illumination while chopping wood, keep chopping wood. If there is something in the act that invites ecstasy, it doesn't need an extra hype or solemn benediction. And there is a wisdom in letting people discover these experiences in their own way, for too many expectations can dampen the spontaneity and sense of release that are part of sport's glory. They can take the fun out of sports in the name of religion.

This sums up well my own feeling about exercise. It really is something you need to find out about for yourself by doing it for, in the last analysis, words are dead – only symbols used to describe what can never by conveyed by description. The reality behind them can only be experienced.

Getting started

Before beginning any exercise programme check how fit you are now. If you are over thirty-five or suffer from high blood pressure, have a family history of heart disease or are recovering from an illness, have a check-up with your doctor to be sure that what you are planning to do is safe for you.

In the past few years a number of complicated tests for cardiac and pulmonary strength have been devised by our ever more high-technology medicine. Most of them are expensive and unnecessary – that is, unless you happen to be recovering from a heart attack.

Do you need an ECG stress test first? Probably not. They are not only over-practised and overpriced, they are also by no means the perfect indicator of heart trouble that we have been led to believe. In one study of people with heart disease given an ECG stress test, as many as 62 per cent of those who showed up as abnormal in the testing did not have heart disease. In any case, if you have any doubts, it is important to have your doctor's approval before beginning a programme of any form of aerobic exercise.

Check out the warning signs:

- *Have you ever been told you have heart disease?*
- *Are you short of breath at even the mildest exertion?*
- *Do you ever have pain in your legs when you walk which goes away when you rest?*
- *Do you often have swelling in the ankles?*
- *Do you get chest pain when you perform any strenuous activity?*

If you have none of these warning signs, there is a simple way to check yourself out for fitness.

Take a walk

Walk a brisk two miles in thirty minutes. How do you feel afterwards? Do you have any nausea or dizziness? No? Then, so long as you have no medical condition that indicates caution, you are certainly fit enough to start at the bottom of a slow, graded programme for runners. If, however, you have any difficulties on the walk, then keep up this two-mile walk every day until such time as you can do it easily in the half hour before you start running (you will be surprised at how rapidly your condition improves even from daily walking). Don't

get discouraged, just keep things up and you will soon be running.

Check your pulse

Put the tips of the first three fingers of your right hand against the artery of the inside edge of your wrist, count the number of beats you get in fifteen seconds, and then multiply by four. Most exercise physiologists who work with weight control suggest that you walk, or carry out whatever other activity you have chosen, at 70-85 per cent of your maximum heart rate (MHR), but some recent studies suggest that exercising at as little as 45 per cent of MHR will do the trick nicely.

Work out your maximum heart rate

To get your maximum heart rate, subtract your age from 220. So if you are 36 years old your MHR would be 220 less 36, which equals 184. From this figure you can calculate your ideal aerobic range by multiplying that number by 0.45 for the low end and 0.85 for the high. Aim for somewhere in the middle unless you are very unfit, in which case go for the lower figure.

After a few weeks you will find you are able to exert yourself much more and still your pulse will remain within the safe range. Besides being sure the level of exertion you are making is safe for you, the main reason for taking your pulse is to discover how much effort you need to make to continue to improve your level of fitness.

What kind of exercise do you need?

There are four different kinds of exercise:

- **aerobic**
- **anaerobic**
- **isometric**
- **isotonic.**

Each can be useful but probably the most beneficial for overall health and vitality – if you only do one kind – is aerobic. The name 'aerobic' was popularized by Kenneth and Mildred Cooper in their books *Aerobics* and *Aerobics for Women*. It means 'living, acting, or occurring in the presence of oxygen'. What makes aerobic activities different from all other kinds of exercise is that they demand your body's efficient use of oxygen throughout the whole time you are doing them.

Aerobic movement

Oxygen is the ignition factor in the burning of energy from the foods you eat. A good supply is always necessary for your body's metabolic processes to take place efficiently. When your cells (particularly the cells of your brain) have an adequate supply, you feel well, have stamina, and don't tire easily. If you tend to feel tired often, get depressed easily, or have trouble thinking clearly, it is likely that your body is not getting all the oxygen you need. In short, you are physically unfit.

Unfit people find themselves breathless after climbing stairs, lack concentration when they get involved in a demanding mental task, and are often too weary in the evening to do anything but plonk themselves in front of a television set.

They also tend to rely on stimulants or depressants such as alcohol to relax or to keep going.

Taking aerobic exercise changes all that. Any sustained rhythmic movement that puts constant demand on your heart, raising your pulse rate to between 120 and 160 beats a minute, and continues to develop your lung capacity will bring about a number of important changes in your body.

Body changes

1 Tone your muscles and improve your circulation.

2 Increase the number and the size of the blood vessels that carry blood from your heart all over the body so you will have better transport of oxygen.

3 Strengthen your chest wall, making you breathe more easily, as air will come in and out of your lungs with less effort. Soon your body will become capable of taking in far more oxygen than it could before. This oxygen will generate energy for sustaining mental and physical effort.

4 Make your bones, joints, and ligaments stronger so they have a natural resistance to injury.

5 Increase the level of enzymes and energy-rich compounds in your body. You will be better able to assimilate and make use of nutrients from your foods.

6 Make your body more efficient. And as the efficiency of your heart increases and you pump more blood with each beat, your basic pulse rate will decline.

Aerobic activities include:

- long-distance running
- steady swimming
- bicycling
- rowing
- cross-country skiing
- long, brisk walks.

Anaerobics

Anaerobic exercise, such as running a hundred-yard dash or gymnastics, involves a high level of effort sustained over only a short period of time. The effort is such that during the activity you run into 'oxygen debt' which means that you use up more oxygen than you take in. This is the opposite of an aerobic activity where, once you are relatively fit, you are able to process oxygen efficiently enough to continue running or bicycling for hours without incurring any oxygen debt. Anaerobic activities can be useful for developing muscle tone and power and for training your body to produce great bursts of strength and movement, but an anaerobic activity cannot be sustained long enough to be of real value to your lungs and heart and so to overall fitness.

Isometrics

Isometric exercises are those you do without any actual movement in your joints. They are muscle-tensing exercises. For instance, try putting your palm against the wall and pushing hard.

Nothing happens in terms of body movement, although the muscles of your arm become very tense. All isometric exercises are based on the idea that you push or pull against objects that are immovable. Tensing muscles in this way brings about an increase in their size in the same way that weight lifting does, for whenever a muscle is put under strain it gradually increases in endurance and bulk. Isometric exercises are often 'sold' to women on the grounds that they are effortless – the lazy way to exercise. In fact, they do require some energy to perform but nowhere near enough to be useful in building overall fitness. They have a disadvantage, however, for contracting muscles in this static way can cause blood pressure to rise. In anyone with a tendency to heart disease this can be dangerous.

Isotonics

Isotonic exercises such as calisthenics, yoga, dynamic weight lifting, ballet bar work, and many sports are more demanding. They call for real movement in muscles and joints and the rhythmic lengthening and shortening of your muscles. For instance, with weight lifting, when you bend your elbows to raise the weight to shoulder level, your biceps contract as the triceps at the back of your upper arm lengthen. Then when you straighten out your arms again, lowering the weight, your triceps contract and the biceps are lengthened. This kind of repeated lengthening and shortening of antagonistic muscles helps you develop muscle strength and tone and freedom of movement in your joints. It is also useful in correcting a muscle area, such as the abdomen or the upper leg, that has become flaccid and flabby.

Some isotonics, such as yoga or stretching exercises, are also important for developing flexibility and suppleness.

The best total exercise programme you can devise for yourself involves some form of isotonics, such as weight training or the stretching exercises described later, done for at least fifteen minutes three times a week, and thirty minutes of aerobics activity, also done at least three times a week. You can alternate doing aerobics one day and isotonics the next if you like. Unless you are determined to become an athlete and the particular sport you have chosen demands work in isometrics or anaerobics, you need not worry about them. Your aerobic activity will build overall fitness, improve your mental and emotional state, and give you energy. Isotonic stretching will give you grace and suppleness and will fill in any muscle-toning gaps your aerobic activity leaves, as well as improving the extensibility of your muscles and tendons. You are after freedom of movement and endurance, not building big muscles.

Extra help for exercise

• *Find a picture of your chosen activity or an inspiring quotation (I like 'Just Do It' in big letters) and pin it up on your bathroom mirror, your refrigerator and your desk for encouragement.*
• *Before you go to bed at night, give yourself a pep talk about your activity the following day and envisage yourself enjoying it.*

• *Lay your exercise clothes out ready for the next day. Many runners agree that the hardest part of a morning run is putting their shoes on and stepping out of the door. After that it's easy.*
• *Make a deal with a good friend to get fit together. Sharing the challenge of reclaiming body power with a friend is much more fun. (It can also give you a chance to moan and sympathize over aches and pains.)*
• *If you choose walking or running as your activity, cajole, borrow or buy a dog to accompany you. Dogs seem to have endless enthusiasm for walks and runs (however bad the weather).*
• *Experiment with different kinds of exercise to find which you enjoy most. Enjoyment is an important factor in making exercise work for you.*
• *Make a note of how you feel on the days you don't take exercise as well as those on which you do, then compare them.*
• *Hunt for a good coach or teacher – especially if you choose to work out at a gym or take an exercise class. The right one can provide encouragement and motivation.*
• *Let yourself daydream about how your body will change for the better in the next few months – the imagination is a potent tool in your quest for more energy.*

Choose the right activity for you. If you love company then solitary jogging down a country lane may suit you less than joining a gym or taking a dance class with friends. If you are shy and easily discouraged by the idea of exercising in public you might be happiest working out with an exercise video in your home.

What sports are best?

There have been several studies of the physiology of exercise, and now it is generally agreed that the best sorts of overall fitness are aerobic activities:

- **running**
- **swimming**
- **rowing**
- **bicycling.**

You can add to that list cross-country skiing, dancing (providing you do enough of it and really get your heart beating and lungs working). Walking is great too if you walk fast and far enough and if you go over hilly ground as well as over flat terrain. For only these activities offer the kind of steady, sustained movement that builds muscle strength, increases the flexibility of joints, and also fortifies the heart and lungs. You may be able to exert yourself by playing tennis or squash or golf, but how well depends on how you play the game and with whom you play. You can win sets of tennis without moving more than a few feet from one place or you can be all over the court and totally exhaust yourself.

Whatever exercise you choose should fulfil the following criteria:

- *It should be sustained and non-stop.*
- *It should last at least 30 minutes.*
- *It must keep your heart beating at 70-85% of its maximum capacity during the time you are exercising. Exercising harder than this can lower energy levels. If you want to get fitter faster, exercise longer not harder.*
- *It should be done at least four times a week.*

Bounce into shape

Rebounding is the perfect solution for anyone who wants to exercise at home, no matter what their fitness level.

Unlike many in-the-home exercise options, rebounding has a particularly high continued use success rate. In case you are unfamiliar with the term, it means bouncing up and down on a mini-trampoline. Apart from being fun in the most natural child-like way, rebounding has some extraordinary health benefits thanks to the forces of gravity exerted on you as you bounce. At the top of each bounce – for a split-second – gravity is non-existent. You experience weightlessness like an astronaut in space. At the bottom of a bounce, gravity is increased by two to three times its normal force. This rhythmic pressure on each of your body's cells stimulates the lymphatic system to eliminate stored wastes – the type of wastes which incidentally are responsible for cellulite. Rebounding is not only great for newcomers to exercise, but is also often used by athletes as part of their training programme – particularly to repair and rebuild muscles after an injury.

Begin bouncing gently so that your heels barely leave the ground. If you feel unsteady, use the back of a chair to support yourself with one arm as you bounce. You might like to bounce to music or even while watching your favourite television programme. As an alternative to bouncing with both feet together, try jogging from one foot to the other. Begin with ten to fifteen minutes a day and work up to half an hour or so as your strength increases. You can also do various exercises on the rebounder to work the muscles throughout your body.

Take to the water

Swimming is one of the best of all the aerobic activities to start with, particularly if you're very much overweight. The support the water gives your body makes you able to put all your effort into participating in the movement, instead of having to direct some at just keeping yourself erect as you do in running. Swimming is also a wonderful way to build beautiful muscles if you are very thin, or conversely to pare down and firm up muscles if you are flabby. This is because swimming develops long muscles in the legs and back, gradually reshaping and reforming any body that has lost its shape.

If you are going to take up swimming, arrange things so you can do it regularly and without fail at least three times a week. The fitness that comes with aerobic exercise is built gradually and depends on consistency. No amount of weekend heroics will accomplish it.

You will need to set yourself a goal – say, at first fifteen minutes of constant swimming from one end of a pool to the other without stopping – and stick to it. If you are troubled by chlorine in public pools, then buy yourself a small pair of racer's goggles. They will keep your eyes protected. Begin slowly. Swim a couple of laps and then stop and, using a watch with a second hand (which a friend can keep for you or which you can leave at the side of the pool), take your pulse.

Work vs effort

It is important to understand the difference between work and effort. Two people may swim a mile in sixteen minutes and do equal work, but if one raises his heartbeat by 60 per cent over what it was in a resting state and the other only by 30 per cent, then their effort has been different. Effort in this sense indicates the effort your heart is making in response to the work your body is doing. In order to increase your level of fitness, you have to keep up a certain level of effort for a specific period of time. The amount of work you will have to do to achieve this, the distance you will have to cover, and the speed at which you will have to swim (or run, walk, dance, or whatever) will constantly alter as you get fitter.

Pulse range

There has recently been a lot of medical research done to find the ideal range of effort. This is measured by the heartbeat rate during exercise. As usual, opinions vary, but there is a pretty good consensus that you need to exercise within a pulse range where your heartbeat rate is between 75 and 80 per cent higher than in its resting state and then to sustain this pulse rate for thirty minutes three times a week.

Taking your pulse can seem a nuisance at first, but it is worthwhile until you get used to exercise and get to know by the feel of things how much effort you are making. After a few weeks you will never need to consult the second hand of a watch again. You will simply know.

Regular breathing

Begin gently. Swim for fifteen minutes

the first three or four times. Then you can gradually add a couple of minutes each week until you work up to thirty minutes, three times a week. At this level, provided you monitor your effort by taking your pulse occasionally, you can be assured of gradually and steadily building fitness. Then if you want to do more for fun, that is up to you. However much you do, watch your breathing while you swim. It is important to breathe regularly, for oxygen is what gives you the power to sustain the physical effort you are making. This is what aerobic fitness is all about.

Buy a bicycle

The same basic principles apply to bicycling. It, too, is an excellent endurance sport that promotes co-ordination and muscle strength, particularly in the lower half of your body. The other good thing about bicycling is that it gives you a feeling of getting good return on energy expended, as a bicycle will carry you a lot farther than a run or swim with the same effort. Cycle in the early morning or on country lanes, then you will be able to keep up a steady pace without having to stop for signals, cars, or pedestrians, and the air is free from dust and fumes. You can take your pulse after, say, five minutes of bicycling, to ensure that you are making the right effort. And you can start off with fifteen minutes' bicycling and then work up to half an hour or more three times a week. Make sure that the seat and the handlebars on your bicycle are the right height for you or you can end up with back strain. And be sure to look after your bicycle well so it offers little

resistance, for although working against unnecessary resistance from a machine may be physically beneficial when you are using an indoor bicycle exerciser, it can be an awful bore and very discouraging. Bicycling is a particularly good sport to take up if you have a family, as children delight in going on bicycle outings. An ideal Sunday afternoon activity is to go on a fifteen or even twenty-mile bike ride together, especially if there is a delicious picnic in the middle.

Walk to fitness

Probably the most neglected of all activities that can build health and fitness, walking can be tremendously enjoyable no matter what your physical condition. In many ways it is the best form of aerobic exercise for most people. The rewards are many, varied, and immediate. There are the delights of feeling fresh, pure air entering your body, the tingle of a cold morning, the wind and rain on your face.

As with most physical activities, the rewards of walking are directly related to the effort you make doing it and to the spirit in which you do it. A gentle stroll without purpose or a grudging constitutional with the dog will do little for you. But taking a brisk walk with good will and a sense of purpose while breathing deeply will put a glow on your skin and help improve your posture, the condition of your muscles all over, and your circulation.

If you choose walking as an aerobic activity, make a date with yourself to spend thirty minutes a day at it.

What to wear
Wear something comfortable and unrestricting. But you do need a good pair of sturdy shoes. They should be stout so that they give you a feeling of security and reliability over even the roughest and wettest ground; thick rubber soles are particularly good because they both grip and act as shock absorbers. Natural fibre socks are better than the synthetic because they are more absorbent. You needn't be deterred by the weather either; walking in the rain, provided you are well dressed for it, can be a delight. A lightweight wind- and water-proof jacket is a great help.

Start off walking briskly – fast enough so that you will be a little out of breath. Feel the rhythmic movement of your body and the way your legs swing freely from your hips. Get into the swing of it all, then after the first week or two increase the time you spend to forty-five minutes and vary your pace. Try not to walk over flat ground all the time – the hills and valleys, the ups and down are what bring real physical rewards.

Walking regularly can bring fitness slowly but surely, without ever taking a pulse or timing anything. A walker can measure her progress by self-observation alone. Ask yourself how you feel and compare your performance walking with that of six weeks or a few months earlier. You will notice that very soon you are walking faster and farther. More important, you are getting ever greater pleasure from the time you spend on the roads and pathways so that before long you won't want to let anything interfere with your daily exercise. You will also probably notice that work has become less of a burden for you, perhaps that you sleep better, think more clearly, and feel more emotionally balanced.

A good thing about walking is that no matter where you are living or visiting, there is always somewhere interesting to go. In town there are always parks and recreation areas, and even industrial areas can be fascinating in the early mornings or late evenings when the air is relatively free of pollution.

Run to freedom

Ideal for anyone who is keen to experience the high-energy benefits of regular exercise quickly. Running is perhaps the most adaptable and practical of all forms of exercise. For anyone who travels often it can be ideal. Running shoes, shorts, a T-shirt and running bra (plus a thin waterproof top and Walkman if you like) take up minimal space in a suitcase. You can also run almost any time and anywhere. Begin by making a circuit for yourself of about a mile. Start out slowly and jog as far as you can. Don't push yourself so hard that you are breathless. At the right pace you should still be able to carry on a conversation as you jog. If you do find you get out of breath, alternate running with walking. Above all be patient. After a week or two, see if you can run the whole mile. When this becomes easy, increase your distance until you can run 2 or 3 miles. If you are really ambitious you might like to try running a marathon. Experts claim that once you can run for 45 minutes you can begin to train for one.

Listen to yourself

The best way to use a graded programme like the one opposite is with flexibility, always adapting it to your own individual needs and level of fitness. If in the early stages you find weeks one, two, and three are very easy for you, then you can try a higher level instead.

So long as your pulse rate when you are running lies within a safe range, what you are doing is right for you. Aim to spend thirty minutes at least three times a week on the road. By all means do more if you want, but to build fitness you need short periods of exercise, half an hour at a time, done often instead of one long period of 1 1/2 hours a week. If, like me, you find you want to run every day, try leaving off Sundays each week. This gives your muscles a chance to restore themselves and to build up their store of glucose again. You will probably find, as many runners do, that your running will be better for your day of rest.

Getting into gear

It doesn't matter what you wear to run, provided it gives you freedom of movement and doesn't inhibit the elimination of perspiration. Clothes made from natural fibres such as cotton and wool, which 'breathe' are much better than those made of synthetics. In summer you probably won't need more than a pair of shorts and a cotton vest or T-shirt. Bare legs give you a sense of freedom when you run and help keep you cool. In winter (oh yes, runners tend to run all year round in all kinds of weather including rain and snow) you will need something warmer – a fleecy lined cotton sweat suit and light sweater are fine. You can add a light waterproof jacket or parka when it rains. When the weather is particularly cold you may need a wool cap or a scarf tied around your head to protect your ears. For night running, wear white or light colours, preferably with reflectors, so you can easily be spotted by cars.

A graded running programme

There are a number of good graded programmes you can follow in some of the good books on exercise: Mildred and Kenneth Cooper's Aerobics for Women; James Fixx's The Complete Book of Running, or Dr Joan Ullyot's Women's Running for instance, or you can try the programme outlined below, which a friend who is a physical training expert, and another friend – a sports medical man – helped me put together.

First week
Take a brisk walk of one mile, breaking into 50- or 100-yard jogs when you feel like it. Walk at a steady pace in between the jogs but never force yourself. Fitness is gained by steady work. You only end up with injuries and anguish when you push too hard. Take a look around you and enjoy your surroundings. Explore the feeling of your body in motion and discover what it feels like to be you.

Second week
Walk/jog a mile, alternating about 100 strides of each at a time.

Third week
Walk/jog 1 1/2 miles, increasing your jogging intervals to 150 strides with 100 strides of walking in between.

Fourth week
Jog for a while at any speed that is comfortable for you. If you find you can't make it all the way without stopping to walk, don't worry. However, by now you should be able safely to tolerate a little discomfort. It soon passes.

Fifth week
Run one mile in less than nine minutes.

Sixth week
Jog/run 1 1/2 miles or more. By now you will be over the hump and beginning to feel all the benefits of your perseverance. You will have started to be aware of your body and to be able to listen to what it is telling you. You will no longer need to monitor your pulse. Now you can even begin to move differently, varying your pace as you go, for your stamina and willpower have increased. You can also start to push yourself a little bit further some days and to let yourself go more slowly than normal if you are feeling a bit low. You will find that you can trust your sense of things.

Onto the fifteenth week
Play about with your speed and distance, increasing your distance when you want. Try to alternate a long run – say four or five miles – with a short run of one or two the next day. By the end of six months of running you will be able to run easily and steadily for from half an hour to an hour, covering between three and nine miles.

Running shoes

Running shoes need to be specially designed to absorb the powerful impact of your feet hitting the road 1,600 times with every mile you cover. They are not cheap but they are an excellent investment, probably the best you've ever made for fitness – provided, of course, you continue to use them. They should not be too flexible. They should be without studs and they need to have a high-density sole. Some of the best soles are made in microcellular rubber. Some soles on running shoes extend up the toe and heel in order to take the rocking motion from heel to toe that running brings. A good pair of running shoes enables you to run on roads without risking shin splints or the injuries to your knees or Achilles tendons that are easy to come by when you wear just an old pair of tennis shoes. The padded instep in your shoes is also useful in absorbing the shock of each step on a hard pavement.

When choosing a pair of running shoes, take your time and be sure they fit properly. There should be enough room inside for your toes to move about. Your heel should be slightly raised as this will help protect you from injuring your Achilles tendon, which can be very painful if you overstretch it. The shoe should lace up with five or six pairs of holes so that when it is tied it will hug your foot comfortably. Ideally, your training shoes should fit so well – they should be comfortable but firm – that they begin to feel as though they are a part of your feet while you are out and about on the road.

Training shoes come in different materials. Some older styles are light leather, which can be very good indeed. The newer designs are in nylon, which dries faster and is easier to care for. Plastic and artificial leathers are not very good because they make your feet sweat.

Socks

Socks are useful because they keep your feet and your shoes dry inside and protect your shoes from odour. I like the bobble socks that don't even come up to the ankle, the kind women tennis players often wear.

The warm-up

Before you start running as with all sports, you need your muscles warmed up, your blood flowing in your veins, and your metabolic rate up. It is not a good idea to get straight out of bed and run. When you have been inactive and your muscles are stiff or cold you are far more likely to pull a muscle or injure a joint. A few exercises or simply moving about the house briskly for five or ten minutes will get your body ready for your run.

Six stretching and firming exercises for runners

Take five minutes or so to do them.

Calf muscles and Achilles tendons: stand about a yard from a tree or wall. Then with your feet flat on the ground, lean into it until the backs of your legs hurt a little. Hold the position for ten seconds and then relax. Do this five or six times.

Tight hamstrings at the back of your legs: keeping your legs straight, put one heel up onto a table or windowsill at waist height (lower, if you cannot reach that high). Now lower your head down to your knee until you feel the strain. Stay in this position for ten seconds, holding on to your leg or foot to steady yourself. Repeat five or six times.

Lower back and hamstrings: lying on your back, arms at your sides, keeping your legs straight bring them up over your head. Now lower them as far as possible above your head, touching the floor if you can. Hold for ten seconds, relax, and then repeat five or six times.

Shin muscles: sitting on the edge of a table, hold a 5-lb weight on the front part of your foot just back from the toes. (You can use an empty paint tin full of stones.) Slowly raise your toes. Keep them there for a few seconds and lower. Repeat several times with each foot until you tire.

Quadriceps: sit on the table and hang the same weight over the toes of one foot so the tin rests on the floor and you don't stretch the knee ligaments. Now straighten your knee, raising the weight. Hold for a few seconds and then lower. Repeat five or six times with each leg.

Tummy muscles: do twenty or more stomach-crunches with your knees bent and your feet flat on the floor, raising your body no more than a foot off the floor. You can either clasp your hands behind your head or stretch out your arms over your head, but do each stomach-crunch by keeping your chin in and curling your body up from the floor to give the muscles of your abdomen as much work as possible.

If you don't have time to go through the whole exercise routine before a run (or, like me, you get impatient sometimes and would rather be on the road), then start your run very slowly and for the first five minutes or so keep it at a slow, steady jog until your heart and lungs get going and your muscles start to warm up. This warm-up is terribly important if you are to protect yourself against injury. And the older you are the more important it becomes. In a few people a condition known as myocardial ischemia, where not enough blood gets to the heart, can occur if they plunge into vigorous exercise without sufficient warm-up. Finally, never run after a meal, a hot bath, or if you are really cold.

The cool-down

Just as important as beginning slowly is how you end your exercise. When muscles have been very active they need help to cool off gradually.

During the cool-down you can shake your legs occasionally, do some stretching exercises if you like, such as bending over from the hips, or simply shuffle along at a slow walk for a while. You will probably find, when you first start exercising, that you have a few aches and pains in your legs, hip joints, or ankles because your muscles are not yet in condition. Muscle ache passes far more quickly than you would think. In a few days you should not have to deal with it any more.

Plan your schedule

Make an exercise schedule for the coming week. Ideally try to include at least three 30 minute sessions of your activity. Begin with 20 minutes and work up to 45 or more. Make time for your exercise by planning in advance.

Getting fit, like getting anywhere, means knowing where you are setting out from. Check your pulse to work out your present fitness level and establish your ideal work-out range. Write this down. Be sure to exercise at this level for optimal rewards. In a month's time you can take your pulse again in order to mark your improvement, and to keep an eye on exercising within your ideal aerobic range.

Set your goal

Make a reasonable goal for yourself and write it under your schedule. Don't invite failure by being unrealistic. Your goal should be a challenge but not an impossibility. When you achieve your first goal, set yourself a new one.

Mark your progress

Keep an exercise log in your workbook to record your progress. Make a note of anything you notice in relation to your exercise session. Not only will this make you conscious of your progress but it will give you the courage and incentive to keep going when you encounter resistance.

Just do it

In the beginning most of us are resistant to exercise. We sometimes feel we have to kick-start ourselves into action and it's not easy. But just as soon as you start to experience some of the benefits of exercise, like having more energy and feeling great about yourself, they will help spur you on. If you continue long enough (and 'long enough' is different

for everyone) one magical day you will find you are actually beginning to enjoy yourself. Then, instead of dreading the next exercise session and finding excuses not to do it, you look forward to it. Of course this does not make you immune to resistance – or excuses.

Get to know your muscles

The cause of all excess tension lies in restricted muscles. It is impossible to be emotionally tense or anxious if your muscles are completely relaxed. Learning to release tension through slow, sustained stretching makes true freedom of movement possible. Muscles are elastic things, able both to contract and to stretch up to one and a half times their relaxed length.

Muscles can be:

- *Contracted, which means it is in the act of causing movement in the skeleton.*
- *In tone, which is in the normal state of an awake muscle where its power is latent but the muscle is ready instantly to contract or stretch as soon as a nerve impulse to do so reaches it.*
- *Relaxed, which should only happen when you are asleep.*
- *Fully stretched.*

In a truly fit body the muscles are capable of moving from any one of these states to either of the others quickly and without strain. In most of us they are not, simply because we do not use them fully so they have become neglected.

Sensuous stretching

Stretching needs to be done slowly and gently. You simply sink into a posture and then gradually let go, allowing gravity to pull as it will. There is a wonderful sensuous feeling about doing this in the different positions, which will leave you feeling not only physically more alive and mentally clear but also emotionally calm and still, much as meditation techniques do.

Breathe normally

It is important to breathe normally while you do the postures and to let yourself relax as completely as you can in each one. The more you practice the postures the easier this becomes. If at first you are not fully relaxed, you may be inclined to hold your breath and to breathe spasmodically. Don't. Neither should you impose any artificial way of breathing on yourself.

When you first begin the postures you may find you feel stiffness or soreness in your muscles as they start to let go of their stored tension. This is a good sign that they are giving up tension. To release stiffness you first need to be aware of it, and it is normal for the awakening process to bring with it mild sensations of pain. But the pain is not the pain of doing something wrong. It is a good ache that comes from letting go. It is also something you are completely in control of in each posture. You can go only as far as is comfortable for you. Then, as your muscles let go a little more, you will find that you can go a little further each time. But never strain. Strain or effort to force anything will only work against the effectiveness of the postures.

What happens when you stretch?

When you stretch a particular muscle you squeeze the blood (especially the veinous blood) out of it. This blood does not depend on the beat of the heart for its circulation. It depends on the contraction and relaxation of muscles that, when they move, compress the veins and capillaries, pushing the blood back in the direction of the heart. Only by this periodic contraction and expansion will any muscle be properly cleansed of the cellular wastes that accumulate in it and only then will it get the circulation of blood needed to bring nutrients and oxygen in optimum quantities to the cells. For as soon as the stretch is finished and your muscle springs back to its normal size, it becomes automatically bathed in fresh blood which cleanses and nourishes it. This is one of the reasons stretching brings with it a wonderful sense of renewal to the whole body.

While dynamic, aerobic exercise brings great benefit to your heart and lungs, tones many of the muscles in your body, and brings you greater vitality, the slow, deliberate stretching of specific muscle groups will give you extraordinary grace, improve the flexibility of your joints, and eliminate muscle tension, which is so limiting not only to your physical wellbeing but also to your personal sense of being free.

To begin

Choose three postures at a time, spending fifteen to twenty minutes a day doing them three to five times a week. You can do them any time, but not immediately before bed or you may feel so invigorated by them that you won't want to sleep. Doing three postures one day and another three the next and so on, you will soon learn them and may find the results and sense of enjoyment they bring give you a desire to spend more time on them. But you should never exceed thirty minutes a day. You don't need more than that and it is far better to do less and have them as something you look forward to the next time than to glut yourself on them one day and skip them when the following session rolls around. Don't rush, go easy and learn to let gravity work for you. The postures are particularly useful when you are tired from work, in the early evening, and are most enjoyable when done with another person or with children. But there is never any sense of competition about how far you can go compared to someone else. Everyone is different and you are only working against yourself. What matters is the continuous releasing of tightness.

Stretching postures

Hip bends for grace

The rewards: This posture eases tension in your hamstring muscles at the backs of your legs, and lengthens the back. Because it reverses the blood flow to the head, it is also good for your skin, face muscles and overall circulation as it brings a feeling of being revitalized.

Here's how: Standing straight, facing a wall, feet a few inches apart and parallel, bend your knees and bend at the hips, dropping your head and back down against the wall, letting your face go limp and your hands and arms hang free in front of you. Now straighten your legs, slowly coming back up with your back against the wall. Rest in this position for one minute (you can gradually work up to four as you get used to it). As a variation, bend one leg for thirty seconds to one minute to give added stretch to the hamstrings of the other leg. With practice, your trunk will gradually go lower and lower with your legs straight. This promotes a free movement at the hip joints for a more beautiful walk and also lengthens the spine.

Wall splits for awareness

The rewards: This passive exercise will make you aware of tensions you never dreamed existed. Practising it regularly can improve your stride, release tensions in your pelvis that interfere with sexual response, and give inner thighs the workout they need to keep them smooth and sleek. It is also excellent for learning how to let gravity work for you instead of expending energy working against it.

Here's how: Sit parallel to a wall with your legs extending out in front of you and one hip right up against the wall. Now lie down, swinging both legs up in an arc along the wall as you turn your body around so that you end up at right angles to the wall with your legs in a 'V' shape. Let your legs fall gently open with the force of gravity to their maximum width. They should be flush against the wall at all times and with your ankles flexed so your feet form almost a right angle with your legs. Relax and let go. You will feel an ache just at the inside of your thigh caused by excess habitual tension. Just be aware of it. You'll find the ache will change in character until it becomes not unpleasant as your muscles start to let go. Gradually your legs will open more and more. Don't force anything – just let it happen. Stay in this position for three minutes with your eyes closed, being quietly aware of the feelings in your body.

Lean-tos for freedom

The rewards: This movement opens the chest cavity, improving your breathing. It can even widen the breadth of your emotional response, bringing you a new sense of freedom all over. It also relieves lower back tension, which can result in menstrual pains, and increases the flexibility of your arms at the shoulders.

Here's how: Standing three to four feet from a wall, arms at shoulder width, place your hands against the wall two feet above your head. Lean on your hands, letting your head and neck drop forward with the pull of gravity and allowing your chest to sink downward so that your back is bowed.

Time: no more than half a minute in this position. Repeat three times.

Stretch back for length

The rewards: This posture eliminates excess tension in shoulders, throat, and pectorals, and is excellent for combating a double chin as well. It brings with it a remarkable sensation of loosening and freedom in the upper half of your body.

Here's how: Using a low table over which you have placed a folded blanket, push the table near a wall and then lie down on your back on it so that your shoulders come just to the edge and your legs are in a relaxed position with your feet flat against the wall. Your head needs to hang loosely over the edge (you will find that you continually have to remind yourself to let go of your head instead of trying to support it). Now interlock your fingers or loosely hold a small stick and try to keep your arms straight as they are extended over your head and allowed to drop with the force of gravity. On coming up out of this position, come up slowly and roll over to one side before lifting yourself.

Time: two minutes, then gradually increase to four.

The neck stretch for beautiful carriage

The rewards: This challenging exercise releases the tension in your neck and promotes a fresh flow of blood to your head. It also lengthens the whole back, relaxes the muscles in your eyes, relieving eye strain, and can also help headache and migraine sufferers by eliminating tension in the neck and shoulders that spurs the pain. It is also great for relaxing if you ordinarily have trouble sleeping.

Here's how: Lying flat on your back, legs stretched out in front, hands by your sides and palms on the floor, bend your knees and lift your legs slowly over your body and head, pushing down with your palms until you are as far onto your neck as possible, keeping your chin well in and head straight. (If your feet don't easily touch the floor, you should use a cushion or low chair to rest them on.) Go easy. Relax and let go as much as you can, being aware of where you are stretching. This exercise contains the whole secret of the effort of making no effort. At first you might feel a bit nervous about the unusual sensations it brings with it but after one or two tries you will be able to let go.

Time: one minute, then gradually increase to five.

Twist-overs for waist and spine

The rewards: This movement lengthens the chest and front shoulder muscles, restoring flexibility at the shoulder joints. It also helps trim down a spreading waistline and midriff. The twisting motion gives elasticity to the spine, making it stronger and more supple and helping to protect it from backache.

Here's how: Lying on your back, draw up your feet and cross your legs, left over right, then tuck your left food under your right calf. Lock your legs in this position and then slowly take your knees over and down to one side to touch the floor, stretching your left arm above the head and gently working your shoulder down to the floor (it may not go all the way to begin with, but it will in time). Now, in a wide and gentle arc, move the same arm around in a half circle until it reaches your side, working your shoulder down to the floor in tiny stops along the arc. Repeat this three times, taking about half a minute for your arm to travel through the arc each time. Change legs and repeat.

Lie-backs for beautiful legs

The rewards: This exercise loosens tension in the muscles all along the front of the legs and slims and strengthens the thighs. It also strengthens the middle and upper back, and used with other back exercises it can help protect you from chronic backache.

Here's how: Sit on your heels with your legs folded under you, back straight, feet far enough apart for your buttocks to rest on the floor. Place your hands behind you, palms on the floor (or, if you are supple enough, bend arms and rest elbows and arms on the floor) and keeping knees together, lean back, stretching out the muscles on the front of the legs while you look down over the front of your body. Go easy. Never strain. As you do this you will find it easier and easier and you can get closer and closer to the floor. If you find it very hard, then place a chair covered with a blanket or a pillow behind you and lean against that until you are flexible enough to go clear to the floor. Be careful – if you get any pain in your lower back you have gone beyond your present limit. Ease forward again until the pain is gone.

Hip looseners

The rewards: This posture helps develop full movement in the hip joint and also stretches the powerful muscles on the inside of the thighs. It leads to more graceful movement and eliminates tensions that interfere with sexual pleasure.

Here's how: Sitting on the floor with your legs straight out in front of you (use a wall for support to keep your back straight if you need to), open your legs as far as they will comfortably go and still let you keep your back straight. Now lean forward from the hips (if you find it difficult to keep your back straight in this position then you are bending at the waist). The movement should only be a slight one but you will feel a pull down the inside of your legs when you are doing it right. If you need to at first, sit on a small cushion instead of directly on the floor so you can gently lever your trunk forward from your hips. Just be sure you don't bend from the waist, for however small the bend from the hips it is doing you good.

Time: three minutes and build up to five.

Side stretches for a slim waist

The rewards: This exercise stretches the side of the body and whittles away excess fat; it also stretches the tendons at the knee joint for better flexibility when you walk.

Here's how: Sitting with your feet straight out in front of you on the floor, draw one leg up and in so that your heel touches the pubic bone, and the sole of your foot rests on the inner thigh. Then draw the other foot in so that the heel touches the ankle of the first foot. Now turn and face the side of the foot touching the pubic bone. Making your spine as erect as possible, stretch out over one knee and let gravity work for you, the centre of the chest just above the knee. (In time the tummy and chest will both rest along the length of the thigh.) Reverse the feet and do the same thing for the other side.

Time: three minutes each side.

Stretch out for slim thighs

The rewards: This exercise trims away excess flab on the thighs and releases restricted movements in the knee joints. In time it can also help eliminate the tension in the lower back that can result in sciatica, and strengthens ankles.

Here's how: Sit on the floor, Japanese style, with your calves alongside your thighs so that you are sitting between your feet. Open your knees to their maximum width and place your hands on the floor in front of you. Gently slide your hands forward until you can rest your head on the floor. (In the beginning your bottom will lift off the floor with the movement but gradually it will stay stationary as you stretch.) Relax in this position for three minutes, breathing normally and letting gravity do its work. With practice, the whole front of your chest and tummy will rest on the floor.

Lower-body stretches

The rewards: This posture will bring with it firmer buttocks, shapelier calves and longer, more supple hamstrings, which improve the whole shape of a leg.

Here's how: Standing with one heel back firmly against the wall to help keep your balance, and the other foot eighteen inches in front, keeping both legs straight, clasp one wrist behind your back and slowly lever your trunk forward by bending from the hips – not from the waist. Do the other side by swapping your leg positions.

Time: one minute each side and build up to two on each side.

RESPECT YOURSELF

STEP FIVE: LOOK INSIDE

Learning to let go

We live in a world of constant activity. It is a world of striving and goals, of planning and remembering – a world of never-ending sensory stimulation, of exciting new ideas and discoveries. Yet amidst all this activity somewhere inside you is a centre of stillness – a wordless, formless space where the seeds of creativity are sown that later become your ideas and your accomplishments. Here in the silence and the darkness you can hear your own 'inner voice'. You can come to know the difference between what you really want, feel and think, and what has been programmed into you by habits, false notions, and values that are not your own. This space, your centre, is also a place of safety and security for you: you can move out of it as you choose, to meet the outside world, to form friendships, to love and to learn. It is a permanent sanctuary to which you can return when you feel overburdened, tired, confused, or in need of new vitality and direction.

Locating this centre within yourself, recognizing its value and then living your life more and more from it are essential parts of staying well and being beautiful – in short, of becoming what you are. The key that opens this particular door for most people is relaxation.

Passive awareness

By relaxation, I don't mean sleeping or flopping down on a bed when you feel you can't go on, or losing yourself in a mindless state in front of the television – although sleep is certainly essential and the other two states have many things to recommend them too. I mean something more: learning to move at will into a temporary state of deep stillness or meditation in which your usual concerns, your habitual thoughts, and the never-ending activity of your daily life are replaced by a kind of alert, yet totally passive, awareness. The relaxed state permits some of the physiological changes normally experienced during sleep to take place to revitalize your body and mind simultaneously. But it is different from sleep. For while your body is deeply passive, your mind is very alert.

For some people this state occurs spontaneously, often between sleep and wakefulness. It is then that their best ideas come or that they experience a sense of harmony in themselves and in relation to the rest of the world. Scientists studying this state of psychophysical relaxation find that the brainwave patterns in it are very different from those of the normally awake state. After tens of thousands of hours of observation of the changes in brainwave patterns in subjects hooked up to EEG equipment, researchers have been able to analyze and describe a number of

interesting altered states of consciousness during relaxation, each with its own brainwave patterns, objective physical manifestations, and subjective feelings. They have discovered that there is an increase in overall awareness and creativity as a person moves from one level of relaxation into the next, deeper one.

This is interesting, for most people have a fear of letting go, thinking that if they give up control of things they won't be able to think clearly and independently or work well, or that someone is likely to put something over on them. In fact, just the opposite is true. When you are able to enter a state of deep relaxation at will, this frees you from patterns of living and thinking to which you tend to be a slave (although sometimes an unconscious one). It enables you to think more clearly and simply and to act more directly when action is called for.

Relief from stress

Relaxation is also the most important key to freedom from the damaging effects of long-term stress. This is something which by now has been well established scientifically. Many studies have been made of people taught a relaxation technique and then monitored as to the psychological and physiological changes that take place after fifteen or twenty minutes of practising it. These studies show that relaxation techniques bring the para-sympathetic branch of the autonomic nervous system into play, calming you, reducing oxygen consumption, lowering blood lactates (high lactate levels are associated with anxiety, arousal, and hypertension), slowing your heartbeat significantly and changing brainwave patterns. They have also shown that repeated practice can lead to improved memory, increased perceptual ability and a subjective feeling in participants that their work and their lives are somehow more creative than they were before.

Deep relaxation benefits

Another interesting benefit from the daily practice of deep relaxation is a reduction of negative habit patterns such as drug-taking (of both prescription and mind-altering drugs), alcohol consumption and cigarette smoking. For instance, research in the United States involving 2,000 students between the ages of nineteen and twenty-three who had practised a form of meditation for periods of from a few months to a couple of years showed that their dependence on alcohol, drugs and cigarettes dropped sharply. The number of smokers was reduced by half in the first six months of doing the practice. By twenty-one months it was down to one third. And these changes were entirely spontaneous – at no time was any suggestion made that relaxation or meditation would change any of these habits.

Cardiologist Herbert Benson did the first studies into the effects of Transcendental Meditation with Keith Wallace many years ago at Harvard, then continued on his own to investigate this state of relaxation. He believes that each of us has what he calls the 'relaxation response' – a natural ability to experience the relaxed state with all its benefits – and that all we need to bring it about is some kind of tool to turn it on.

Possible tools

- transcendental meditation
- yoga
- breathing exercises
- zazen
- silent repetition of a word
- autogenic training
- long-term strenuous exercise
- biofeedback.

Each can be useful for silencing everyday thoughts and for temporarily shutting off habitual ways of seeing the world and doing things – for creating a pathway between your inner and outer world. All of them are different, and for you some will work better or be more enjoyable than others. That is why it is worthwhile to try a few different techniques until you discover which ones you prefer.

Practising one or two techniques every day will make you aware of the enormous power your own mind has – power to alleviate suffering and bring a sense of wellbeing, power to change those things you want to change but which seemed impossible to change before, power to expand your whole awareness of your world of work, pleasure, and relationships. Meanwhile, almost automatically you will reap the well-documented physical and psychological benefits of stilling your mind. But regular practice is important.

Discipline for freedom

We live in an age where discipline is often looked down upon as something that impedes spontaneity and freedom, something old-fashioned and stifling to life. We all tend to rebel against it. But it has been my experience, and the experience of a great many professionals working in the field of humanistic in-depth psychology, that the kind of discipline needed for daily practice of meditation or deep relaxation tends not to stifle one's ability to be involved in the spontaneous business of life but to free it. This is something you will have to find out for yourself. At first it may take a little effort to get up the fifteen minutes earlier each morning to practise a technique and to take fifteen minutes out of your busy afternoon or

early evening to practise again, but you will find it is well worth it. The most common excuse is that you don't have time. The reality of the situation is that practising twice a day for fifteen to twenty minutes will give you time, not take it from you, for you will find that you do everything with greater efficiency and enjoyment, that far less of your energy is wasted in fruitless activity. Every minute you spend in a deeply relaxed state will yield a fourfold return in the energy you need in your outer life.

Here are a few useful techniques to try. Some are directed more towards the body, such as Jacobson's progressive relaxation and many of the breathing techniques described later; others, such as Benson's relaxation response or zazen, focus more on the mental processes. But it is important to remember that there is no real

separation between the two; mind and body are not different entities, they are merely different ends of the same continuum. Each technique affects both. It could not be otherwise.

You might find it helpful to have any instructions for the techniques featured below and overleaf read to you by a friend, at least until you get to know them yourself, or to make a cassette recording of them to play while you are relaxing. Remember to leave enough time after each instruction for you to carry it out.

Progressive relaxation

A technique based on the work of Edmund Jacobson, this is an excellent way to begin if you have never done any sort of relaxation or meditation technique before, because it gives most people some sense of what relaxation feels like even the first time they try it. As you repeat your technique again and again, you will find that you enter a progressively deeper state of relaxation.

The whole practice demands about 15 minutes (it is best done at least twice a day) with a break of from two to five minutes of stillness while you experience the relaxed state you have achieved.

The first few times you try the technique, you may find you have trouble picturing all the images as they come or preventing your mind from wandering. It doesn't matter if you don't 'see' anything. Some people are more visual in their imagery and others more feeling; both work superbly well, just approach the exercise from your own point of view. When you find your mind wandering (which is a common occurrence because one's concentration is not used to focusing so intensely, or because being a new technique or a new feeling causes

a little anxiety) ask yourself 'Why is my mind wandering?' Pursue that thought for a couple of minutes, then go back to the exercise and continue it as best you can. All difficulties will iron themselves out automatically after you have practised the technique often enough.

1 Find a quiet room, preferably one without too much light, and sit in a comfortable chair that gives support to your back. Place both feet flat on the floor and close your eyes. This technique can also be done lying down if you prefer

2 Become aware of your breathing and just watch the air come in and go out of your body without doing anything.

3 Take a few deep breaths, and as you breathe out each time slowly repeat the word 'relax' slowly and silently to yourself.

4 Focus on your face and let yourself feel any tension in your face or eyes, your jaw or tongue. Make a mental picture of tension – you could picture a clenched fist, a knotted rope, or a hard ball of steel – then mentally picture the tension going and everything becoming relaxed, like a limp rubber band.

5 Feel your face and your eyes, your jaw, and your tongue becoming relaxed, and as they relax, experience a wave of relaxation spreading through your whole body. (Each step takes about ten seconds.)

6 Tighten up all the muscles in your face and eyes, squeezing them as hard as you can. Then let go and feel the relaxation spread throughout your body again.

7 Now apply the same instruction to other parts of your body, moving slowly downwards from your head to your neck, shoulders, and upper back, arms, hands, chest, mid and lower back, your abdomen, thighs and calves, ankles, feet and toes, going through each area until every part of your body is relaxed. With each part, picture the tension in it mentally and then picture it going away; each time, tense the muscles in that area and then let them go and feel the relaxation spreading.

8 When you've relaxed every part of your body, sit quietly in this comfortable state for up to five minutes.

9 Now let your muscles in your eyelids become lighter ... get ready to open your eyes and come back to an awareness of the room.

10 Open your eyes. Now you are ready to do whatever you want.

Zazen

One of the simplest ways of meditating, this technique involves nothing more than just being aware of your breathing. But don't be deceived by its simplicity. It is a potent tool for stilling the mind and regenerating the body. And concentrating your awareness on the breath is not as easy as it sounds.

The exercise, like most techniques, is best done twice a day, morning and evening. A beginner will usually notice positive results by the end of a week but they become increasingly apparent the longer you go on doing it. Some Buddhist monks do this exercise for two or three years before beginning any other form of meditation.

1 Find yourself a quiet place where you will not be disturbed. You can sit cross-legged on the floor with a small cushion underneath you or you can sit in a chair if you prefer, but your back should be straight. (This straight-back position is a requirement for many meditation techniques since it creates a physical equilibrium which makes calm mental focus possible.) Let your hands rest quietly on your lap.

2 Close your eyes. Take several long, slow breaths, breathing from your abdomen so it swells out with each in breath and sinks in again when you breathe out.

3 Now rock your body from side to side and then around in large, gentle circles from your hips to the top of your head. Rock in increasingly smaller circles until you gradually come to rest in the centre.

4 Now breathe in and out through your nose quietly without doing anything to your breathing (that is, don't try to breathe deeper or slower or faster, just breathe normally). With each out breath, count silently to yourself. So it goes: in breath, out breath, 'one'; in breath, out breath, 'two'; and so on up to ten, counting only on the out breath. When you get to ten go back and begin again at one. If you lose count halfway it doesn't matter. Go back and start the count at one again. Counting isn't the whole point, but only a tool for focusing your mind on your breath.

If you are like most people, the first few times you do the exercise you will find you lose count often and you are often distracted by thoughts or noises. Each time some random thought distracts you, simply turn your mind gently back again to counting the breaths. Distractions don't change the effectiveness of the meditation.

5 After fifteen minutes (sneak a look at your wristwatch if you must), stop. Sit still for a moment, then open your eyes and slowly begin to go about your everyday activities again.

Benson's relaxation response technique

Herbert Benson, who wrote *The Relaxation Response*, discovered that the same measurable physical benefits that accrue from practising Transcendental Meditation, which depends on the silent repetition of a mantra (a word sound), can be had by repeating any word over and over while the eyes are closed and the body is in a quiet state.

Meditation by concentration on a mantra or word sound has a long tradition.

Some mantras are said to be sacred words that have particular sound vibrations which transmit particular powers. Each tradition has its own mantras such as Guru Om, Om mani padme hum, La ilaha illa 'Ilah, or in the Catholic religion, Hail Mary, full of grace, the Lord is with thee. Whether their magic aspects are true or not the technique works beautifully to replace the habitual chatter that runs through one's mind, such as worries about things past and things yet to come.

Benson suggests you find a word that is pleasing to you. It could be anything – say, garden, peace or life. He likes the word 'one' as it is simple and has the connotation of unity about it. (The teacher Krishnamurti once remarked that any word would be better than the fruitless and often destructive thoughts that normally run through our minds; then he wryly suggested 'Coca-Cola'.) Here's how:

1 Find a quiet place where you won't be disturbed for fifteen to twenty minutes and a comfortable chair that supports your back.

2 Sit down and close your eyes. Give yourself a moment to settle in and you are ready to begin.

3 Simply sit there, feet on the floor and eyes closed, quietly repeating your word over and over to yourself: 'one...one...one...'

4 Whenever your mind wanders or you are disturbed by a sound or thought, simply turn your mind gently back to repeating the word again.

5 That is all there is to it. After fifteen to twenty minutes, stop repeating the mantra and get ready to open your eyes.

6 Open your eyes, stretch, and go about your everyday activities. This is a particularly useful technique once you have practised it a few times because you can do it in so many different places, such as in a waiting room or on a commuter train or bus. I know a lot of men and women who have made it a part of their daily trek to and from work with tremendous benefits.

Total body relaxation

Like Jacobson's progressive relaxation, this technique is useful in getting rid of physical tension rapidly as well as in preparation for using creative imagery. It is also a technique that is often used in self-hypnosis. Unlike many relaxation or meditation exercises, it is done lying down. Once you get the hang of it and have done it a few dozen times, it becomes so efficient that the whole process from alert wakefulness to deep relaxation can demand no more than a couple of minutes. This is hard to believe at the beginning, but it is so. I have used it for years in bed each morning before I get up and each evening before I go to sleep, together with imagery or visualization about things I want to change in my life. I also use it in the middle of the night if ever I am awakened instead of just lying in bed

fitfully trying to go back to sleep again. If you do total body relaxation during the day, it is often useful to place a small pillow under your knees while you lie back, and place your arms quietly at your sides or folded lightly over your abdomen.

This exercise is done entirely in the mind. No physical movements are necessary as you go through the body. You are telling your body to let go. That is one of the reasons it is useful for making you aware of how much of an effect your mind can exert on your body. When you begin to practise, don't be discouraged if you feel you are not really very relaxed. Don't try to do anything – just let it happen.

Total body relaxation

1 Lie down in a quiet, preferably darkened room. Get comfortable with a pillow or two under your head and one under your knees too if you wish. Now close your eyes and take a few deep breaths, letting them out completely before you begin.

2 Think of your feet. Forget everything else and just concentrate on your feet. Now mentally tell them to let go; say to yourself silently, 'My feet are relaxing and getting heavy – heavy and warm, warm and relaxed. They are sinking into the bed.'

3 Now go on to your ankles. 'My ankles are getting heavier and heavier, more and more relaxed – relaxed and floppy, floppy and warm and heavy. I let them go completely.' Now go on to your calves and then to your thighs. 'My calves are getting heavier and heavier, warm and heavy, heavy and relaxed. They are sinking into the bed – heavy and relaxed, relaxed and floppy. I let them go completely.'

4 *Now you give the same directions to each part of your body, moving from toes to head, one part to the next part, relaxing each part as you go – hips, back ('I let go vertebra by vertebra all the way up my spine') – then come around to the front to the abdomen. ('My tummy is warm and relaxed, all soft and floppy, sinking heavily into the bed.') Then chest, neck, shoulders, head, face, tongue, jaw, and eyes. Now do your arms, forearms, hands, and fingers until every part of your*

body is given the direction to let go. 'My whole body is completely still ... warm and relaxed ... heavy ... quiet and at peace ... relaxed and warm. I can feel it in my mind.'

5 *Now you are ready to use whatever visualization you want, or you can let yourself sink even deeper into relaxation by counting backwards from ten to one, saying with each number, 'I am sinking deeper and deeper into a state of warm relaxation...deeper and deeper.' When you reach one, stay for a few minutes in this peaceful, relaxed state, feeling the calm all through you. Then, when you are ready to finish, say to yourself, 'Now I am going to open my eyes and get up feeling pleasantly fresh and well.' Open your eyes and get up.*

The breath of vitality

Even more important than the food you eat is the air you breathe and the way you breathe it. They can affect how you feel emotionally and physically, how your skin looks (for cells of the skin are dependent for their metabolic processes on a constant supply of enough oxygen), how much vitality you have, and even how clearly you can think.

Because breathing is the only one of your body's functions that can be either completely involuntary or voluntary, it can form a bridge between your conscious and unconscious functions. This makes it possible to look at your breathing to find out how you are feeling and what is happening to your body. It also means you can use breathing to change your energy level or your mood.

Breath energy

Throughout history the breath has been associated with energy, force, and power of both a physical and metaphysical kind. In the Bible, the word translated as 'spirit' can also be translated as 'air'. It is the invisible life force, the energy the Chinese call chi and attempt to manipulate in acupuncture treatments. The Sufis refer to it as barales. It plays an important role in their techniques of meditation. The yogis call it prana, and claim it is responsible for the extraordinary control they can exert over their minds and bodies. Prana means breath, respiration, life, vitality, wind, energy, and strength. It is also used to mean soul as distinguished on a more simple level. Some physicians and therapists such as the late Captain William P. Knowles have had excellent results when treating chronic chest complaints, fatigue, depression, and nervous disorders, simply by teaching patients the art of breathing fully. Making changes in the way you breathe or using specific methods of breath control can also help you do a lot of useful things such as increase your vitality, calm your emotions when they are disturbed, and clear an overtaxed mind.

The breath of emotion

The link between the way you breathe and your emotional state is well established. Not only do your emotions affect your breathing (remember the last time you were frightened and you gasped for breath; how when you are excited your breathing becomes shallower and faster than usual), but how you breathe can bring on or turn off emotional states too. Here's an experiment that shows this. Start to breathe very shallowly so only the shoulders and top of your chest show any signs of movement, and pant in and out quickly for about forty-five seconds. At the end of that time your heart will be pounding and you will have all the feelings of anxiety and fear. Or try it the other way around. The next time you are in a difficult situation and you feel you might lose control, stop. Take three or four long deep breaths from the abdomen and let them out slowly. Then take another look at the challenge. You'll find your mind and feelings a lot calmer.

Full breathing

When you breathe, breathe with your whole chest and abdomen too. Most of us breathe only with the top part of our body, which means we are not fully lowering the diaphragm and expanding

115

Use the following exercise for five minutes twice a day to increase your lung capacity, slim your middle, purify your blood, and help you learn the art of fuller breathing. You can also use it whenever you feel tense or need to clear your head:

1 Resting your hands on your rib cage at the sides, just above the waist, breathe out completely. Now inhale gently through the nose, letting your abdomen swell as much as it will to a slow count of five.

2 Continue to breathe in through the nose to another count of five, this time letting your ribs expand under your hands and finally your chest too (but don't raise your shoulders in the process).

3 Hold your breath for a count of five, now slowly let it out through your mouth as you count slowly to ten, noticing how your rib cage shrinks beneath your hands and pulling in with your abdomen until you have released all the air. Repeat four times.

the lungs and so are not making use of their full capacity. This kind of restricted breathing stifles emotional expression and is often linked with anxiety, depression and worry. To check for abdominal breathing, put your hands on your tummy. Does it swell when you breathe in and sink when you breathe out? It should. Lying flat on a firm surface, practise breathing fully and gently until you get the feel of it.

Make sure that with each out breath you let out all the air you take in. By exhaling more of the carbon dioxide, you will get rid of more of the cells' waste products and you will be able to make full use of each new breath of air as it is taken down into your lungs.

Take up some kind of aerobic exercise – such as running, bicycling, or dancing – that demands full use of your lungs every day.

Sensuous breathing
This technique, which was taught to me by one of Britain's top bioenergetic therapists, is a wonderful way of rediscovering the feel of your body. The therapist uses it to encourage the unblocking of any repressed emotional or physical tensions. She also claims that it increases your ability to experience heightened sexual pleasure all over the body.

1 Lie on the floor on your back and relax as much as you can, letting your arms and legs flop. Close your eyes and feel your body against the floor; do you notice any tension in any part of it? Shoulders? Back? Legs?

2 Now focus inside your body and ask yourself where you feel any movement in your muscles because of your breathing. Anywhere you feel tense, imagine you're breathing into that spot, imagine you can exhale through that part of your body and as you do, experience the breath relaxing your sore muscles as it filters through them.

3 Then, when you are relaxed, experiment with the movements which are part of natural free breathing. They are beautiful movements.

4 When you breathe in, feel your pelvis tip back gently so there is a slight arch to your back while your abdomen and chest rise, ribs and back expand, and chin tilts forward just barely.

5 Then, when you exhale, your pelvis moves down again so your spine almost touches the floor, your back contracts, and your chin and head move back again exposing the front of your neck a bit more. This natural movement is a wavelike motion that flows without hesitation from each in breath to its following out breath and so on. Practice it, exaggerating the tiny movements at first until you get the feel of it and then it will flow naturally.

The decanter

This exercise stimulates the nervous system and at the same time stills a restless or anxious mind. I like doing it after I have been working in an immobile position for a long time – for instance, when I have been at my desk writing for several hours. I do it just before I get up to move about.

1 Sitting comfortably in a chair with a straight back or cross-legged on the floor, imagine that your body is like a decanter, the bottom of the decanter being your pelvis and hips and the top of it your head. Pretend that you are going to fill it with energy in the form of air.

2 Now, breathing in slowly, imagine it filling up gradually. After you have taken in as much air as you can comfortably hold and are getting to the top, hold your breath as long as necessary to become aware of the feeling of fullness.

3 Then exhale slowly and imagine that it is emptying as you do.

4 Repeat this five to ten times. (If you find yourself becoming lightheaded, it is nothing to worry about. This often happens if lungs are not used to being fully used. But don't ever force your breathing.)

Tension taker

This exercise is useful to do whenever you find yourself under stress or feel you are getting tense.

1 Stand comfortably with your arms at your sides and inhale through your nose slowly. Hunch up your shoulders as high as you can, clench your fists and, standing on tiptoes, tense your body harder and harder, concentrating on your centre – the navel area – to help you keep your balance.

2 Hold your breath and sink back onto your feet, loosening your shoulders and letting them drop. As you unclench your fists, exhale through your nose very slowly, pushing down on your palms and on your shoulders.

3 Do this five or six times.

Revitalizer

This exercise was taught to me by a friend who teaches yoga. It is wonderful if you are feeling drowsy from sitting too long or are very tired. It revitalizes you very quickly.

1 Let all the air out of your lungs – then even more – and then even more.

2 Now take a deep breath from your abdomen so it swells as you breathe in. Exhale immediately through your nose, jerking in your abdomen momentarily and then jerk it in again, pushing out even more air.

3 Repeat this five times until your lungs are completely empty.

4 Now take in a long, slow breath, retain it for a count of five, and slowly exhale it all away.

5 Repeat the whole exercise five times.

Prana power

This is an interesting exercise which makes use of the breath to do all sorts of surprising things such as banishing minor aches and pains caused by tension. If practised regularly it can also help keep the skin of your face looking smooth and wrinkle-free. It is a simple yogic technique for directing prana, or breath energy, to whatever part of your body needs it.

1 Sitting in a relaxed position with your spine firmly supported, or lying on a firm bed, slowly breathe in deeply, imagining the life force you are taking in as you do. Hold your breath for a few seconds.

2 Then, as you begin to breathe out, imagine directing the energy to whatever part of your body you want to affect for the better. For instance, see the skin on your face as soft and unlined and direct the energy there, or direct it at your shoulders to make them lose tension and so forth.

3 Repeat the process for three to five minutes at a time. If you are using it for smoothing away lines on the face, you need to do it twice a day. It is good to do just after a relaxation or meditation exercise if you can.

Yoga for union

According to yogic theory, there are three basic sources for the expression of human life: the subconscious or instinctive self, the intellectual or reasoning self, and the mind out of which intuition, inspiration and creativity spring. In most of us, they are not balanced. One or another, or even all three, are under-developed, over-active, or uncontrolled. No matter what the imbalance, it inevitably leads to frustration and dissatisfaction, for part of you is either left out or left busy battling against the rest of you. This is where intrinsic yoga can play an important role.

The meaning of the word yoga is *union* – or in modern terms, *integration*. Intrinsic yoga arises from within through the breath rather than being imposed upon your body from outside. This approach is deceptively simple, yet suitable for anyone, whether you have been practising yoga for many years or have never done any in your life. Intrinsic yoga is not about the accomplishment of the exercise or asana you are practising. It is concerned with increasing your awareness of the experience in your body and with helping you explore a sense of being at ease. Intrinsic yoga is also about – how you feel about an exercise and how you experience it. Each exercise is done from within, with your mind focused upon your breath. Because your body is working in unison with the breath, you begin to experience a new sense of wholeness – the kind of integration of mind, body and breath that is the core of yogic practice. You also develop a feeling of well-being that helps to keep things in perspective.

Let's get started
One of the fundamental aims of yoga is

to improve the condition of the spine. All the exercises here aim to do this. They begin by centring on the breath – but not changing it, simply being aware of our breathing, aware of the cool air entering the nostrils and the warm air leaving them. As you become aware of the breath, your out-breath begins to lengthen naturally and makes you feel relaxed. You feel your shoulders becoming a little heavier, and then the rest of your body.

Now let's begin. Never strain in any of the exercises. Always stop if you feel discomfort. If in doubt about anything, seek medical advice before beginning. The movements of intrinsic yoga are designed to follow one another gracefully, all the while building on your breath.

The practice is divided into three stages, allowing you to learn the full programme slowly over a week. For the first three days, practice stage one. In the following three days, add the new movements in stage two, and on the seventh day, add the movements in stage three. You then have a full programme of intrinsic yoga to work with daily.

The exercises are written so they can be read aloud by a friend or put on tape if you like until you learn them since it can be difficult to practise and exercise while attempting to read from a book. They are deceptively simple yet infinitely profound because they work so closely with the breath – that great interface between your inner and outer world, each breath gently flowing into the next.

Relaxation position

Lie on the floor in a relaxation position. It is only on a firm surface that the body can relax fully. Be aware of the symmetry of your body – visualize an imaginary centre line. Sense that your limbs radiate out from that line as you stretch out your legs and take your arms equally away from the sides of your body – palms upwards. Straighten your legs: you may be aware of an arching under the lower spine. This often happens, so bend your knees and rest them together, taking your feet far enough apart so that the knees can stay propped against each other without effort. Now feel your lower back gently flatten on the ground. If you still feel tension, tilt your pelvis a little, tipping the pubic bone up towards the ceiling, and letting the muscles and the hips relax. You should now feel that the lower back is eased as much towards the ground as is comfortable for you. Close your eyes. Relax your jaw, separating your teeth and letting your tongue rest behind the lower teeth.

Now be aware of the back of your neck. It should be long, with your chin drawn gently towards your chest. This may be a strange feeling at first but it will allow the back of your neck to relax into a beneficial position. Your arms are away from your sides, palms upwards. This lets your shoulders soften. Be aware of

the weight of your shoulders as they begin to relax. Feel them softening and drifting towards the ground.

As your body begins to let go, stop for a moment to see if there are any other areas of tension. Imagine that you can breathe into each of these areas. Then, as you breathe out, visualize the tension evaporating. This is a very useful method of relieving pain or discomfort in any area of your body. And, once you get the hang of it, you can create it any time.

Now bring your right hand in to rest over your left collar bone and sense the breath coming in or out gently under your hand. This has the effect of taking the air to the uppermost part of your lungs, where stale pockets of air tend to accumulate through lack of use. Concentrate on the in-breath for four breaths. Now bring your left hand in to rest over your navel, and be aware of breathing out from beneath that hand. As you breathe out gently draw your tummy muscles inwards and upwards under the rib cage to allow the outward breath to leave the lowest part of your lungs. Try to keep your breathing relaxed, concentrating on the next four out-breaths, and then on both in- and out-breaths. As you observe your breathing, you will find there is a natural pause between the changes of breath. Enjoy that pause and wait until your body is ready to breathe in or out again. Stay centred on your breathing. It may be difficult to get the feel of it at first, but practise it as much as possible, for once you begin to experience it you can use it at any time to relax. Now return your arms to the floor and you are ready to begin intrinsic yoga.

Stage one

Flamingo

Focusing on your breath, when you next breathe out, draw up your tummy muscles, and slowly ease the right knee towards your chest during the out-breath. As you breathe in, reach up for your knee and hold onto it. On your next out-breath, again pull up your tummy muscles and, without using your hands, ease the knee towards your chest, then use your hands to ease it a little further. Start your in-breath and then soften the grip on that knee, exhale – tummy muscles – moving the knee towards your chest again using your hands. Inhaling, soften the grip, then do one more movement in the same three stages – the breath, move the knee, lastly using your hands. Now, when you are next ready to inhale, release the knee and return your foot to the floor with your knee bent again. Now do the same on the left side. Exhale, drawing up the tummy muscles, bend your left knee towards your chest, and, inhaling, hold onto the knee. Follow the same procedure, exhaling – in three stages again – no strain, softening the grip, inhaling and so on for three breaths. Concentrate on the effect of the breath on your movement rather than achieving it. As you draw your right knee down, you are exerting pressure on the ascending colon, and on the descending colon with the left knee, which acts as a tonic to the digestive system, excellent for a sluggish colon or constipation. Return your foot to the ground on an in-breath.

Now work with both knees in exactly the same way. After drawing up the tummy muscles while exhaling, tip both knees towards the chest, and so on. You will find there is very limited movement of the knees without using your hands. Work with three breaths, and return your feet inhaling. Separate your feet, leaning your knees together, and check that the

lower back is eased down, or again tilt your pelvis as before. Return your arms to the sides of your body, keeping your concentration on your breathing, and checking that the back of your neck is still lengthened.

Rainbow

With palms down, arms at your sides, when you are next ready to breathe, slowly take your arms up towards the ceiling and then start to soften them, bending at the elbows so that they come over to rest on the floor well away from the sides of your head. Check that your elbows and the backs of your wrists actually touch the ground. If not, move your elbows further down towards your feet until they do. When you are ready to exhale, gently straighten the arms in the air once more, and slowly return them to your sides in time with your out-breath. Observe the natural pause between the breaths, keep your chin down, and continue to work for six more breaths. While doing the exercise not only will you be softening your shoulders, you will also be relaxing mentally through the discipline of working your mind, body and breath in unison.

Shoulder bridge

Having finished the Rainbow now take the feet and knees to hip-width to ensure that you don't strain the muscles of the back or abdomen. As you inhale, lift your breast-bone and then very gently allow your hips to come off the ground – just a small, gentle, lift, not too high. When you are ready to exhale, gently draw up the tummy muscles and slowly lower the middle spine to the ground, and then allow the rest of the spine to ease down, and the back of the neck again to lengthen. Pause there, relax your chest and, holding onto your

knees, relax into the dormouse position, shown above. You might like to rock gently from side to side to massage your back muscles and coax them to relax. Lower your feet when you are ready, and adopt the relaxation position again.

Crocodile

Lying on the floor knees bent, bring your feet together, pressing the knees and ankles together. Take your arms away from your sides, palms down. Imagine that you have a coin between your knees and another between your ankles which you need to keep there. When you exhale, draw up your tummy muscles, and very slowly ease your knees out towards the right, both knees absolutely level so that the left foot comes off the floor almost immediately. Be sure to keep your left shoulder down. Inhaling

under your collar bones, slowly return your knees to the centre. Exhale – tummy muscles – lower the knees to the left, right foot coming clear of the ground this time and right shoulder staying down. Don't aim to lower your knees too far. Instead concentrate on the knees staying level and together. Pause for a moment before inhaling again and returning your knees to the centre. Work with two more breaths to each side unless there is any discomfort. If you are not sure if your knees are level, glance down at them to check. Relax with each out-breath, feeling the effect of the exercise on your body – the gentle stretch down the sides of your body, and the rotation in the lower spine. When you finish the movements, ease your knees towards your chest once again, letting the muscles along the spine soften and relax. Release your knees, and separate your feet into the relaxation position again.

Crocodile – variation no. 2

When your muscles have relaxed, separate your knees and your feet to at least hip-width. This time you will be doing a movement similar to the previous one, but aiming to rotate different areas of the spine to ease away tension. We all accumulate tension along the spine, partly through poor posture and partly through sitting in badly

designed chairs that exert downward pressure on the spine. That pressure and tension need to be relieved to keep the spine healthy.

First tune into your breath. Your arms should be away from your sides, palms down. Your in-breath is under your collar bones and the out-breath from the abdominal area. As you draw your tummy muscles up, breathe out slowly and ease both knees towards the ground on the right-hand side. Check that your feet are far enough apart not to inhibit

the lowering, or allowing the legs to touch. The left shoulder stays down on the ground. Pause and, when you are ready to inhale slowly, return your knees to the vertical position. Exhale – tummy muscles – lowering both knees towards the left. Feel it working on your outer hip joints and thigh muscles as well as rotating the spine. Inhaling, return your knees again. Work twice more to each side – again, only if comfortable – observing the pauses and softening the muscles during the pauses, especially after the exhalation. Experience the movement and its effect as well as the relaxation that follows it. When you finish the exercise, take your knees to your chest yet again, rocking in a circular motion if it feels good, or even in a figure-of-eight to ensure the massage reaches your sides and the base of your spine.

Unsupported cobra

Roll over onto your stomach, bringing your arms back to your sides with your palms up and your toes turning inwards, so that your legs roll gently outwards, with your comfortable cheek turned to the floor, i.e. the side you instinctively turn your head to. Be aware of relaxing, of your shoulders softening, and of the base of the spine as it relaxes and eases. Aim to take your breath down to the base of your spine, taking energy into that area, and breathing away any tension. The muscles of the lower spine are softening.

The most important point to remember during this exercise is to keep the back of your neck long and relaxed. One of our greatest mistakes in modern life is to shorten the back of the neck. When we are driving cars we all tend to lift our chins – particularly women who often have difficulty seeing over the bonnet otherwise. The design of much modern furniture also makes us shorten the back of the neck, which can cause headaches, migraines and stress that spreads into the shoulders and eventually transmits to the spine. You can often improve these problems (even what appears to be a totally separate back problem) by simply lengthening the back of your neck, and taking that awareness into everyday life, not just when you are practising yoga.

Now bring your forehead to the floor, with your palms down at your sides. Your feet need to be hip-width apart. You will be extending the crown of your head forward as you inhale so that the back of your neck stays long as you lift. When you are ready to inhale, extend the crown forward and then upwards a little as you lift your head and shoulders only as much as you are comfortable with, keeping your arms passive at your sides. When you are ready to exhale, slowly lower and relax, turning your less

comfortable cheek to the floor. Allow the muscles to relax at the back of your neck, your shoulders and your spine. Observe your breath. If the movement is a strain rest, otherwise when you are ready, once more return your forehead to the floor. Extend the crown as you inhale, and begin to lift your head and the shoulders – with your chin down. Ease down exhaling, and once more turn your comfortable cheek to the floor with your palms upwards, toes inwards and heels falling outwards. Allow all the muscles that you have been using to relax, and feel your breathing returning to normal.

Very gently roll over onto your back again. To compensate for the cobra movement bring your knees to your chest in the dormouse position and either rest with your knees above your chest or rock gently – feeling the spine 'alive', warm and relaxed. The cobra is also a tonic for the respiratory system and good for asthma sufferers – as indeed is all the breath awareness of intrinsic yoga.

When you feel the muscles have softened, keep your knees above your chest with your arms gently around them, and exhaling – tummy muscles – draw both knees closer to your chest as you did in the Flamingo. Then, keeping your knees drawn towards your chest after exhaling, inhale, being aware of the abdominal massage. Exhaling, relax the muscles but do not soften the grip, and take one more inhalation, relax again exhaling, and release your knees inhaling. Separate your feet into the Relaxation Position, chin drawn downwards, and focusing on your breath while it slows down.

Stage two

Crocodile – extended version
Tune into your breathing again, centring yourself, your in-breath under the collar bones, out-breath drawing the tummy muscles upwards. The pauses become evident, and also the feeling of great peace, of being in the momentary stillness before the breath changes. The feet and knees are pressed together as before. Exhale – tummy muscles – slowly lowering both knees towards the right, keeping the left shoulder down, but the left foot leaves the ground. Return, inhaling, and repeat to the left in the same way. After returning to the centre

on an in-breath, work again to the right but, if you are comfortable, stay in position for up to three breaths initially,

being aware of your breathing. Feel your spine gently lengthen, as you inhale under the collar bones, and the muscles soften as you exhale – even in this twisted position. Make sure the knees stay level and together. Return when you are ready, inhaling and, if you are happy, work to the left again in the same way. Experience the movement and the breath. When you return to the centre, take your knees to your chest once again and listen to your body as to whether you should rock gently or not. Return to the Relaxation Position in your own time, and feel the warmth in the muscles that you have been working. Let that warmth soften the muscles still more. Observe your breath slowing down and relax.

Crocodile – variation no.2 – extended

version

In the next crocodile movement your knees and your feet must be well apart. The same extension applies as for the previous version, i.e. holding the position for a maximum of three breaths initially, using the breath to relax into the exercise, and becoming conscious of where you feel the breathing in your

body. As with the previous extension, only stay in position if you are comfortable and return to centre on an in-breath. After the exercise, yet again, take your knees to your chest, and relax, perhaps rocking in a circular motion or a figure-of-eight to massage the muscles. Explore the feeling in the muscles along your spine, and out towards your sides as you rock. Return to the Relaxation Position in your own time and check that the lower spine is eased down. If not, tip the pelvis as before. Relax.

Half-scissor

At this stage we are going to add in one more exercise which will work towards the very base of the spine. It is particularly beneficial for sufferers of sciatica, as it helps to relieve tension in this area, but it must be used very gently and only gradually built up if you feel it is

helpful for you.

Tune into your breath and straighten out your legs. Arms away from your sides, palms down. When you are ready to breathe in gently lift the left leg no more than a foot off the ground. As you

exhale, cross the left leg over your right leg towards the floor on your right, keeping your left leg low and both legs straight. When you are ready to inhale, take the leg back to its starting position, keeping it low to the ground and straight. Exhaling, lower it to the ground. When you are doing this exercise you need to roll the hip of the leg you are working up off the ground as much as you can, but always keep both shoulders on the ground. Work with the right leg when you are ready – in four stages. Inhale, lifting the leg a few inches, exhale crossing it over (letting the right hip roll to follow it), right shoulder down. Inhale bringing the leg back, and exhale lowering it to the ground again. Only if it is comfortable repeat the exercise, taking care not to strain, but working in the four stages for each movement. When you are ready, take your knees back to your chest and relax in the dormouse position as before, following your instincts about rocking to ensure the very base of your spine softens – feel the warmth in the muscles.

Stage three

Stage Three encompasses all of the above, but adds the sequence of the Cat movements.

The cat
This exercise is effective in alleviating backache and stiffness, and digestive

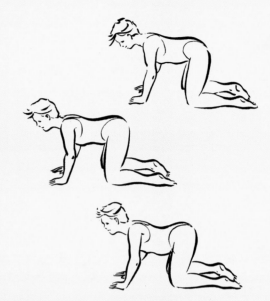

discomfort.
Come to a kneeling position (if you have knee problems you can put a folded blanket under your knees or, indeed, practise the same kind of movement while sitting on a chair). You need to have your hands directly under your shoulders, and your knees under your hips. Knees and hands should be shoulder-width apart. Your elbows must be slightly bent throughout the exercise, because to straighten them would create tension in the back of the neck, and to bend them any more would mean they would take too much weight. If the hands become uncomfortable, make fists and turn the knuckles towards the floor. Tune into your breathing pattern and let your spine relax, as well as your

neck and shoulders.
When you are ready to inhale, begin by extending your crown first forward and then upwards just a little, then move

your chest down and lastly lift your hips. Exhale, drawing up your stomach muscles and tuck your tail under, round the lower back, middle back, then drop

your head a little.

Inhale, extending the crown again while the rest of the spine stays still; then your head raises gently, your chest moves down, and your hips lift. Exhale – tummy muscles – tail under, rounding the lower spine, middle then upper spine and lowering your head. Elbows still slightly bent. On the next inhalation extend the crown, allowing the movement to travel down the length of your spine as before until the hips lift. Exhaling, the movement moves up the length of your spine until your head lowers. Lean your hips back towards your heels just until the stretch reaches your upper back –

elbows still bent.

Inhale, extend the crown and again feel the movement travel down your spine, and exhale once more as the movement travels up your spine and lean your hips back again. If you are comfortable move to one more breath, feeling every inch of your spine moving with every breath. When you finish, lie back down and for

the last time take your knees to your chest and feel the muscles softening along the length of your spine. When they have relaxed, once more adopt the Relaxation Position and rest for a minute or two, feeling all tension slip away from your body. It is a good idea to practise the Cat in front of a mirror, as often we are not aware that an area of the spine is not moving as it should until it can be seen working.

When you feel ready to come up to a standing position, do so very slowly and then take a few deep breaths. Always stretch gently – particularly if you are going to drive soon after your practice – just to make sure you are not too relaxed to concentrate!

Try to lay aside a special time for yoga. I like to do my yoga in the evening as it is so relaxing. Other people prefer first thing in the morning. Try to practise a little every day, even if it is only for five minutes. You can begin to feel more peaceful and centred very quickly. It has been said that the rise of yoga in the West is directly attributable to the instant benefit felt from very little practice. Dedicate a regular time of day to practice, and announce to the family or whoever is around then that this is your time. Take the phone off the hook. Forget to answer the door. Then people will learn to respect this time. At first they may think you are a bit strange to want to isolate yourself in this way, but when they begin to notice a greater peace emanating from you (which has spin-off effects on those around you), they become happy to give you that space – and to reap its benefits.

STEP SIX: STOP CHECK

Claim your right to energy

There is one question I find I am asked more frequently than any other. How do I get more energy? In working through the preceding steps you have (although you might not have noticed) learnt all about the best possible ways of increasing and supporting your energy levels. Yet some of us still find ourselves drained and fractious despite our best efforts and intentions. This step is about how to break through some of the energy barriers still blocking our way, from underlying conditions such as food allergies to environmental pollutants which can undermine our natural energy rights.

There is one great energy secret, however, which you must learn for yourself. Everyone has experienced the ability to summon up energy almost magically when it is most needed to cope with particularly demanding situations – the appearance of a second wind when you have been up all night nursing a sick child; the athlete who discovers he can call forth extra strength on the last lap of a long race. We can summon up energy to do what we passionately want to do. The more passionately you live your life, the more energy you will generate. Do what you love, love what you do, and be honest about it. Living the high-energy life is ultimately about learning to listen to the whispers of your own soul and to live out the truth of who you are and what you really value.

Collar the energy thieves

Our world is full of energy thieves. Excessive noise, environmental poisons and allergy-provoking chemicals in our air, water and food: all these things can drain us of energy. Eating junk foods is another big-time energy thief. Even changes in the weather can drain our energy. So does heavy emotional stress from anxiety, resentment or depression. Such delinquent influences also lower your immunity, make you vulnerable to catching colds and 'flu and susceptible to premature ageing and the development of degenerative conditions. For lasting high energy the energy thieves in your life need to be cornered, collared and dealt a fatal blow.

Environmental hazards

Here are just a few of the energy-stealing environmental hazards the body has to overcome:

- *Aluminium from anti-perspirants, pots and pans and antacids*
- *Anabolic steroids*
- *Antibiotics*
- *Cadmium and lead in cigarette smoke*
- *Cleaning solvents*
- *Contaminated foods*
- *Lead solder from canned foods*

- *Mercury from fillings in teeth*
- *Non-steroid anti-inflammatory drugs*
- *Oestrogens from oral contraceptives and HRT*
- *Pesticides and herbicides: DDT, DDB, dioxins and halogenates like PCB and PCP which act as oestrogen mimics and screw up our reproductive systems*
- *Solvents like formaldehyde, acetone and toluene.*

Heavy work for your liver

The organ at the centre of clearing the body of environmental pollutants is the liver. When your liver is working well and is not overburdened with potentially destructive elements, your body remains clean, your immune system is free to function well, and your energy levels can soar. When the liver is not working well neither is the immune system.

If you are chronically tired, here's how you can take steps to protect your body from pollutants as much as possible and give your liver some extra support to do its job well:

- If you use paints or solvents always wear a mask.
- If you smoke, stop; if others around you do, stay away from them.
- Always choose biodegradable cleaning products and forget the chlorine bleaches. Avoid as many environmental pollutants as possible.

- Don't cook foods in plastic containers in a microwave.
- Explore having the amalgam fillings in your mouth replaced with safer alternatives.
- Stay away from all drugs – prescription and otherwise – unless they are absolutely necessary.
- Exercise moderately but regularly – long walks are a great way to energize liver functions.
- Grow your own foods in the garden organically and take the 10 Day Spring Clean every three months (see pages 24-47).

Light up for energy

Light matters for energy too. When you don't get enough full spectrum UV light entering the eyes in winter, or when you are constantly indoors, you may experience big drops in levels of melatonin – an important brain hormone which regulates our body clocks and influences our moods. This can lead to a condition known as Seasonal Affective Disorder or SAD. Your energy seems to drain away and you get depressed or suffer disturbances in sleep and appetite. The remedy? Try exposing yourself to plenty of full-spectrum light, artificially. Next time you replace a lighting fixture in your home or buy a desk lamp, go for one which uses full-spectrum tubes instead of the usual tungsten bulbs. If you suffer greatly from light deprivation, consider buying a full-spectrum light box. Studies have shown that exposing SAD sufferers to full-spectrum light by having them sit in front of a light box for several hours a day lifted the spirits of 60 to 80 per cent of the people tested.

ENERGY DRAINERS	WHERE FOUND/SYMPTOMS	HELPFUL HINTS
Electromagnetic pollution	Caused by static from electrical appliances, VDU displays, TV, radio and portable phones, microwave ovens, electrical dial-face clocks. Symptoms include mental and emotional confusion and hormonal imbalance.	Don't sleep under an electric blanket. Unplug TV in the room in which you sleep. Sit at least 1 m (3 ft) away from a VDU and 2 m (6 ft) from your TV. Give away your microwave oven.
Heavy metal pollution: e.g. from lead, aluminium, mercury, cadmium	Lead from car and industrial fumes, water from lead pipes. Cooking with aluminium pots, drinking orange juice packaged in aluminium lined boxes, using certain antiperspirants. Mercury from tinned tuna and amalgam dental fillings. Cadmium from instant/non-organic coffee and other crops grown on contaminated soils. Heavy metals interfere with energy-producing enzymes in the body leading to fatigue as well as mental and physical disorders.	Replace aluminium cooking pots/kettles. Drink spring water such as Volvic. Use green supplements and add seaweed to soups and salads to chelate (bind) and eliminate the metals. Eat apples (pectin helps bind and remove heavy metals from the body).
Weather	Unusual winds and shifting barometric pressure cause depletion in negative ions resulting in depression, fatigue, irritable behaviour. Lack of adequate UV light, such as during the winter, causes Seasonal Affective Disorder (SAD).	Use an ionizer in the room in which you work and by your bed at night. Consider full-spectrum lighting.
Office pollution	Concrete buildings, plastic furniture, and synthetic decor deplete negative ions. Stale air recycled through conditioning and heating systems contains bacteria which challenge the immune system. VDUs (see above). Fluorescent lighting disturbs the nervous system, photocopier and printer chemicals cause allergic reactions. General office pollution symptoms: fatigue, headaches, irritated eyes, skin rashes.	Use ionizers and replace fluorescent strip lights with full-spectrum ones. Keep photocopiers and printers in a room separate from the one in which you work. Take a break from your VDU for a few minutes every hour. Use radiation control screens.

The sneaky inner thieves

Negative emotions like fear, resentment, depression and low self-esteem do a great deal to interfere with the full expression of who we really are – especially when they are long-term and especially when they remain unconscious. So does compromising yourself by living your life by somebody else's rules rather than your own. There is nothing wrong with a good bout of anger if it is felt consciously and expressed, but when anger turns inward, it can become resentment which gets filed away deep within us – sometimes so far down we are not even conscious that it is there. When our basic life force and creativity become hampered and self-defeating, psychological states come into play. We can experience long-term hopelessness or depression, bouts of anxiety and also physical illness. Unhappiness and lack of passion for life undermines all aspects of our lives. It is important to become aware of whether these things are operating in your life, and if so, how. Read on and see if any of the following applies to you.

Anxiety waste

Few emotions drain vitality like anxiety. While you dash about (either physically or in your mind), feeling unsafe and unstable and trying like mad to make everything seem alright, you waste enormous amounts of energy. Living with anxiety often leads to nothing ever being fully achieved. This, in turn, results in further anxiety and depletion of energy.

Wherever there is anxiety there is a high level of electrical, electro-positive magnetic activity and chemical acidity in the body. This affects the sympathetic nervous system and encourages further feelings of fear, irritability, nausea, headache, as well as an inability to concentrate, and can produce muscle pain and insomnia. Even minor attacks of nervousness can dramatically undermine your work performance and make it almost impossible to enjoy yourself. Chronic anxiety in someone's life is frequently related to food allergies. Realigning your diet can help a lot with it. So can physical exercise, which calms electrical and chemical over-activity, replacing them with more balanced energy.

Get into anger

Resentment is another emotional drain. Anger immediately felt and expressed keeps your energy flowing. Think of when you were a child and you got angry at a friend. It was quick to come and quick to pass, so you could get on with whatever you were both doing. As adults, however, we tend to swallow our anger, turning it into resentment. Anger in itself can be the driving force to achieving a goal. But when anger is held in, instead it can slowly turn into depression or resentment.

Harboured resentment corrupts your view of life and of yourself. To get rid of it means taking a long hard look at the resentments in your life and gradually letting go of them.

A very useful exercise is to write a letter to any person towards whom you feel particularly resentful or angry (even write to life itself). List all of their offences and tell them exactly how you feel about them. Then, when you are ready (it may be now or six weeks from now), at the bottom of the letter write: I (your name), hereby forgive you (the person's name) entirely for the above grievances. In so doing I bless you and wish you well and release all my ill feelings. When you have finished, read this letter out loud to yourself. Then leave it behind – or tear it up and burn it.

What do you fear?

In a measurable, physical way, fear freezes you into inactivity and makes all things seem impossible. Chronic fear, usually unconscious, can lead you to make the wrong choices because you feel the need continually to compromise on fundamental issues such as what you really want and value. This is dangerous thinking. You can quickly find yourself caught up and helpless – a victim to circumstances over which you have no power. Becoming aware of your fears and just writing them down can help diffuse a lot of their power. If they are great, get professional help from a counsellor.

Women and depression

According to recent research, women are twice as susceptible to depression as men. One obvious factor is the female biological make-up with its hormonal cycles that contribute to mood swings. But there are also social factors. According to the American Psychological Association, the structure of our society, which tends to place women in more passive roles than men, creates a sense of impotence, making women more prone to dissatisfaction and depression. The APA's Task Force on Women and Depression also found that 37 per cent of the women suffering from depression that were studied had been victims of significant physical or sexual abuse by the age of twenty-one.

How about depression?

Depression is believed to be the most common cause of chronic fatigue. Like anxiety, it can sometimes grow out of a biochemical imbalance. For example, living on a diet of processed convenience foods depletes your body of the minerals essential for brain chemicals, like noradrenaline, that are needed to keep your spirits high. Sometimes depression develops as a result of blocked emotions which you may not even be aware you are feeling – like grief or sadness. Often depression arises when you turn your anger in on yourself in a misguided attempt to stop yourself from doing harm to anyone. In any case, once you feel depression, you get caught up in a vicious circle where your low-energy state only further feeds the negative state, and vice versa.

Where long-term depression is present, a person's creative power is blocked. This is something that I know a lot about since in my early twenties I suffered from depression badly. It was the kind of depression which appeared to have no specific cause – the kind for which the doctor suggests either anti-depressant drugs or psychotherapy. Anti-depressant drugs are not only dangerous because of

their side-effects, they also, I believe, miss the point. You do not want to cover over depression, instead you want to release the energy locked within yourself so that it can be transmuted into creativity within your life.

To achieve this, try a fresh approach:

1 Unlock your imagination so that you begin to see depression not as an illness or insurmountable obstacle in your life but rather as something for you to work with and transform so that the energy trapped beneath it can be freed for creative use.

2 Alter the way you are living by detoxifying your body (see Step 2), identifying and clearing away any biochemical problems such as food allergies or candida overgrowths (see below), and then slowly, yet with determination, build a new lifestyle for yourself that serves your purposes – whatever they may be.

3 Find a creative outlet for the enrgies that emerge and be willing to listen to what they are telling you, even if it means you find you have to change things in your life such as a job or relationship that is not working.

EMOTIONAL ENERGY SNATCHERS		
Draining relationships	Any relationship based on illusions that each person has about the other wastes a great deal of energy. Such relationships often involve a sense of being crushed or held back by the other person.	As you clear away old perceptions and ideas you are more able to recognise any relationship that doesn't serve you, and adjust it to fit the real you or else spend less time with the person concerned.
Fear	Freezes you into inactivity and avoidance. Forces you to make compromising life choices. Inhibits the immune system, making you more susceptible to illness.	Identify your fears by writing them down. Decide which are valid and take action to allay them.
Compromise	Continually sacrificing your own needs or desires in favour of what others want from you, or what you believe is required of you socially, drains energy.	Identify the signs of compromise such as your use of the words I should and I feel guilty if I don't. Pause before you promise to do something you don't want to do and think again.
Resentment	Feeling wronged by someone can lock you into a self-limiting, energy-blocking prison.	Express your feelings of anger or pain directly to the person concerned. If this isn't practical or appropriate, try writing them in a letter.
Depression	Suppresses metabolic processes, decreases energy levels, lowers self-esteem.	Check out your diet for sensitivities, start exercising and try out some of the herbal helpers (see overleaf and also see Step 9, Depression).
Low self-esteem	Lack of self-esteem encourages a defeatist/victim attitude which drains energy. If also invites a lack of respect and appreciation from others around you.	Take a good look at the reasons you devalue yourself and ask if they are valid. Then write a list of your achievements and good qualities. Make a conscious effort to acknowledge these. Take action to increase your self-esteem – take up exercise.

Natural helpers

From a physical point of view there are some wonderful natural substances and plant helpers you can make friends with. You can explore what they have to offer you in helping to shift emotional gears should you find yourself plagued by depression, anxiety, fear or low self-esteem. Here are some of my favourites:

- **GABA** *Gamma-aminobuteric acid* is a natural metabolite – a substance found in the body – which your body makes from the amino acid-glutamine. It is important for brain chemistry since it has a calming ability.

- **Kava** *Piper methysticum* is a root used in the South Pacific to make a popular drink which for centuries people have taken in order to calm themselves and to promote good will and peace between friends and neighbours. It is a wonderful plant: it really does impart a sense of peaceful contentment and is especially good for counteracting the negative blocked feeling that comes with depression and anxiety.

- **St John's Wort** *Hypericum perforatum* is the centuries-old wise-woman herbal remedy for female depression.

- **Siberian Ginseng** *Eleutherococcus senticosus* is not a real ginseng at all but rather an adaptogenic plant which has been well tested by Russian scientists for its ability to enhance people's stamina, increase resistance to illness and heighten energy over a long period of time. It is also useful for chronic depression, anxiety, fear and low self-esteem.

Face the body snatchers

In Charles Dickens' *A Christmas Carol*, Jacob Marley, Scrooge's dead partner, appears to him as a ghost:

'You don't believe in me,' observed the Ghost. 'I don't,' said Scrooge. 'What evidence would you have of my reality beyond that of your senses?' 'I don't know,' said Scrooge. 'Why do you doubt your senses?' 'Because', said Scrooge, 'a little thing affects them. A slight disorder of the stomach makes them cheat. You may be an undigested bit of beef, a blot of mustard, a crumb of cheese, a fragment of an underdone potato. There's more of gravy than of grave about you, whatever you are!'

Scrooge was right. Biochemical changes brought about by what you eat, how well you eat, and how often you eat, can affect your brain and alter consciousness, producing imaginary fears – even, for some people, hallucinations – and can cause depression and anxiety as well as

LIFESTYLE ENERGY DRAINERS	
Convenience foods	Processed foods contain altered fats, regine flour and sugar, as well as artificial additives, flavourings and preservatives, all of which provoke biochemical chaos and can result in mental confusion and depression, bad skin and increased susceptibility to illness as well as degenerative conditions.
Addictions	Addictions to substances such as cigarettes, narcotics, alcohol, chocolate, sugar or caffeine upset the bodys metabolic balance, depleting it of essential nutrients and leading to chronic fatigue. They also waste energy by channelling it into dead ends instead of freeing it and enabling you to make creative use of it.
Overeating	Eating more than your body needs stresses the digestive system, depleting enzymes so that foods are badly broken down and poorly absorbed – deficiencies result. Digestion in itself requires tremendous amounts of energy and eating too often and too much causes fatigue.
Crash dieting	Fad diets are poorly balanced and deplete the body of vital nutrients, often resulting in fatigue and deficiency diseases such as anaemia. They also make you fat and flabby as you regain the weight you lost.
Sedentary lifestyle	Undermines your body's potential to produce electromagnetic energy and can result in calcium and magnesium being leached from your bones and tissues. This can wreak havoc with nails and hair, too. It can also deplete you of hormones needed to prevent premature ageing and can encourage depression.

chronic fatigue. Let's look at some of the energy-sensitive nutrition-related areas which affect mind, body and spirit and at what can be done to overcome them.

Check out your blood sugar

A common energy drainer is low blood sugar – known as reactive hypoglycaemia. It happens when your body is not able to metabolize carbohydrate efficiently and is often the result of years lived on convenience foods, most of which are stuffed with hidden sugars and refined flour.

Carbohydrates are essential to provide us with the energy we need. But for high-level, lasting energy you need to choose the right kind. Complex carbohydrates such as the wholegrains, brown rice, vegetables, fruits, and wholegrain breads we looked at in Step 3 are the real energy-makers. These are 'good guy' carbs.

Refined or simple carbohydrates like white bread, white rice, most breakfast cereals and sugars are the 'bad guys'.

Simple disasters

In the West, we consume an astounding one-third of our calories in the form of refined sugar. Many experts believe that, as a result, between 65 and 80% of us experience blood sugar problems.

Glucose is the body's primary source of energy, and is especially important for

brain function. We need to maintain our levels of glucose in the blood within a very narrow range. But drinking drinks or eating foods which contain glucose is, strangely enough, the worst thing you can do to accomplish this. To balance blood sugar the body uses a number of elaborate feedback mechanisms and is highly dependent upon the secretion of appropriate quantities of insulin. When sugar levels get too high a release of insulin from the pancreas brings them back down within the normal range.

Pancreatic burnout

This is all well and good when you are eating slow-release complex carbohydrates. But when you eat refined sugar over and over again this can produce a trigger-happy pancreas which keeps pouring out insulin to try to regulate glucose levels in the blood, and produces blood sugar chaos. In time this way of eating can actually exhaust the pancreas altogether. The result? Chronic fatigue, through chronic reactive hypoglycaemia, plus all sorts of symptoms that can come with it. In some people, low blood sugar can bring about the onset of diabetes.

The good news about low blood sugar is that if you suspect you have it, the dietary changes needed to clear it are bound to do you good whether you have low blood sugar or not. Here they are:

Banish coffee, cut out refined foods including sugars and fruit juices, and eat only small quantities of fruit. Get into the way of eating outlined in Step 2. One more thing: consider supplementing your diet from a good chromium source every day (see Step 7, Low blood sugar, for more help).

Chromium is a gift from the gods when it comes to overcoming hypoglycaemia. 200mcg of chromium polynicotinate or chromium picolinate is usually recommended taken one to three times a day.

Thyroid threats

Another body-based energy snatcher is hypothyroidism. As well as chronic fatigue, some of our most common problems – headaches, falling hair, skin troubles, and even a tendency towards infections – can be the result of low thyroid functioning.

Check out your thyroid

The thyroid gland regulates metabolism in every cell of your body and has a lot to say about how much energy you have in your life. When your thyroid gland is under-active this can predispose your body to a lot of undesirable effects:

- Overweight caused by slow fat burning
- Dry skin
- Dry, coarse hair and hair loss
- Constipation
- Thin or brittle nails often with transverse grooves
- Depression, together with weakness and fatigue
- Shortness of breath
- High cholesterol and triglyceride levels
- Capillary damage, water retention and cellulite
- Loss of sex drive
- Infertility, premature birth and stillbirths.

Do-it-yourself thyroid check

- *Before you slip into bed shake down a thermometer to below 92° F and place it beside your bed.*
- *In the morning as soon as you awaken slip the thermometer under your arm and let it rest in your naked armpit for a full ten minutes.*
- *Stay as quiet as you can during this time, with your eyes closed, just resting.*
- *Read your temperature and record it along with the date in your workbook.*
- *Repeat the same procedure for at least 3 – preferably 5 – mornings in*

a row, ideally at the same time each day. (Do not carry out this procedure during the first three days of your menstrual period, but any other time will do.)
- *Normal basal body temperature is between 97.6° F and 98.2° F. If your temperatures are lower than that this may reflect hypothyroidism and require that you see a doctor – preferably one who is aware of the work of doctors such as Broda Barnes (see Resources, page 253).*
- *The best treatment consists of using a supplement either of specific thyroid hormones or (far better) whole thyroid (such as Armour Thyroid) daily, although in some people dietary improvement itself, plus regular exercise, can enormously improve hypothyroidism.*

Are you yeast free?

Yeast is another energy-sapper. The common yeast Candida albicans lives harmlessly in the gastrointestinal tract of all of us, along with a lot of other micro-organisms, some of which actually support high-level health. Candida is the yeast which, if it proliferates in the vaginal tract, can cause thrush.

Candida overgrowth factors

Here are some factors which are most common in people with chronic yeast syndrome. Do many of these apply to you?

• Impaired immune function
• Sensitivity to dampness and smells
• Emotional mood swings, confusion and depression
• Recurrent vaginal yeast in women and recurrent problems in the prostate in men
• Frequent use of cortisone-related drugs and ulcer drugs
• Frequent or long-term use of antibiotics for recurrent infections or the treatment of acne
• Chronic digestive problems such as bloating or wind
• Food reactions such as food allergies
• Long-term fatigue
• Recurrent skin fungus problems such as athlete's foot, or nail problems or genital itching
• Cravings for sweets, breads or alcohol
• Eating a lot of sugar
• Diabetes mellitus.

The good news is that most of the things you can do to improve the overall quality of your diet, such as cutting out junk fats, sugar and highly processed foods (all of which candida thrives on), alter the internal environment and discourage the proliferation of this yeast/fungus. However, if you suspect a significant level of candidiasis, experts offer advice which is useful to follow since it does not contradict the general guidelines for good eating and has made an enormous difference in the lives of many people who have been made miserable by this condition:

Anti-candida foods

Stress these in your diet:

- meats (preferably organic)
- chicken
- turkey
- eggs
- fish
- wholegrains except wheat
- pulses
- nuts and seeds
- butter
- extra virgin olive oil
- lemon
- fruit
- vegetables

Foods to avoid:

- sugar in any form
- fruit juices
- dried fruit
- honey
- baked goods containing yeast or made from wheat flour
- simple carbohydrates such as most breakfast cereals, white bread, white rice and pasta
- mushrooms
- cheeses
- vinegars
- alcoholic drinks

Candida check

- *Drop the drugs: don't take antibiotics, steroids, birth control pills, or standard drug-based HRT (unless there is a real medical necessity).*
- *Change your diet: don't feed candida on foods it thrives on. This means avoid like the plague any refined carbohydrate foods like white flour and refined sugars, such as corn syrup and glucose, fruit juices and honey. Also steer clear of milk products, baked foods made with wheat flour, and all foods to which you suspect you might be allergic or sensitive.*
- *Never eat foods which may have a high yeast content: avoid alcohol, cheese, peanuts, dried fruits, grapes and yeast breads.*
- *Eat lots of fresh vegetables: (except yams, parsnips, corn and potatoes): eat as much as you like of fish and game, lamb and wholegrains, except wheat.*
- *Limit fruits: to no more than two pieces a day, chosen from apples, berries, pears and bananas, until symptoms have gone.*
- *Check for food sensitivities: food sensitivities are common with candida. The things you crave are frequently what the yeast itself craves. Try to identify any possible sensitivities and weed them out. This can help a lot.*
- *Drink pau darco: this tea from the South American tree has a long folk use in the treatment of infections probably thanks to its lapachol content. Both lapachol and other compounds from pau darco have demonstrated anti-candida effects. Drink some several times a day.*

- **Add a grapefruit seed extract:** *and a good probiotic supplement to your diet.*
- **Go for help:** *if these things do not make a significant difference then seek out a good nutritionist or nutritionally-orientated doctor who is genuinely knowledgeable about the treatment of candida. It is not enough to simply give a fungicidal drug, which is the usual treatment. While it can suppress the candida when you are taking it, often when you stop doing so it regrows, so you are soon back to where you started.*
- **Take heart:** *once the candida is under control you will probably be able to eat everything you like so long as you continue to steer clear of unnecessary drugs and highly processed convenience foods. But be patient. It takes time for nature to balance your body from inside out.*

Food sensitivities

Sometimes called food intolerance or even food allergies, these sensitivities, which were first identified way back in the 1930s by the famous allergist Dr Albert Rowe, are an alarmingly common cause of chronic fatigue. Rowe called the kind of chronic fatigue which arises from food allergies – and often includes muscle and joint aches, depression, sleepiness and poor concentration – allergic toremia. Later he realized how widespread this condition is and renamed it allergic tension-fatigue syndrome. Today, unfortunately, many doctors faced with chronic fatigue in their patients forget that somewhere between 50 and 85 per cent of these people, when tested, will be found to be food-allergic.

Allergy with a difference

Food allergies are quite different from ordinary allergies, where you have an antibody response to something you have come into contact with. The curious thing is that often what you happen to be allergic to, whether it be wheat or alcohol or chocolate, you will find you have a craving for. Wheat is one of the most common foods to which people are allergic.

Food allergies happen when for any number of reasons your body reacts badly to the food you eat. This reaction may or may not be mediated by the immune system and therefore may or may not be picked up by a doctor trained in traditional methods of spotting allergies.

Beware leaky gut

Many things can cause a bad reaction to food. It can be a response to the protein or starch or additives the food contains (such as colourings or preservatives). In some cases it is a high sensitivity or a drug-like reaction to the food. In others the intestinal mucosa may become damaged causing what is known as leaky gut syndrome, where long chain proteins or starches or unwanted chemicals are drawn straight through the gut wall into the blood-stream where they have no business to be.

Food allergies used to be relatively uncommon. Now they are becoming so widespread that many nutritionally-trained doctors estimate that more than 50% of people in the Western world suffer from symptoms associated with food reactions.

Tests for food allergies

There are various ways to find out if you are food-allergic. You can use an elimination diet which usually consists of lamb, chicken, potatoes, rice, bananas, broccoli and pears eaten with nothing else for a period of one or two weeks. If you are food-allergic, your symptoms should disappear by about the sixth day of the diet. After a week or two on the elimination diet you then 'challenge' your system very carefully by continuing with the same elimination diet but adding every other day a new food – on its own – to which you suspect you may be allergic. Then watch to see if any symptoms reappear. This takes a lot of time and care, and means recording everything carefully. Gradually, provided only one suspected food is introduced at a time, you can eventually identify the culprit foods and then eliminate them completely from your diet from then on. (For more help, see Step 7, Allergy.)

Energy soars

When you eliminate foods to which you are allergic your energy levels rise and rise. If then you suddenly introduce a food to which you are allergic you will get a reaction either immediately or within the next two to three days.

There are also lab tests designed to identify food allergies, but they tend to be expensive and the average doctor usually knows little about them. Typical skin scratch tests used by many doctors to identify what are known as IgE allergies – that is those which involve a particular antibody – are pretty useless when it comes to checking for food allergies as they will only pick up between 10 and 15% of them.

What do you crave?

Biscuits, bread, pastry and pasta? Suspect wheat.
Cheese, butter, yoghurt? Suspect milk.
Chocolate? Suspect sugar, chocolate, or processed fats.
Coffee or cola? Do you drink more than 2 cups/glasses a day? Suspect caffeine.
Orange drinks, oranges, orange sorbet? Suspect oranges.
Ice cream or creamy desserts? Suspect milk, sugar or junk fats.
Pizza, tomato sauce, spaghetti? Suspect tomatoes
Wine? Suspect grapes, sugar or yeast.

Digestive enzyme helpers

The healthy body produces its own enzymes, each of which has a specific job to do like breaking down fats or breaking down proteins or cellulose in the foods you eat. Crash dieting, chlorine in drinking water, poor eating, stress or deficiencies of specific minerals or vitamins needed for your body to produce these enzymes can mean that your enzyme supply becomes depleted and that you are therefore unable to break your foods down properly. Digestive enzymes such as amylase, protease, lipase and bromelin are essential to break down the foods you eat into usable nutrients. Supplements of these enzymes can often be especially helpful for anyone with a food allergy as well as anyone who is experiencing difficulties with digestion or chronic fatigue. (See Resources, pages 253-4.)

Anaemia needs checking

Another common cause of long-term fatigue is anaemia. Anaemia is often the result of low levels of iron which in turn produce a deficiency in haemoglobin, the iron-containing part of red blood cells responsible for carrying oxygen to the cells all over the body and for removing waste carbon dioxide from them. If you suspect anaemia, go and see your doctor and ask him or her to do a *serum ferritin* lab test to find out about your body's iron supplies. (A routine blood analysis is simply not accurate enough.) If you find you do need extra iron, be choosy about what kind you take, since many of the iron tablets you buy over the counter or which are commonly prescribed by doctors are both poorly absorbed and can cause constipation. (See Resources, page 253.)

Source your iron

There are two alternatives: 'heme' iron which comes from animal sources only – especially liver – and 'non-heme' iron which comes from plants. Heme iron is much better absorbed and does not depend on having sufficient hydrochloric acid in the stomach to use it. Non-heme iron is only one-fifth as easily absorbed. It is also easily removed from the body before absorption by the presence of fibre in the diet, calcium, preservatives etc, while heme iron remains unaffected.

Eating good organic liver several times a week is about the best way of all to build your iron reserves, provided of course that you are not a vegetarian. Liver has been shown to have all sorts of blood-building and health-building properties. When it comes to liver, if you can possibly afford it, eat organic. If you are a vegetarian, consider taking a plant-based liquid supplement. (See Resources, pages 253-4.) If you are anaemic it is also a good idea to take the other blood-building nutrients in extra quantity – vitamin B12, folic acid and vitamin C as well as a good green supplement such as Pure Synergy (see Resources, pages 253-4). (For more help, see Step 7, Anaemia.)

The metabolic body snatchers can all be big energy-drainers. The annoying thing about them is that more often than not someone with one problem, say food allergies, is likely to have low blood sugar as well. That is the bad news. The good news is that what is useful in collaring one of the body snatchers will also help you get rid of another. What is good in tackling all of them is simply detoxifying your body.

Junk the junk

When we eat convenience foods over a period of time two things happen. Firstly, we end up with subclinical nutritional deficiencies of vitamins and minerals because so many essential nutrients have been lost in the processing and storage of these foods. Secondly, wastes accumulate in the tissues. What the body tends to do with toxic wastes is tuck them away in fat cells so the more wastes you hold in your body the more fat cells you are likely to accumulate to store them in.

Any body burdened with a high level of wastes channels much of its available energy into trying to handle these toxins rather than into keeping cells functioning efficiently and providing you with ongoing energy. In broad terms this means that you are likely to experience flagging vitality over the years and to feel that you simply can't make the effort to change things for the better. Before you do anything else on your road to creating a high-energy lifestyle, you need to junk the junk food:

- microwave meals
- pizzas
- highly processed breakfast cereals
- pasties
- cakes
- biscuits
- colas and diet colas
- fruit drinks
- flavoured yoghurts
- trifles.

Get rid of them all.

Forget the guilt, look to the rewards

The first barrier to overcome is attitude. Stop blaming yourself and look to strengthening your overall state of health and raising your energy levels instead.

Here are some of the junk-free diet bonuses:

- *Greater emotional balance*
- *Abundant energy*
- *Sparkling eyes and clear, glowing skin*
- *Strong shiny hair*
- *A leaner, firmer body*
- *A clear mind*
- *A fresh, positive outlook on life*
- *Relief from constant hunger.*

Drink like a fish

Few of us drink enough. On average, in a temperate climate we need about (3.6 litres) 6 pints of pure, clean water a day for optimal health, although few of us consume even as much as (1.2 litres) 2 pints. Provided you are not suffering from a kidney or liver disease, keep a large bottle or two of pure, fresh mineral water on your desk and make sure you consume your quota of this clear, delicious health-giving drink.

Get into water

One of my favourite energy-enhancing and energy-balancing techniques is the use of hot and cold water applications on the surface of the body. Using water in this way has the remarkable ability to energize you when you are down as well as calm you when you are over-stressed. I use if often and swear by it. The use of hot and cold water – it is a practice known as contrast-hydrotherapy – can stimulate adrenal functions, alleviate inflammation, enhance hormone production, firm skin, balance the nervous system, strengthen muscles and energize the body and psyche. The greater the contrast between the temperature of the water applied to the skin and body temperature itself, the greater the effect contrast-hydro produces. Using hydrotherapy for energy is easy provided, of course, you are generally healthy and not suffering from a heart condition. It is a simple matter of developing new habits. Hot water is applied to the whole body for three or four minutes in the form of a hot bath or shower, followed by thirty to sixty seconds of cold water. This procedure is repeated three times. The application of cold water need only be long enough to ensure that the blood vessels constrict sufficiently, and this has been shown to take place in as short a period as twenty seconds.

Contrast-hydro makes you feel great – but it is important to start slowly, increasing the length of your exposure to hot and cold water gradually. It can be done in the shower by taking a three-minute hot shower followed by twenty seconds to one minute of cold, repeating this three times beginning with hot and ending with cold.

Hot and cold protocols

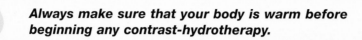

Always make sure that your body is warm before beginning any contrast-hydrotherapy.

See that the room is well heated. At no time during hydrotherapy should the body become chilled.

Always begin with a hot application and end with a cold.

Begin slowly with 2-3 minutes of hot application followed by 20 seconds of cold. As your body accustoms itself to contrast-hydrotherapy you can increase the time of the cold application up to 1 minute.

After water contrast-hydrotherapy dry your body well and make sure that you do not become chilled.

Don't use contrast-hydrotherapy if you have any kind of organic disease, nervous disorder, high blood pressure, insulin-dependent diabetes, if you are very weak, or suffering from hardening of the arteries.

Always check with your doctor before beginning any natural treatment to make sure that it is appropriate for you to use.

Low energy checklist

- *Stop doing everything yourself.* Start delegating, both at work and at home, and whenever you can, get someone else to do what needs to be done. Reach for the top but never struggle in vain.
- *Take a close look at your values.* What really matters to you? You can't have everything. Make choices. Otherwise you could end up a workhorse who's ultimately not very good at anything.
- *Don't say yes to everything.* When something is asked of you, give yourself time to consider the request before you immediately agree. Is it something you can handle with relative ease? What are you going to have to lay aside to do it? What is it going to cost you in terms of time?
- *Forget the hero image.* You are only human. And you'd be surprised how much pleasure it can bring to other people when they feel they can do something for you for a change. Express your needs and many of them are likely to be satisfied. Lock them away behind the perfectly 'together' superhuman image you project and you go it alone.
- *Guard your time jealously.* Limit the time you spend on inessential things such as seeing people you don't really care about just because you feel it is expected of you. Cut back on the chores you feel you have to do. Do you really have to? Or could somebody else do them for you? Or could they remain undone for the sake of your peace of mind?
- *Sort your priorities.* Take a look at what is absolutely essential to your life and what is marginal. Write them down in your journal then make sure the time and effort you spend on each thing is in line with these priorities. Take an active role in deciding how you will spend your time and live your life. Don't just let it happen.
- *Create a routine.* From day to day you need to make sure you have time to relax and to take care of yourself and time to spend with the people you love. Recreation and having fun are as important as hard work, responsibility and success.

Make sure you get the balance right.

STEP SEVEN: HEAL YOURSELF

Fuel-up

Raw juice is the most perfect fuel for your body. Its high water content means that it is easily assimilated and tends to cleanse and nurture the body, and it is the richest available source of vitamins, minerals and enzymes. Not only is it the best possible tonic for promoting all-round health and general well-being, each juice has specific therapeutic properties and this chapter shows how you can use raw juice as a quick fix to treat a range of common complaints.

Modern medical science tends to have a nuts and bolts approach in prescribing drugs to treat the symptoms of illness, frequently without paying attention to the underlying causes of the condition. Natural health practitioners try to take a holistic view, seeing the body as a complete organism with many parts, all of which must operate synergistically for the whole being to be healthy. Illness is the result of disharmony, or a chemical imbalance in the body caused by nutritional deficiency.

Here are suggestions as to which foods you should eat (and which ones you should avoid) in order to alleviate the misery of a number of all-too-common complaints. The suggestions are followed, in each case, by a list of appropriate juice recipes. Most of the conditions described below will respond rapidly when you drink the recommended juices, but do remember that these are only recommendations, not prescriptions. Any attempt to treat a medical condition should always come under the direction of a competent physician.

Acne

A lot of acne is the result of eating a diet high in sugar and low in fibre. When the body is not eliminating waste properly, the pores of the skin become blocked. It is very important to make sure that you eat plenty of vegetables that are rich in fibre (not wheat or wheat bran as in wholegrain bread as this tends to clog up people who suffer from acne and skin problems). Steer clear of processed convenience foods (they are full of the kind of hydrogenated fats you find in margarines) and stick to using olive oil for your salads and wok frying. Do a detox and use a diet which emphasizes fresh vegetables and fruits. Avoid dairy products.

Carrot juice is very beneficial for acne, but the green juices are supreme. Drink lots and lots of fresh carrot juice, to which you add as much green as you can manage, as often as you can manage it. The best sources of green are cabbage and kale, beetroot and turnip tops, watercress and spinach, parsley and dandelion leaves.

All juice recipes make approximately 280ml/10fl. oz/half a pint of liquid. Use a centrifugal extractor (see Resourses, pages 253-4), except for those requiring a food processor or blender.

CARROT AND APPLE
This is the most basic juice cocktail; use it as the springboard for experimentation. Start by combining equal parts of the two juices and experiment until you find the proportions that suit you.

**4 carrots
1 apple**

CARROT HIGH
**5 carrots
4 sticks celery
1 clove garlic**

CHLOROPHYLL PLUS
**A handful of dandelion leaves
A handful of parsley
A handful of spinach
1 whole apple
A small bunch of grapes**

GINGER SPICE
**3 large carrots
1 whole pear
A small chunk of fresh ginger**

GREEN FRIEND
**3 whole apples
2-3 dandelion leaves or a couple of large kale leaves or beetroot tops
A handful of mint**

Allergy

All allergies, from the classic antibody antigen reaction that causes the release of histamine, to food allergies which can act quite differently, must be treated holistically. That means diet, rest, stress management and the elimination of any possible trigger foods or environmental chemicals.

Most allergic reactions occur when the body is over-acidic. A high alkaline diet, such as a high-raw diet, plus lots of alfalfa sprouts or juice (which is rich in mineral salts) can help to create the right internal environment. Celery will also help you become allergy-free. Grapefruit, orange, cantaloupe and parsley are rich in the bioflavonoids; spinach, kale and sweet peppers are rich in B6, which can be particularly helpful for many sensitivities; garlic, spinach and cauliflower are a good source of molybdenum, a trace element that tends to be deficient in people who are sensitive to the sulphites and MSG.

CELERY STICKS
3-4 sticks celery
4-5 carrots
1 clove garlic

Juice as usual and drink immediately.

PARSLEY PASSION
Another vegetable rich in mineral salts is parsley. Drinking parsley juice daily can bring relief to people troubled by allergies.

1 bunch parsley
3-5 carrots
2 apples
2 small cauliflower florets

RED COOL
The addition of a cube or more of ginger makes Red Cool red hot.

1 beetroot
2 apples
4 carrots
1 (or more) 1cm cube of fresh ginger

SPROUT SPECIAL
This juice is rich in natural phyto-hormones that help protect the body from the damage that petrochemically derived pesticides and herbicides can foster. It is also enormously rich in life-enhancing enzymes.

4 carrots
1 whole apple
1 cup sprouted seeds (mung beans, alfalfa, chickpeas, adzuki beans, etc)

Sprinkle some grated ginger on top or a little cinnamon and serve over ice.

Anaemia

Anaemia occurs either when there is a decrease in the total number of red blood cells, or in the volume of the blood, or when red blood cells become abnormal in shape or size. This condition tends to make you pale and weak and inhibits your resistance to infection. It often creates insomnia, leading to irritability and depression and causing chronic fatigue. There are a number of different underlying deficiencies that are present when one is anaemic; iron is important in order to be able to form new red blood cells, and folic acid and vitamin B12 help to rebuild red blood cells. If anaemia persists, consult your doctor. It could possibly be the result of abnormalities in the production of haemoglobin itself.

Green drinks and green foods are essential for anaemia sufferers. They are rich in folic acid and many of them are rich in iron, particularly watercress, spinach, beetroot tops, dandelion leaves and the brassicas. Vegetables which are particularly beneficial include parsley, green pepper, beetroot tops, carrot, kale, spinach and asparagus. Berries can be very useful, particularly for women (they are good for menstrual cramps, morning sickness and calming labour pains, not to mention sea sickness, yeast infections and poor circulation).

Try to drink as many green drinks as possible. To each glass add a teaspoon of spirulina, which is extremely rich in B12, and shake or blend well.

BEET TREAT
Profoundly powerful, this juice will give you sustained energy throughout the day.

> 1/2 whole beetroot (plus tops, if possible)
> 2 carrots
> 1 apple
> 1 stalk celery
> 3 cm cucumber

DANDELION PLUS
> 4-5 carrots
> A handful of dandelion leaves
> 1 bulb of fennel
> lemon juice

DOUBLE WHAMMY
> 4-5 carrots
> A handful of dandelion leaves
> 2 whole pears

EASY DOES IT
> 1 large green apple, whole
> 2 stalks celery
> 8-10 lettuce leaves

Juice as usual and drink before bedtime, or when you are feeling particularly tense.

GREEN ZINGER
> 2 kale leaves or beetroot tops or a handful of spinach
> 4-5 carrots
> A small handful of parsley

RED FLAG
> 3 small ripe tomatoes
> 4 carrots
> A handful of spinach

Arthritis

Both osteoarthritis and rheumatoid arthritis have been successfully treated with juice therapy, which is particularly beneficial if the patient has not been on long-term drug treatment. Osteoarthritis affects the bones and joints with symptoms such as swelling of soft tissues, local tenderness, restricted movement, bony swellings and crackings of the joints as well as stiffness after resting. The more the joint is used in osteoarthritis, the worse the pain generally becomes. Rheumatoid arthritis produces inflammatory conditions in the joints and the structures surrounding joints, as well as a feeling of weakness, often with low-grade fever, long-term fatigue, pain and stiffness. Rheumatoid arthritis is increasingly considered an auto-immune reaction where the body has actually developed antibodies against its own tissues.

In both osteo- and rheumatoid arthritis, certain things are essential. Firstly, that you cut out foods from the nightshade family such as potatoes, aubergine, tomatoes, and peppers. Secondly (in the case of osteoarthritis) that you avoid citrus fruits such as limes, lemons, oranges and grapefruits. In the tradition of natural medicine these are believed to contribute to the inflammation.

With both forms of arthritis, it is important to avoid all convenience foods and refined foods such as white sugar, white flour, processed foods that contain chemical additives, and alcohol. Consider the possibility that you might have some sort of a sensitivity or allergic reaction to food, perhaps to wheat or to dairy products. Try eliminating wheat flour and everything made from it as well as all dairy products from your diet for three weeks and see if it makes a significant difference. In the case of rheumatoid arthritis it can be useful, if you are not a vegetarian, to eat more cold water fish such as tuna, sardines, salmon and mackerel which contain the essential fatty acid known as omega-3. Many people with arthritis fare better on a low-fat vegetarian diet.

Vegetables to incorporate into your juices include carrot, beetroot tops, broccoli, turnip, grapes, kale, cabbage, all dark green vegetables, apple, and ginger. Pineapple is particularly good for rheumatoid arthritis since it contains the enzyme bromelin which has anti-inflammatory properties.

Dandelion juice is excellent, especially for rheumatoid arthritis. Pick the dandelion greens carefully, from places which are not likely to have been sprayed and are not along the verges of roads where they may have picked up heavy metals such as lead from air pollution. Cut off the leaves and wash them well before putting them through the juicer. If you are used to drinking green juices you can actually drink dandelion juice on its own, or mixed equally with carrot. It also mixes well with a little watercress. If you are not used to drinking green juices, it can be useful to start with a delicious sweet juice such as carrot and apple and then gradually increase the levels of dandelion you are putting into it. Dandelion also has the ability to create an amazing high once the juice is assimilated into the liver, which usually takes about half an hour. But go easy, for if your digestive system is not used to green juices this can be too much of a shock. Start with small amounts and increase gradually.

GINGER BERRY
1 (or more) 1cm cube of fresh ginger
1 medium bunch of grapes
2 cups blackberries or raspberries

Juice as usual. You can also add some sparkling mineral water to this, or some ice; it makes a delicious and refreshing long drink on a hot day.

GREEN GODDESS
This juice makes you smile like the Mona Lisa

60 ml (2 fl oz) of carrot juice
60 ml (2 fl oz) of apple juice
60 ml (2 fl oz) of beetroot juice
60 ml (2 fl oz) of broccoli juice
1/2 tsp kelp powder
1/2-1 tsp chopped fresh parsley
A squeeze of fresh lemon juice

GREEN WOW
2 green apples
4 stalks of celery
6 Chinese leaves
Juice of 10cm of cucumber

PINEAMINT
Especially good if taken at bedtime for settling the stomach.

1 small pineapple
A small bunch of fresh mint leaves

Remove the skin of the pineapple and cut into convenient spears. Juice as usual and serve over ice for a long summer drink.

PINEAPPLE GREEN
To 180ml (6 fl oz) of freshly extracted pineapple juice add one or more of the following:

1 tsp-1 tbsp of powdered wheat
   grass, green barley
spirulina or chlorella

POPEYE PUNCH
1 whole apple – including seeds
4 or 5 carrots
A small handful of spinach
1 cucumber

RED GENIUS
4 carrots
1 large raw beetroot
3cm section of cucumber

SPROUTING O' THE GREEN
2 cups of alfalfa sprouts
2 cups of mung bean sprouts
1 carrot
A few sprigs of parsley
2 apples

TOP OF THE BEET
1 apple
5 carrots
3 leaves of beetroot top
A handful of parsley

Asthma

The theory is that asthma comes in two forms. One kind is said to be caused by specific allergens either in the air or food; the other is said to have no particular cause. Most experts in natural medicine, however, find that there is always an allergic element, as there is also always an emotional one in any kind of asthma or other condition in which the symptoms include spasms of the bronchial tubes and swelling of the mucous membranes.

Perhaps the most important remedy is to eliminate from the diet any foods that create mucus in the body. This means not eating dairy products, coffee, tea, chocolate, wheat, and convenience foods. Many asthmatics find they do best when they eliminate from their diet not only wheat but other grains as well (except for buckwheat, which is not a true grain, and brown rice or millet).

Asthmatics seem to be more affected by food allergies than other people, which can result in inflammation of the bronchial tubes that causes an even stronger reaction to smoke, pollen and air pollutants such as sulphur-dioxide. Asthma also appears to weaken the adrenal glands, so handling it means living on a low-allergy diet in which at least 50 per cent of the foods that you eat are taken raw.

Juices that are rich in magnesium, which relaxes the bronchial muscle, are particularly useful, including turnip, watercress, kale, turnip greens, parsley, collard greens, carrots, asparagus and beetroot tops. A couple of tablespoons of lemon juice added to any glass of fresh raw juice is a traditional treatment for asthma, as are molasses, which can be a useful additive to a glass of any juice. Other additives which are equally useful include fresh ginger, onions, and garlic (in small quantities, if you wish to keep your friends).

CARROT HIGH (SEE PAGE 153)

GLORIOUS GRAPEFRUIT
Apparently there is a world glut of pink grapefruits, which make a frothy, sweet and sharp juice that is wonderful to drink for breakfast. Peel the fruit, but remember to leave as much of the white pith as possible to put through your juicer. Two grapefruits will yield slightly more than half a pint of juice.

HI MAG
  4-5 carrots
  2 florets of broccoli
  2 dandelion leaves, beetroot tops, spinach or kale leaves

Juice and season with a twist of lemon and a pinch of salt.

HI NRG
  1 apple
  2 carrots
  1 stalk of celery
  Soya milk to taste

LESLIE'S COCKTAIL
Bananas are not totally unjuiceable if you use very ripe fruit. Put them through your juicer first, then the apples, which will help to flush the thick banana through the machine. Alternatively, use a blender to make the breakfast of champions. This recipe also works well with melon in place of apple.

  180ml (6 fl oz) of fresh apple juice
  1 ripe banana
  1 tsp each of spirulina, chlorella, and green barley powder

POTASSIUM PUNCH
A tribute to N.W. Walker, the American raw food pioneer and evangelist of detoxification; drink it religiously!

  3 carrots
  2 stalks celery
  4-6 leaves of lettuce or winter greens
  A few stalks of fresh coriander or parsley
  A handful of spinach or watercress (or dandelion leaves)

Cellulite

Orange peel skin – the lumps and bumps that are so hard to get rid of, even in slim women – can be shed provided you take a total body approach to the issue. Women with cellulite are often constipated, even if they have one bowel movement a day, and they also tend to have poor lymphatic drainage, so that wastes are not eliminated properly. In addition, many women with cellulite suffer from poor liver function and an under-active thyroid.

Foods that are rich in bioflavonoids such as sweet peppers, tomatoes, cabbage, parsley and citrus fruits (incorporate the pithy, white covering inside the peel in your juices) are important because they help strengthen the capillaries so you don't get leakage and the pockets of water that create peau d'orange flesh. Vitamin C is also important to strengthen the capillaries, as is zinc. If you want to shed cellulite permanently, shift the percentage of raw foods in your diet so that you are consuming between 50 and 75 per cent of your foods raw. Use skin brushing, cut out all convenience foods which are replete with junk fats and chemicals, and eliminate coffee and tea.

Remember that cellulite is slow to form and slow to clear, but it will go away provided you are persistent. These juices will be beneficial:

GINGER BERRY (SEE PAGE 156)

GINGER'S BEST
  1/2 cantaloupe melon
  1/2 cm slice fresh ginger
  1 lime (peel, leaving pith)

HI MAG (SEE PAGE 158)

PINEAPPLE GREEN (SEE PAGE 157)

POTASSIUM POWER
  1 yellow or green melon, such as cantaloupe, honeydew etc.
  1 over-ripe banana
  A pinch of grated nutmeg
  6 cubes ice (made with spring water)

Scoop out the flesh of the melon, place in a food processor or blender, add the banana, blend well, pour into a glass over the ice cubes and sprinkle with a pinch of freshly ground nutmeg.

WATERFALL
  5cm section of cucumber
  1 whole apple
  3 carrots
  1/2 smallish beetroot

Colds

The common cold has for generations been considered by natural health practitioners to be the body's means of eliminating waste when it has become overloaded. When you feel yourself coming down with a cold eliminate all dairy products from your diet and all foods with sugar in them and do a Juice Blitz.

Juicing for colds has two goals. The first is to strengthen the immune system, and for this you need lots of greens – kale, parsley, green pepper, watercress – which contain plenty of anti-oxidants such as bet-carotene (don't forget your carrots too) as well as vitamin C, chlorophyll and all of those as yet unexplained plant properties which are so strengthening to the body. The second purpose of juicing for colds is in

BEETROOT, CARROT & ORANGE
Beetroot enriches the blood and provides an excellent tonic for the kidneys. The sweetness of orange juice in this recipe will help you become accustomed to the earthy flavour of beet.

> **1 smallish beet**
> **4 carrots**
> **1 orange**

Save one of the carrots to put through the juicer last, as it will help to clear the machine.

CARROT HIGH (SEE PAGE 153)

GINGER SPICE (SEE PAGE 153)

HI MAG (SEE PAGE 158)

PINEAPPLE GRAPEFRUIT DRINK
> **1 small pineapple**
> **1 peeled grapefruit**

RED GENIUS (SEE PAGE 157)

SALAD JUICE
> **4-5 carrots**
> **4 sticks celery**
> **3-4 radishes**

SWEET AND SPICY
> **2 whole apples**
> **2 x 1cm cube fresh ginger**
> **1/2 small pineapple cut into convenient-sized spears**

Juice as usual, adding as much ginger as you like, and sprinkle with a little ground cinnamon.

many ways the most important and that is elimination. This means using juices from vegetables and fruits which help eliminate waste from the system. These include lemon, apricot, garlic, parsley, ginger, watercress, kale, radish, spinach, apple, pear and tomato.

ATOMIC LIFT-OFF
This gives an immediate lift when you are feeling low. It's also a wonderful chaser for shots of tequila!

> **4-6 ripe tomatoes**
> **1 lime**
> **A pinch of cayenne pepper, or dash of Tabasco**

Juice the tomatoes and the lime (removing the skin but leaving the pith) then sprinkle with a dash of cayenne pepper.

Constipation

Constipation is the hidden condition that, according to natural health practitioners, is so widespread that it would be hard to quantify it. These experts insist that very few of us are actually cleansing our colon as thoroughly as we should. Most people find that when they begin to take juices and eat a higher percentage of their foods raw, their constipation clears by itself and they begin to have two or three bowel movements a day. It is essential to overall health that the bowels function really well, for if faecal matter stays in the colon then harmful substances from the natural bacteria that live in the bowel can contribute to the development of many specific ailments such as haemorrhoids, varicose veins, hernias, cellulite, flatulence, obesity, insomnia, bad breath, indigestion and diverticulitis. Constipation also plays a part in the development of degenerative diseases, from cancer to coronary heart disease, diabetes and even long-term depression.

One of the best natural remedies for constipation is rhubarb. Rhubarb is a vegetable but is usually thought of as a fruit. It is rich in calcium, phosphorus, iron, sodium, potassium, vitamin A, folic acid, vitamin C and magnesium. Raw rhubarb, like spinach, also contains oxalic acid, which you don't want to get too much of. Therefore rhubarb is not an ingredient we would use daily in any of our juices. Rhubarb is useful for intestinal parasites and for intestinal wind, and rhubarb juice

applied externally is traditionally used to treat leg ulcers, bed sores and wounds. However, rhubarb juice and spinach juice should not be taken by anyone who suffers from kidney stones, because of their high oxalic acid content.

Getting over constipation is usually a simple matter once you begin to juice, but there are a number of juices that are especially useful during the transition stage. Rhubarb, apples, spinach, prunes and pears all have a natural laxative effect.

APPLES AND PEARS
Apples and pears are closely related and make a sublime combination when juiced together.

2 pears
2 whole apples

Juice as usual and drink straight away as this oxidises very quickly.

BEET TREAT (SEE PAGE 158)

BLACK WATERMELON
You have two choices on how to prepare this, you can juice the skin of the watermelon as well as the pink flesh and then add the molasses and stir in. Or, you can take only the pink flesh, put it into a blender or food processor, add the molasses and blend.

1/4 small watermelon
1 tsp-1 tbsp blackstrap molasses (unsulphured)

CARROT, BEET, CELERY, TOMATO
3 carrots
1/2 beetroot, peeled
2 stalks of celery
2 tomatoes

GINGER'S BEST (SEE PAGE 159)

RHUBARB RADIANCE
Drink at night before bed.

2 large stalks rhubarb
3 medium apples

SPINAPPLE
When you mix apple with spinach you have an amazing combination for cleansing the digestive tract and improving elimination quickly, probably because spinach (which is high in oxalic acid) combines with the pectin in the apple's mineral salts to form a unique compound that has remarkable cleansing actions. Some practitioners in natural medicine claim that it actually clears old encrusted faeces that has accumulated over months and years in the colon making it possible to eliminate it from the body.

3 whole apples
A handful of spinach

Drink twice a day; especially important just before bedtime.

SPROUT SPECIAL (SEE PAGE 154)

TROPICAL PRUNE
1 small pineapple, peeled and cut into convenient-sized spears
2 fresh prunes – when prunes are not in season, substitute one pear

Juice as normal, then grate a pinch of nutmeg on to the top and serve.

Depression

Feeling depressed is not just a psychological condition. Very often that sense of purposelessness, emptiness, feelings of worthlessness and guilt, come from a bio-chemical imbalance in the body. Internal pollution is a major cause.

The neurotransmitters – hormones in the brain which control feeling – are derived from the food we eat, so the food has got to be good. Serotonin (derived from the amino acid tryptophan) is a particularly significant neuro-transmitter. When there are adequate levels of serotonin in the brain the mood tends to be elevated and sleep normal; low serotonin levels are associated with mood distortions and interrupted sleep patterns. A meal rich in complex carbohydrates helps the body absorb tryptophan, and therefore promotes the production of serotonin.

Bananas, figs and dates are rich in tryptophan. Carbohydrate in the form of a piece of toast and a banana before bed can help tremendously to induce sleep and also create a sense of calm peacefulness (provided, of course, that you are not allergic to the grains from which the toast is made).

To banish the blues permanently, increase the levels of raw food in your diet to between 50 and 75 per cent each day. Meanwhile make your juices rich in dark green vegetables full of magnesium, potassium, iron, calcium and folic acid. A deficiency in any of these can contribute to depression, as can a deficiency in fatty acids, which is why it can be useful to add linseeds to your juices. Don't be discouraged if it takes a little time to deep-cleanse your body and replenish the nutrients you may be lacking. It is well worth the effort.

CHLOROPHYLL PLUS (SEE PAGE 153)

GINGER SPICE (SEE PAGE 153)

HI MAG (SEE PAGE 158)

LINUSIT PERFECT
This recipe is replete with valuable essential fatty acids – both omega-6 and omega-3 – which are often deficient in people who have been surviving on the typical Western fare of convenience foods. It must be made with freshly ground vacuum-packed linseeds or flaxseeds for these precious fatty acids are highly unstable and go rancid quickly.

2 whole apples
1/2cm slice of ginger
3 carrots
1 tbsp linseeds or flaxseeds

Juice the fruit, carrots and ginger as usual. Place the linseed in a coffee grinder and grind finely. Then add to the glass of juice, stir well and drink immediately. Alternatively you can put the linseed into a food processor, grind and then pour the freshly made juice in and blend for 3 seconds.

PINEAMINT (SEE PAGE 157)

RED GENIUS (SEE PAGE 157)

SALSA SURPRISE
2 large ripe tomatoes
3 carrots
2 sticks of celery
A small bunch of parsley
1 clove garlic

Digestion

Digestive troubles come in many forms, from minor problems such as a bloated feeling after a meal, to abdominal pain and wind, nausea, and more serious ailments like gastric ulcers, diverticulitis, and colon troubles. In all these circumstances, it's important to avoid taking in any substances that can irritate the gut, such as coffee, alcohol and chocolate. Occasionally stomach troubles come from hypochlorhydria – a deficiency of hydrochloric acid – in which case pineapple and papaya juice are excellent since they are rich in the protein-digesting enzymes bromelin and papain.

Among clinical reports of juicing, none is more impressive than the results that Dr Garnett Cheney of Stanford University reported for his treatment of gastric ulcers using juices alone. Dr Cheney prescribed for his patients fresh raw green cabbage juice, prepared and drunk immediately. It contains anti-peptic ulcer factors which have a really quite remarkable effect.

Cabbage juice tends to benefit most digestive upsets. It's not exactly delicious, however, and it can be helpful to mix it with pineapple juice to soften the flavour. Ginger is also good for digestion and has been used for thousands of years to counteract nausea, travel sickness, and morning sickness. Bananas have been shown to help protect the stomach from excess hydrochloric acid. Most people with any digestive upset that is not a serious medical condition requiring treatment find that simply getting into a habit of drinking juices clears up the problem. The following juices are especially good for that purpose:

GINGEROO
Carrot and apple juice tastes even better if you ginger it up a little.

> **1 (or more) 1cm cube of fresh ginger**
> **1 whole apple**
> **4 carrots**

GINGER SPICE (SEE PAGE 153)

PINEAPPAGE
This may seem like a weird combination, but it's one way to sweeten the mega-nutrient fix of fresh cabbage.

> **1/4 large pineapple cut into spears**
> **1/3 green cabbage**

RED FLAG (SEE PAGE 155)

RED GENIUS (SEE PAGE 157)

Eczema

An annoying condition that's often hard to get rid of, where the skin becomes red, swollen and itchy in the beginning, then later thickens to produce crusted, scaly patches, eczema has many causes. Allergies are often a prime factor, which makes it important to use an elimination diet and to check for any food allergies. With eczema, as with any skin condition, it is important that your elimination works properly so that your skin is not forced to eliminate waste the hard way.

Certain nutrients are also very important in the treatment of eczema. Sweet peppers, tomatoes, cabbage and parsley are all excellent sources of bioflavonoids, which help reduce inflammation and control allergy, as well as enhancing the capillary function so you get a better flow of nutrients and elimination of waste from the skin. Citrus fruits are also good, provided you incorporate the pithy, white covering inside the peel in your juices. Zinc is particularly important. It's usually found in good quantities in carrots, garlic, parsley, and ginger. Carrot and parsley are also prime sources of beta-carotene, as are kale and spinach.

CARROT AND APPLE (SEE PAGE 153)

CHLOROPHYLL PLUS (SEE PAGE 153)

GINGEROO (SEE PAGE LEFT)

GREEN WOW (SEE PAGE 157)

PARSLEY PASSION (SEE PAGE 154)

SPRING SALAD
3 florets of broccoli
4 carrots
2 stalks of celery
1 clove of garlic
1 tomato

Eye health

The health of the eyes depends more than anything else on the quality of anti-oxidant protection that your body gets. Free radical damage is a major factor in the development of both minor eye problems, such as short-sightedness, to major problems, such as cataracts and glaucoma. For the eye to remain healthy it needs to be able to maintain a normal balance and concentration of such minerals as calcium, potassium and sodium within the lens. When free radical damage occurs the cellular mechanisms by which nutrients are pumped to the eyes and excess sodium and wastes removed no longer work so well. Beta-carotene, one of the most important of all of the bioflavonoids, is an anti-oxidant that helps protect the eye lens from ultra-violet damage.

Yellow, orange and dark green vegetables which are rich in beta-carotene as well as vitamins C and E, the B complex, zinc, calcium and phosphorus are very important for eye health. Ginger, garlic and parsley are rich in zinc, another mineral element that has been shown to be helpful. There is anecdotal evidence that drinking lots of carrot juice will improve eye sight, particularly night vision. Here are some favourite recipes for eyes, designed to help keep them in tip-top condition.

BEET TREAT (SEE PAGE 155)

CARROT AND APPLE (SEE PAGE 153)

DOUBLE WHAMMY (SEE PAGE 155)

GREEN WILD
2 whole green apples
2 stalks celery
1/4 lemon
1 (or more) 1cm cube of fresh ginger

HI MAG (SEE PAGE 158)

ORANGE TONIC
2 oranges
1 (or more) 1 cm cube fresh ginger
sparkling water

Juice the ginger and orange as usual, pour into a glass and top up with sparkling mineral water. This is particularly delicious in winter.

PINEAPPLE GREEN (SEE PAGE 157)

SPIKED CELERY
4 stalks celery
4-5 carrots
1 clove garlic

Fatigue

One of the underlying causes of fatigue can be iron depletion. Spinach juice is a far better way of boosting iron levels than taking tablets, which tend to be highly constipating and are not really absorbed very well. The iron in natural foods and juices such as spinach, or any of the green leafy vegetables, and also in legumes, poultry, wholegrains, liver and molasses, is highly bioavailable, i.e. your body has no trouble making use of it. Remember that replenishing the body with essential nutrients takes time and so be prepared to work with natural foods and juices for several weeks before you start to see lasting relief from chronic fatigue.

Again, make sure that 50-75 per cent of the foods you eat each day are raw and make sure you get lots of chlorophyll-rich foods. Cereal grasses are good, as they are high in minerals, vitamins and enzymes and also have a wonderful ability to enliven the liver and thereby to create more energy. Chlorophyll also helps protect from infectious diseases. You can take wheat and barley-grass juice as a supplement in powdered form added to vegetables and fruit juices or go the whole hog and get a cereal grass juicer and grow your own cereal grasses (see Resources, pages 253-4).

Magnesium is another important mineral when it comes to fatigue. Low intracellular magnesium makes the body very prone to infection, food allergies and chronic conditions. Good sources of magnesium are any of the dark green vegetables, wholegrains, seaweeds, molasses, legumes, fish and nuts.

ATOMIC LIFT-OFF (SEE PAGE 160)

CITRUSUCCULENT
1 ripe grapefruit (or pink grapefruit)
1/2 ripe lemon
2 ripe oranges

Peel the fruit (leave the pith) and juice as usual.

DANDELION PLUS (SEE PAGE 155)

GINGER BERRY (SEE PAGE 156)

GINGEROO (SEE PAGE 165)

GLORIOUS GRAPEFRUIT (SEE PAGE 158)

GREEN ZINGER (SEE PAGE 155)

HI MAG (SEE PAGE 158)

HIT THE GRASS
A handful of fresh mint
A small pineapple, peeled and cut into convenient sized spears
A handful of any fresh cereal grass such as wheat or barley

Juice the mint and pineapple in your ordinary juicer, then juice the cereal grass in a wheat-grass juicer. Whisk together. Alternatively, pour the fruit juice into a food processor or blender and toss the cereal grasses in, blend with the blade until highly blended, then pour through a strainer to remove the indigestible fibre. Serve over ice. This can also be made using a teaspoon to a tablespoon of any of the freeze-dried cereal grasses such as barley grass or wheat grass.

PARSLEY PASSION (SEE PAGE 154)

SECRET OF THE SEA
4 carrots
2 whole apples
2 sheets nori seaweed

Juice the apple and carrot then pour into a blender along with the seaweed. Blend thoroughly and serve. This is even better if you toast the seaweed under a grill or near a flame or hotplate, very briefly – it takes no more than 10 or 15 seconds to do on both sides. You can then break it up into the juice and blend.

SPROUT SPECIAL (SEE PAGE 154)

Hangover

The inevitable consequence of over-indulgence is waking up feeling dehydrated and nauseous, with a brain that feels as if it's banging against the side of your head when you move. You need to replenish your bodily fluids, renutrify exhausted muscles and get your head together. Fruit juice is strongly indicated. Citrus juices, being full of natural sugar and vitamin C, are the most immediately effective remedy, but they may be a bit harsh if your stomach is delicate. Watermelon, being exceptionally mild, is ideal.

There is an art to hangover management and the key to it is regarding detoxification as the corollary of intoxication. All drugs provoke a strongly acidic reaction in the body which causes the symptoms of a hangover and the first step to recovery is to correct the body's chemical imbalance. Plain old carrot & apple juice is effective for re-balancing and it's easy to take when you're feeling weak. Beet juice will greatly assist the repair of any possible damage done to your liver and kidneys.

APPLES AND PEARS (SEE PAGE 161)

BEET TREAT (SEE PAGE 155)

CARROT AND APPLE (SEE PAGE 153)

MERRY BELON
Berries are one kind of fruit that combines really well with melons and the array of flavours gives lots of scope for experimentation. Try galia & raspberry, honeydew & blackberry or the classic watermelon & strawberry.

1 slice of watermelon, 3cm wide and cut into chunks to fit your juicer
6 strawberries, washed and with their green stalks removed

In hot weather, a good tip is to freeze the berries before juicing them.

VIRGIN MARY
A Bloody Mary without the vodka, the flavour of this refreshing tomato-based cocktail benefits from a few drops of Tabasco. Add a clove of garlic and it becomes a Vampire Mary; a fresh jalapeno or other hot green chilli pepper turns it into a Scary Mary.

2 ripe tomatoes
2 carrots
1/2 beetroot
1 stalk celery
1 cucumber

Insomnia

Insomnia can have many causes. Drugs such as beta blockers or thyroid medication, even caffeine and alcohol can all disrupt sleep. So, ironically, can sleeping pills, if your body becomes addicted to them.

Getting regular exercise – taking long walks rather than going to aerobics – can help enormously to reduce the nervous tension that prevents sleep. Sometimes sleep is disrupted by hypoglycaemia, so make sure you don't have a blood sugar problem (see Low Blood Sugar below). Eliminate coffee, tea, alcohol and junk foods – including diet colas – from your life once and for all. Eat your biggest meal at lunchtime, as everyone sleeps better (and longer) when their stomach is not full. Consider using one of the well-

proven natural tranquillisers such as Valerian, Passiflora (Passion flower) or Wild Lettuce. You can make a night-cap cocktail to help increase the levels of serotonin in the brain: blend a pinch of one of these natural tranquillisers into it.

Magnesium, vitamin B6 and niacin have to be present in order for the amino acid tryptophan to be able to turn itself into serotonin. Carrots are a rich source of all three. Calcium induces muscle relaxation and so does folic acid which in sufficient quantities prevents leg twitching and calms nervous tension. The green drinks, from dandelion to parsley and spinach, are excellent sources of folic acid and calcium. Seaweed is also a good source of magnesium. Many people (except those with low blood sugar) need an extra boost of fruit sugar before going to bed to trigger sleep. Pineapple and grape is a wonderful combination for this. Others include:

GREEN GODDESS (SEE PAGE **157**)

HI MAG (SEE PAGE **158**)

LAZY LETTUCE
2 whole apples
5 lettuce leaves

PINEAMINT (SEE PAGE **157**)

SMOOTH AS SILK
This recipe is rich in natural fruit sugars, potassium, magnesium and the amino acid tryptophan which can be turned into serotonin in the brain. It is also absolutely irresistible.

2 cups blackberries, either fresh
or frozen
1 ripe apple
1 whole banana

Juice the berries and the apple. Put the juice and banana into a food processor or blender and blend until smooth. Drink 45 minutes before bedtime.

SPICY CARROT
This juice is a great source of minerals such as magnesium, potassium, calcium, iron, sulphur, copper, phosphorus and iodine, as well as anti-oxidants, beta-carotene, vitamins A, C, E and niacin, vitamins D and K. It will also soothe a slightly delicate stomach. Braeburn and Cox's are ideal for this juice, but any sweet apple will do.

4 carrots
2 spears of pineapple
1 Braeburn or Cox's apple
A pinch of ground cinnamon
A pinch of ground nutmeg

Pineapples vary considerably in size. You'll need half a small one or a quarter of a big one. Remove the fibrous skin with a sharp knife and cut into long spears that will fit into your juicer. The cinnamon and nutmeg can be sprinkled on top of the freshly-extracted juice, or stirred into it as you prefer.

SPROUT SPECIAL (SEE PAGE **154**)

Low blood sugar (hypoglycaemia)

Low blood sugar, where the body tends to secrete insulin which in turn makes the blood sugar level drop depriving the brain of its main 'food', glucose, is a condition that underlies much of the chocolate munching and coffee drinking that people indulge in in order to keep themselves going.

The vegetable juices are better than the fruit juices until blood sugar is stabilised. If you're hypoglycaemic, don't drink fruit juices unless they are well diluted with mineral water, and then only a couple of times a week. Try adding a little turmeric or cinnamon to your juices. Both these spices have long been used to help stabilise blood sugar. Foods which are rich in chromium will help regulate glucose metabolism in the body. These include spinach, apples, green peppers, wholegrains, clams and liver. Use foods which are rich in manganese such as carrots, celery, beetroot, beetroot greens, turnip greens, pineapple, liver, eggs, green vegetables and buckwheat.

An antidote for a sweet tooth is lots of green drinks, but you will have to get yourself used to drinking them since they are about the last thing the hypoglycaemic wants. Once you do get used to it you will find that blood sugar stabilises and you have energy to spare, day in and day out. All of the green juices are excellent, such as:

DANDELION PLUS (SEE PAGE 155)

GREEN FRIEND (SEE PAGE 153)

GREEN ZINGER (SEE PAGE 155)

LEMON ZINGER
1 whole apple
1/2 a lemon
Sparkling mineral water

Juice the apple and the lemon – leaving the white pith on the lemon – pour into a glass and top up with sparkling water and ice.

PARSLEY PASSION (SEE PAGE 154)

SECRET OF THE SEA (SEE PAGE 168)

SPICY APPLE
2 apples, whole
1 lime
A pinch of cinnamon

Juice the apples and the lime (leave the pith on the lime), sprinkle with cinnamon and serve.

TOSSLED CARROT
5 big carrots
1 whole apple
A pinch of turmeric

Juice the carrots and apple, pour into glasses and sprinkle with turmeric.

Migraine

Dr Philip Kilsby, a remarkable doctor who believed in supporting the body to heal itself using juices and raw foods, experienced 99 per cent success in the treatment of migraine, using juices, lots of raw fruits and vegetables, and a few dietary supplements. The only case of migraine he had not been able to cure was that of a woman who turned out not to have migraine but a brain tumour.

Kilsby taught that all migraine, regardless of cause, is centred in a liver that is over-worked trying to keep the body internally clear. So Kilsby took stress off the liver by removing from the diet foods that people are commonly allergic to such as red wine, other alcohol, salad cream, red plums, soft cheeses, figs, aged game, chicken liver, canned meat, salami sausages, pickled herring, aubergine, soy sauce and yeast concentrates, as well as chocolate, wheat, milk, the food colouring tartrazine, sugar, coffee and peanuts.

Kilsby then put his patients on a detox programme and followed it with a regime in which he insisted his patients drink a juice rich in green vegetables twice daily. He found that his patients experienced migraines of decreasing intensity until, once their bodies were detoxified, the migraines altogether ceased.

Migraines result from contraction followed by rapid dilatation of the blood vessels in the brain, and this can be triggered by certain foods. Biofeedback can be helpful: this involves training yourself to visualise your hands as warm, thereby drawing blood away from the head and taking pressure off the area that is involved in the migraine. The herb feverfew can also be useful to many people.

If you suffer from migraine banish all chemicals, including artificial sweeteners such as aspartamine, from your diet. Include in your juices some of the fruits and vegetables which are known to reduce platelet stickiness, since foods that inhibit blood clotting are known to reduce migraine. These include garlic, cantaloupe, and ginger.

DANDELION PLUS (SEE PAGE 155)

GINGEROO (SEE PAGE 165)

GREEN FRIEND (SEE PAGE 153)

GREEN GODDESS (SEE PAGE 157)

SPRING SALAD (SEE PAGE 166)

SPROUT SPECIAL (SEE PAGE 154)

Pre-menstrual syndrome

PMS comes in many forms and causes many symptoms, from irritability, depression, tension and decreased energy, to backache, breast pain, changes in libido, abdominal bloating, oedema and headache. There are certain things that all PMS sufferers need to watch. It is essential to clear sugar out of your diet as well as cut down on any

other form of refined carbohydrates, including white flour and honey. Avoid coffee, tea and chocolate, for two reasons – first because they contain methylxanthines, which have been linked with a number of the symptoms associated with PMS, and secondly, because anything containing caffeine can have a very negative effect on such things as breast tenderness, anxiety and depression.

It is also a good idea to eliminate all milk products and wheat from your diet for seven days prior to menstruation. At the same time increase your intake of certain nutrients such as magnesium, B6 and the B complex, as well as beta-carotene. Bromelin too can be helpful since this enzyme is believed to help relax the smooth muscle tissue of the body. Go for the green juices, which are rich in all these things. If you have water retention, turn towards watermelon, grape, cucumber and dandelion, each of which has a splendid ability to eliminate excess water from the system. You are likely to find that all the juices that are good for PMS are also useful for someone who is wrestling with menopausal symptoms such as hot flushes. In both PMS and menopausal cases it can be helpful to follow a way of eating where 50-75 per cent of your foods are taken raw during the 7-10 days before a period or whenever the symptoms seem to be at their worst.

BLACK WATERMELON (SEE PAGE 161)

COOL AS A CUKE
  1 cucumber
  1 clove garlic
  1 tomato
  dash of dill

Juice the vegetables and then sprinkle with ground dill and serve over ice.

GINGER BERRY (SEE PAGE 156)

GREEN ZINGER (SEE PAGE 155)

HI MAG (SEE PAGE 158)

PINEAPPLE GREEN (SEE PAGE 157)

SECRET OF THE SEA (SEE PAGE 168)

SPRING SALAD (SEE PAGE 166)

SPROUT SPECIAL (SEE PAGE 154)

WATERFALL (SEE PAGE 159)

Stress

Stress is a complicated condition to treat as it has many causes and takes many forms. However, whenever the body is under prolonged stress the tissues tend to become more acidic. There is nothing better and more life-changing that you can do when your system is too acid than to drink fresh vegetable and fruit juices to alkalinise it. Detoxification helps eliminate the constant tension, anxiety and frustration that so often go with stress, as well as its common consequences such as gastro-intestinal difficulties, high blood pressure, dizziness, loss of appetite or excessive appetite, and headaches.

While it is important to practise some sort of deep relaxation or meditation if you are suffering from prolonged stress, the effect of dietary change alone, through incorporating a juice-high regime into your lifestyle and, as always, making between 50 and 75 per cent of your foods raw, can literally transform your life within a fortnight. Useful nutrients to incorporate in your diet include pantothenic acid, which occurs in good quantity in green leafy vegetables such as kale, dandelion and broccoli; potassium, which is found in bananas, parsley and spinach; zinc, a good source of which are carrots and ginger; and magnesium, which also occurs in the green foods.

EASY DOES IT (SEE PAGE 155)

GINGEROO (SEE PAGE 165)

GINGER SPICE (SEE PAGE 153)

GREEN FRIEND (SEE PAGE 153)

HI MAG (SEE PAGE 158)

HIT THE GRASS (SEE PAGE 167)

SILKY STRAWBERRIES

Strawberries are surprisingly potent when it comes to supporting a body that is under stress. Just 100gms of strawberries contain as much as 80mg vitamin C, as well as all the other vitamins except for B12 and D, plus valuable minerals. Strawberries have a natural diuretic action and are very calming to the liver. They also contain salicylic acid which, according to experts in natural medicine, is good for any sort of kidney or joint complaint.

2 cups strawberries
1 ripe pear
1 ripe banana
A handful of fresh mint leaves

Juice the strawberries and pear as usual then place in a blender with the banana and mint and blend until smooth. This drink is particularly delicious when made from a frozen banana; it takes on the taste and consistency of a natural ice-cream.

SPROUT SPECIAL (SEE PAGE **154**)

Urinary infections

Cranberry juice is excellent for any sort of kidney and urinary infections. Cranberry is also thought to be good for under-active thyroid, partly because it has traditionally been grown, particularly in the United States, in iodine-rich bogs. Cranberry juice on its own is much too strong for most people to handle. However, it mixes beautifully with any number of gentler juices like melon or apple. It will also add extra zest to basic vegetable juices like carrot. Cranberry is known for its cleansing properties, helping to rid not only the digestive system but other organs of the body of waste and bacteria. It is also said to be very good for skin problems such as acne.

CRANBERRY COCKTAIL
1 cup of cranberries
lemon juice
1 cup of sweet grapes or 2-3
apples

Put the grapes or cranberries and apples through the juicer then add a squeeze of fresh lemon juice before serving. If you don't have fresh cranberries you can use frozen ones.

Water retention

Water retention or oedema is a sign that the metabolism is not working properly and the body needs to be deep cleansed and rebalanced. It can be caused by many things, from hormones in birth control pills and Hormone Replacement Therapy, to hormone changes during the premenstruum and pregnancy. It can also be caused by food allergies and liver problems.

Encouraging the body to eliminate excess water from its tissues is a two-fold process. First, use natural diuretics such as nettle, dill, watermelon, grapes and cucumber that gently encourage the loss of excess water. Second, detoxify the system as a whole. If swelling in the ankles is severe and prolonged it can indicate serious problems such as heart failure, so you need to check with your doctor. Check also for any possibility of food allergy if you have prolonged water retention, and decrease the amount of salt in your diet. The sodium/potassium balance in your body determines to a great extent whether the body eliminates excess fluids properly. Cut sugar from your diet.

Fight water retention by increasing the number of potassium-rich foods that you eat and from which you make your juices. These include: bananas, prunes, raisins, figs, seaweeds, fish, green vegetables, whole grains, kale, broccoli, spinach, Swiss chard, and all the other green foods, plus carrot and celery. You may be deficient in vitamin B6, which can interfere with the kidneys' ability to eliminate waste. Foods rich in B6 include molasses, brown rice, liver, eggs, cabbage and fish. Garlic, too, is one of the traditional foods for eliminating oedema from the tissues.

BLACK WATERMELON (SEE PAGE 173)

COOL AS A CUKE (SEE PAGE 173)

DANDELION PLUS (SEE PAGE 155)

GREEN FRIEND (SEE PAGE 153)

GREEN ZINGER (SEE PAGE 155)

POTASSIUM POWER (SEE PAGE 159)

SECRET OF THE SEA (SEE PAGE 168)

REVIVE YOURSELF

STEP EIGHT: SELF-INDULGE

You deserve it

To an astute eye, your body can reveal almost everything about you. It can tell how you think and feel, how you eat, how you exercise (or don't!) and how much physical care you give yourself.

Every woman has her own perfect form. She has a natural shape of body and face that is unique to her. When this perfect form has not been obscured by excess weight, poor muscle condition, blemished skin, or such things as cellulite that develop when toxic wastes and fat are stored in the body, it is a true expression of you. If, however, your body has been ignored, treated carelessly, or has become distorted over the years through excess weight and general neglect, then the form that should be expressing you in all clarity serves only to obscure you.

This is the case with many women. They are carrying too much weight, or they have neglected themselves, believing wrongly that to look after their skin and nails, hands and feet, hair and face is a useless self-indulgence. This step is all about the things that can help you rediscover your own unique form if you have lost it as well as what will help you keep it if you haven't – nail care, foot care, bathing, and aromatherapy. In short, it's all about looking after your body. And caring for your body is caring for the new you.

Cellulite

Cellulite exists, whether one wishes to call it cellulite or something else and whatever a few doctors may say. It is real enough for the woman who, in spite of being lean and well, reaches down and pinches her thigh only to find it puckers, ripples, and looks like the skin of an orange.

Cellulite is the result of a build-up of wastes in specific areas of the body. They tend to settle in a woman's body in the areas which, as a result of female hormones, tend to collect fat as part of the secondary sex characteristics – thighs, hips, buttocks and so forth.

There are two situations that attract cellulite. First, it occurs in parts of the body where the circulation is poor through inactivity and the muscles are flaccid, for instance in the hips and upper thighs of women who spend each day sitting at a desk and get no exercise. Second, it appears where the

opposite extreme is true – in areas where tension has led to chronic spasm of the muscles. This not only interferes with proper circulation of blood and lymph to the cells, so that they are never properly nourished and wastes from them are not properly eliminated, it also irritates adjacent nerves and soft tissue structures, which in turn results in yet more spasm. Slowly, a congested area forms, since cell nutrients and wastes are only sluggishly exchanged and vascular dilation and constriction in the area is erratic. Gradually, wastes accumulate and a kind of tissue sludge is formed. There it tends to remain, for each condition in the area tends only to reinforce each other in a vicious circle.

Causes

Anything that puts into your system more pollutants from the air, food, and water than it can efficiently deal with and eliminate quickly:

- *Too much of the wrong kind of exercise*
- *Prolonged stress*
- *Faulty digestion*
- *The long-term use of diuretics*
- *Vertebral lesions in the pelvis*
- *Chronic constipation.*

It is interesting that 75 per cent of cases of cellulite in women have started during a period of drastic hormonal change in their lives. Dr Pierre Dukan, author of La Cellulite en Question *(La Table Ronde edition) has compiled statistics of cellulite sufferers. He has found that:*

- *12 per cent of cellulite begins at puberty*
- *19 per cent when a woman first takes the Pill*
- *17 per cent during pregnancy*
- *27 per cent at the first indications of menopause.*

Women on the Pill, who suffer from irregular periods, and those who suffer any severe or long-term stress are perfect targets for tissue sludge. The pituitary gland is affected both by shock and stress. Because it is largely responsible for triggering the secretion of female hormones, when its function is disturbed or upset, hormonal secretions are modified and often increased and cellulite develops.

How to keep cellulite away

Don't take into your body too much of the wrong kinds of food:

- refined carbohydrates
- over-processed, precooked, or pickled foods
- prepared meats
- alcohol
- coffee.

Instead, drink the following:

- spring water
- fresh, unsweetened fruit or vegetable juices
- herb teas sweetened with a teaspoon of honey.

Smoking is also taboo when it comes to the prevention of cellulite, for two reasons: it robs the system of vitamin C, and nicotine in the system interferes with the circulation.

Cellulite essentials

- *Proper nutrition*
- *Regular exercise*
- *Breathing properly*
- *Deep relaxation*
- *Meditation practised daily.*

What to do when you have already got cellulite

Treat yourself to a 10 Day Spring Clean to encourage waste elimination and improve the rate of cellular exchange.

There are some vegetable and fruit juice combinations that are particularly good for clearing tissue sludge from the system. Try to drink at least two glasses a day. Also make sure you get plenty of water in order not to put too much strain on the kidneys, which will be dealing with some pretty concentrated wastes as your system begins to clear.

THE 3 Cs
Carrot – 4 ounces
Celery – 2 ounces
Cucumber – 2 ounces

CARROOT
Carrot – 3 ounces
Beetroot – 2 ounces

APPLE PINCH
Carrot – 4 ounces
Celery 2 ounces
Apple – 2 ounces

GREEN LIFE
Carrot – 4 ounces
Watercress – 1/2 ounce
Cabbage – 1 1/2 ounces

PURE ORANGE
Orange – 4 ounces

HERB TEAS
Herb teas that are particularly good for cellulite sufferers include:

- Maté tea is a tonic for the kidneys, a tension soother, and is so satisfying to drink that you feel less inclined to eat. It is nice taken plain or with a squeeze of lemon in it.
- Solidago tea (wild goldenrod) is an excellent natural diuretic and a mild stimulant.
- Nettle tea is another diuretic and tonic, and it is an excellent tea for the lymphatic system.

Cellulite creams, lotions and oils

External treatment is almost as important as internal treatment – breaking down the pockets of cellulite physically so that stored wastes in them are released and can be eliminated from the body.

The active ingredients in the best of the cellulite creams, lotions and oils include a number of potent herbal extracts to help enhance circulation, encourage lipolysis (fat burning), restore integrity to damaged capillaries, decrease waterlogging and improve firmness. The trouble with all of the creams and potions is that, like the special treatments for cellulite you can get from a doctor or a beauty therapist, they will only work together with a total body programme.

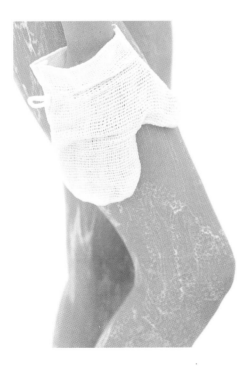

Making your own

If you can get to a good herbalist's shop, you can make one of your own, however, which works even better than most of the fancy ones at a fraction of the cost.

ALOE VERA PLUS

Take 1 small bottle of aloe vera liquid (350ml). Add to it 25ml of liquid extract of fucus vesculosus and 25ml of kola liquid extract. Shake well. Keep refrigerated. Apply twice a day to cellulite-prone areas of the body after a bath or shower; then, using one of the special anti-cellulite gloves or mits or rollers, gently go over affected areas of your body.

DIY massage oils

To 4 ounces of almond or hazelnut oil (or make it 2 ounces wheatgerm oil, 2 ounces safflower or sunflower oil), add the contents squeezed from eight 100 IU capsules of vitamin E that have been pierced with a pin (this will provide 200 IU of the vitamin per ounce). Then add the contents of two 25,000 IU vitamin A capsules. Shake well.

L'origans

To 4 ounces of almond, hazelnut, or apricot oil add 10 drops of oil of lavender, 5 drops of oil of juniper, and 20 drops of oil of rosemary. Shake well. Lavender is mildly antiseptic and softens the skin while rosemary has natural diuretic and stimulant properties.

The medium is massage

Massage is important. It helps stimulate local circulation, loosen the waste products from their hold, and get rid of the pitted, orange-peel look. But it has to be done properly.

First, always use an oil or creamy cellulite product or talcum powder to help your hands slide. Begin with effleurage – meaning a light stroking of the skin in the area to be treated, hand over hand, always beginning above the area affected (to improve the flow of blood to the area), stroking towards the heart. The only time you should work in a direction away from the heart is when you are in a very tense state, when it will help calm and relax you.

Now the circulation is improved you can begin to knead the area without fear of causing damage. Work hand over hand, taking hold of your flesh with the whole palm of your hand and fingers (not just the fingers) and pulling it away from the bone, squeezing it rhythmically at the same time. Continue this for a minute or two and then, using the base of your thumb and the knuckles of your hands, push them gently but firmly into the troubled areas, twisting them in a circular motion at the same time. This movement helps break up the pockets of tissue sludge and release their contents into the circulatory systems, from which they can be eliminated from the body. Use this motion for no more than three or four minutes in

each area or you risk irritating the tissue and undoing all the good you have done. Finally, finish off with the same sort of effleurage with which you began in order to help carry wastes away.

You may notice after massaging yourself for a week or two that the condition seems to get worse: your thighs are flabbier and your bottom more puckered than ever. Don't despair. This is a good sign. It means the treatment is working. Tissue sludge almost always goes through this stage before it is finally reabsorbed into the system and eliminated from the body.

Take to the waters
Another useful external treatment for cellulite is hydrotherapy. There are two types. The first uses powerful jets of water directed onto the surface of the skin. The second involves the alternate plunging of the body into hot and cold water.

If you have a hose that can be attached to the bath tap or a flexible shower head with a fairly good water force you can benefit from self-treatments while you are showering or bathing. Direct a jet of warm water against the problem areas from a distance of four to six inches (depending on the strength of the jet), moving it systematically backwards and forwards across the hips and buttocks and up and down the legs in a snakelike fashion. Then do the inside of your thighs and calves and the bottom of each foot. Finish off by passing the jet, held a bit further from the skin, across the shoulders, chest, abdomen, and down the back.

Sweating it off

A sauna taken weekly will greatly speed any anti-cellulite programme. However, if you suffer from a serious respiratory ailment or heart disease you should use a sauna only on doctor's orders.

Rules for the sauna

1 Give yourself plenty of time. It will benefit you most if you take it leisurely so you have time for several sessions in the heat, with short rests in between and a rest of at least thirty minutes, preferably an hour, after you are through.

2 Never take a sauna until at least two hours after a meal and never take a sauna during a juice fast.

3 Never take a sauna if you have symptoms of any illness.

4 Wear little or nothing in the sauna – a towel wrapped around you is more than enough.

5 Stay in the sauna room for only five minutes at a stretch. Then plunge into cold water or take a cold shower and rest before going back in.

6 Don't water the stones during your first session and be sparing with the moisture you put on afterwards.

7 Lie down in the sauna room if you can, or sit quietly.

8 Be sure to get half an hour's rest at the end to let your body readjust to the normal temperature of the room. Never drink alcohol just before or after the sauna.

9 Don't towel yourself dry afterwards.

Seek professional help

There are many practitioners nationally.

Rolfing

By stretching and making elastic the distorted connective tissue in the muscles and skin and by repositioning ligaments and tendons which have become tightened or bunched in compensation for these distortions, rolfing causes the joints to move more freely and the muscles themselves to take on a different quality, look and feel. This naturally helps to eliminate cellulite – it restructures the whole body.

Connective tissue massage

The other treatment that can be particularly useful in treating a body that has seriously lost its form is connective tissue massage (CTM).

CTM is a specific form of massage performed primarily with the fingers and thumbs and designed to affect total body shape by altering the structure and organization of connective tissue. Connective tissue gives structure to your body and acts as binding and support for organs and muscles.

But connective tissues can become distorted by poor alignment, injury, age, or other factors (poor nutrition among them) so that the circulation of lymph and fluids to and from the cells becomes sluggish. Then you get areas of stasis, such as cellulite, sagging muscles, and poor elimination of waste, which can lead to rapidly ageing skin and bulges and bumps where they shouldn't be. CTM breaks down these sluggish areas, bringing improved blood flow and altering the physical look of your skin and flesh.

Aromatherapy

Aromatherapy is the art of using essences of plants to treat the skin, the emotions, and the body as a whole. It is one of the most interesting areas of beauty care. For each plant essence has its own unique qualities, yet like a piece of music or a painting will evoke slightly different responses from different people depending on their personalities, needs, and tastes. Learning about aromatherapy, the essences themselves, and some of the things you can do with them is sheer delight. It is also a wonderful way of looking after your skin, calming your nerves when you are overwrought, and creating interesting atmospheres in your living and working environment.

Etheric oils
Plant essences are the free, light, almost etheric essential oils taken from plants in their prime of life. Although they are technically known as essential oils, they have little in common with the fatty oils we know, like olive oil or lanolin. For centuries they have been used for blending perfumes and making incense for religious rites. They are found in tiny droplets in specific parts of different plants in a concentration of between 0.01 and 10 per cent; in roots and barks (calamus and cinnamon, for instance), flowers (jasmine and rose), leaves (rosemary and basil), and the rinds of fruit (lemon and orange). Highly volatile, these substances are what give a plant its distinctive smell. They seem to contain the vital essence of the plant that is probably responsible for their beneficial effects.

These effects are so varied and so profound that it is hard to list them all. Many essences stimulate the generation of new cells. (Lavender and orange blossom are particularly good for this.) Some, like fennel, contain plant hormones similar in their chemical structure to oestrogen. Mixed with a good carrier oil they make an excellent anti-wrinkle treatment. Others have different phytohormones that can be of equal benefit to both dry and oily skin. Many essences profoundly affect the psyche as well, both when they are rubbed on the body and when they are simply inhaled. All essential oils are powerful and, therefore, used only in minute quantities diluted in other oils. Most are easily absorbed into the skin, probably through the hair follicles, which contain sebum, an oily liquid with which they appear to have a natural affinity. From there they can be carried either by the bloodstream or via the lymph and interstitial fluid (the liquid that surrounds all the body's cells) to other parts of the body. Experiments with animals, for instance, have shown that when an essence is applied to the skin it can reach an internal organ in half an hour.

Do-it-yourself aromatherapy

There are a number of ways of using plant essences. You can dilute them in oil and apply them to the face and body for skin treatments. You can use them in the same mixture on the face, at the back of the neck, and on the base of the spine for their effect on the psyche and nervous system. You can inhale them directly from the bottle or breathe them in the form of steam from a humidifier or pot of very hot water to which a few drops of essence have been added. They can also be used in your bath but always in the minutest quantities – ten to fifteen drops. Some essences will be absorbed into the skin more rapidly, depending on their volatility and the carrier oil in which you have put them.

Essential oils should never be applied directly on the skin. Many of them are so powerful in their action that to do so would cause a burn. Also, their potency is such that they actually work better in minute quantities, highly diluted.

Oils for the skin

When making an oil to apply to the skin, you need two things – the essences which you wish to use (one or more of them mixed together) and a carrier oil in which to put them. The carrier oil depends on your taste and purse. Sweet almond oil and apricot oil are excellent. So is hazelnut oil, which gives a high degree of penetration on the skin. Less expensive, but perfectly adequate, are cold-pressed sunflower oil, safflower oil, olive oil, and peanut or ground-nut oil. Whatever oil you choose, it should be cold-pressed to preserve the quality of essential fatty acids it contains and it should be fresh. Once mixed, an oil should be tightly capped and kept under refrigeration. A couple of capsules of vitamin E squeezed into the oil when you mix it will keep it from going rancid quickly because of the vitamin's anti-oxidant properties. The proportion of essence to carrier oil should be one to fifty by weight.

Pomades

You can also make a pomade or a cream from the essences. You will need beeswax, your carrier oil, and your essences. Take half an ounce of beeswax to two ounces of carrier or to twenty drops of essence. Heat the beeswax and oil in a double boiler and remove from the heat when the wax has melted. Whisk briskly to blend the two thoroughly. When the mixture begins to solidify as it cools, add your essence (not before or too much of it will evaporate), and the contents of a vitamin E capsule. Use the same ratio of essence to carrier here (one to fifty) but include the weight of the beeswax in your calculations of the carrier.

Fragrant waters

Finally, you can make fragrant waters by using four or five drops of essence shaken well into a pint of distilled water. Put this into one of those little spray bottles used for misting plants and you can have a room freshener or scenter far better than anything you can buy. Or splash it on after a bath.

Another way to scent a room is to add a few drops to a humidifier or to a pan of boiling water just taken off the heat.

Build a collection

It is a good idea to start with three or four essences and then experiment, each time adding more oils to your collection as you get to know them. Some of the best to start with are jasmine, sandalwood, geranium, neroli, lavender, and cinnamon.

Always keep your essences in a cool place (the refrigerator is ideal) and in dark glass bottles. Essential oils are highly volatile and all-too-easily destroyed through proximity to heat and sunlight. They have to be treated like something very precious.

SKIN	
To improve circulation	Juniper, camphor
For broken veins	Cypress, neroli
For oily skin	Lavender, lemon, geranium, sandalwood, bergamot, cypress, juniper
For dry skin	Geranium, rose, sandalwood
For dehydrated skin	Clary, sage, geranium, sandalwood
For fine, sensitive skin	Neroli, rose, lavender

BODY MASSAGE	
Soothers when you are tense	Lavender, geranium, camomile
Pepper-uppers when you are down	Cinnamon, bergamot, patchouli, jasmine
For mild aches and muscle pains	Lavender, rosemary

FOR BATHING	
Add a few drops when running the bath	Camomile, neroli, jasmine, lavender, patchouli, ylang-ylang, rose, sandalwood, rosemary, frankincense, cardamom, melissa

PSYCHIC ESSENCES	
Dilute in the carrier and rub them on the face, back of the neck, and the base of the spine. Or put a few drops in a humidifier or pan of steaming water and let it waft into the room. Or add a few drops to water and spray like an air freshener	
To calm you when angry	Ylang-ylang
To brighten you when depressed or grieving	Lavender, geranium or sandalwood
To clear your head for mental work	Melissa, orange blossom
Aphrodisiacs	Jasmine, ylang-ylang, sandalwood, rose

How and where to buy your essences

Herb stores sometimes sell them, as well as the carrier oils and beeswax. Some health food stores sell beeswax and most have the carrier oils. Beware of so-called essential oils that are synthetic. They are not good for aromatherapy and won't work. Neither will essences that have already been diluted in oils and which are sold in little bottles for perfumes. Read labels carefully and ask questions. Be particularly cautious when buying the following – they are very often not real but synthetic: jasmine, lily of the valley, lilac, frangipani, cucumber, clove, carnation, musk, orange blossom (neroli), rose, ylang-ylang, and violet.

Suppliers

For the addresses of suppliers in your area, look in the yellow pages of the telephone directory under these listings:

- *Aromatherapy*
- *Beauty salons and consultants*
- *Essential oils suppliers*
- *Herbalists*
- *Homoeopaths*
- *Perfumers' raw materials.*

Hands and nails

Your hands probably reveal more about you than any other part of your body. Yet hands are often the most neglected part of your body. As a result they age rapidly and are hard to rejuvenate once you have let them go.

Hands love moderate temperatures, hand creams, and massage. They hate water, detergents, household chemicals, harsh weather and unprotected, prolonged exposure to the sun, which encourages the development of liver spots – high concentrations of melanin in clusters as a result of the skin's reaction to the ultraviolet rays.

The health of your nails depends on two things: adequate diet and protection from environmental damage.

Eat for nails

A healthy nail should be strong but flexible, smooth and rich pink in colour. If yours are not, the first thing to do is to revise your eating habits. Nails, like hair, need protein, B-complex vitamins, minerals, trace elements (particularly zinc, calcium, iodine, sulphur, and iron), and vitamin A to grow healthy and strong.

A good overall nutritional programme to keep nails healthy includes lots of raw vegetables and lean protein, whole-grains, seaweeds or kelp tablets, green foods such as spirulina and chlorella, plus one teaspoon of blackstrap molasses a day. It is good added to yoghurt, cereal, or even herb tea. There is one substance however that surpasses all others when it comes to creating strong, beautiful nails: silica.

The second most widely available element on the planet, silica in its organic form is an element essential to human health and life.

A woman's daily requirement of silica is rather high at 20-30mg.

There is only one extremely rich source known to man of this precious yet much neglected nutrient: horsetail – the beautiful and primitive *equisetum arvense* – one of the world's earliest forms of plant life.

The horsetail plant has a remarkable structure, with two types of aerial stalks, one of which is fertile and looks after the plant's reproduction and the other which is sterile. It is the sterile stalk which can be harvested to produce organic silica supplements. In it is found the element silica bound together with 10 other trace elements for great nails and hair.

Environmental dangers

Breaking nails and unsightly hands can be caused by outside influences too – soaking your hands in detergents, bath salts, disinfectants, chlorine in swimming pools, strong lotions and soaps, cutting or filing your nails too far in at the sides, and damage done to the embryo nail (the matrix) by digging into the cuticles during a manicure. The answer to external threats is preventative care, which takes three forms: gloves (of all kinds, worn as often as possible), proper treatment, and creams.

Hand essentials

- *Nourishing creams – rub into your hands just before bed and then cover with a pair of cotton gloves for the night.*
- *Barrier creams – ideal protectors for daytime use. They usually contain silicone. They are water-resistant and also good for guarding the hands against chapping in cold weather. They*

don't need gloves to do their work, but these creams should be renewed each time you put your hands through any kind of vigorous treatment.

- *Sunscreens* – *use whenever your hands are exposed to ultraviolet light in quantity. Many women end up with unsightly spots on their hands simply because they neglect this when they are out in the sun.*

The do-it-yourself manicure

1 Take off all the old varnish using an oil-based remover by soaking a large piece of cotton in the remover, placing it on the nail for twenty seconds to dissolve the varnish, and then sweeping it away from the base to the tip (never the other way, as this pushes varnish and remover under the cuticle where it can do damage).

2 Filing is one of the most important parts of a manicure. Bad filing can cause nails to split, and good filing can actually help to stop splitting. The right way is to use the smooth side of an emery board and file from side to centre, keeping the board at an angle of 45 degrees to the nail. Never saw backwards and forwards, as this creates heat, dries what little moisture there is in the nail layers, and can cause peeling. It is important to finish the nail well afterwards. You do this by bevelling it or stroking the nail lightly up and down with the emery board to coax the nail layers together. Remember that when nails are cut straight at the top with rounded or squared corners, they are less likely to split.

3 Massage a generous amount of cuticle cream or oil into the cuticle and nail area with round movements of your thumb, and then soak your fingertips in a bowl of warm water, to which you can add a little ordinary vegetable or bath oil.

4 Gently ease back your cuticles with your fingertips. Dip an orange stick wrapped with cotton into cuticle cream or remover and work away any dead skin and clean under the nail, but gently; never poke into the area where the nail comes away from the finger.

5 Don't trim your cuticles if you can help it. This can infect the nail.

6 Dry your hands and massage cream or oil well into the skin; wheatgerm oil, nut oil, and avocado oil are all particularly beneficial to hands. Start at the end of the fingers, one at a time, massaging towards the wrist. Knead the palm with the fingers of your other hand.

7 *'Squeak' your nails. This means putting a little nail varnish remover on cotton and running it over your nails to remove all the grease.*

8 *Stroke on a nail strengthener if you need one (if your nails are brittle, you don't) and leave it to dry. Then put on a layer of acetone-free base coat.*

This will help protect and strengthen nails from coloured varnish if you want to add it later.

9 *Colour can change the shape of your nails dramatically. A sleek strip of dark colour down the centre of the nail will lengthen it. Fill the whole nail with colour if it is perfectly shaped. If you have very heavy or wide nails, start at the centre of the moon and brush outward and inward to the tip to give the impression of longer, almond-shaped nails. Whatever you do, start with a line of colour going down the centre and then one on either side. Never put too much varnish on the brush or it will take ages to dry and form ridges of colour. Apply at least two coats. Once they are dry, apply a top coat of clear varnish to protect from chipping and to give a high gloss. You can also spray or stroke on some quick-drying solution to reduce waiting time.*

10 *It is good for nails to be left without varnish whenever possible.*

Trouble shooting

When nails don't grow fast enough
Exercise your hands and fingertips. Drum them on the table as if you are playing the piano. This helps improve circulation to the fingertips and carries nourishment to the nail matrix via tiny blood vessels. Open and close your stretched hands quickly. You can do this at any time of the day. To loosen your fingers, place the fingers of your outstretched hand flat against the palm of your other hand and push gently several times. Do the same with the other hand. To exercise each finger, close one hand around the other and push gently to either side. Relax your hand and take each finger at a time with the index and middle finger of your other hand. Pull gently as you slide the finger between the two other fingers. Look at your diet to see it is adequate, particularly in vitamin A, protein and the sulphur amino acids.

Brittle nails that break easily
Stay away from nail hardeners that contain formaldehyde – they will only make brittle nails more brittle. What will help is one of the protein conditioners. Leave nails free of varnish and apply one of these or simply white iodine daily. See that you get adequate zinc and B-complex vitamins, particularly B6.

Nails that peel and split and don't seem to grow
Look at your diet as described above. In this case try a formaldehyde-based hardener, applying it carefully so you don't get any on the skin. Be sure to bevel the ends of the nails when you file them. Steer clear of water except very

briefly to wash your hands – it will soften the nails too much. Wear gloves when gardening, washing, working and out in the weather.

Broken nails

There are many excellent nail-mending kits that either cover the break with fine paper and then varnish or which offer a glue that is strong enough to hold a broken tip when it is replaced.

Red hands

Exercise your fingers as much as possible. Cover your hands with a rich oil or cream and alternately dip them in hot and cold water twice a day. Apply a green-tinted moisturizer over your hand cream to hide the redness.

Clammy hands

Take exercise. Make dips in cold water. Use a silicone-based hand cream. Spray an antiperspirant on palms afterwards.

Rough hands, stained hands, and callouses

Hard lumps of skin will smooth away with a pumice stone rubbed with soap. Wash dirty areas with a brush, then rub the pulpy part of half a lemon on the skin and add loads of hand cream (the nourishing variety) before your hands have dried completely. Repeat in a few hours and continue in the same way until they are smooth again.

Feet and legs

Feet are more important than most people realize. When they ache, not only are your posture and movements affected, so is your complexion and your energy level. Nothing brings a haggard, older look to an unlined face like sore feet. Also, one of the most common complaints with which doctors are faced is fatigue. And often behind this fatigue lies an unnoticed foot problem.

Little wonder, when you consider that city dwellers walk an average of ten miles a day. All your weight is borne by twenty-six little bones, some of which are the most delicate in the body.

Learn to look after your feet well and you'll reap immeasurable benefits in looks, health, and high spirits. Foot care is also the first step towards having beautiful legs.

Choose your shoes

The shoes you choose affect far more than the look of your feet. Poorly fitting shoes, shoes with too rigid a sole or too high a heel may play an important part in the formation of cellulite on the thighs and in the development of varicose veins. If your shoes fit and heel height is right for you, then you stand a good chance of avoiding them. It is also a good idea to vary the height of your heel throughout the day by carrying an extra pair of shoes with you to work or shopping.

When you wear a heel that is too high you throw your posture off balance. This makes you tire more easily and tilts your pelvis in such a way that sacral muscles are forced to remain in a state of continual spasm. As a result, you can end up with a hollow in your back and agonizing backache, particularly around the time of your periods. If your heel is too low for your foot, it is not so serious,

but this can result in overdeveloped calves or muscle ache in the back of the legs.

If you want to wear a really high or stiletto heel, or clogs, do it only occasionally. The rigid soles of clogs act as splints, immobilizing the feet so they and the legs don't get a proper workout when you walk. They are also responsible for a lot of twisted ankles and the development of deformities.

Too loose a shoe of any kind rubs against the heels and toes and is responsible for a lot of corns and callouses.

Legs from the inside

Varicose veins are the most serious enemies of leg looks. The hidden constipation that results from living on the average Western diet lacking in natural fibre from wholegrains and raw vegetables is one of the prime causes, for unelimated wastes in the intestines put constant pressure on the blood vessels supplying blood to and from the legs.

Long-term overweight is another factor in the development of varicose veins, as is inactivity. The small valves in the legs that open and close alternately to keep the blood flowing in the right direction depend on firm and well-toned muscles for support.

To avoid the problem, follow a good diet of natural unrefined foods, don't let yourself become over-fat, and get plenty of exercise – swimming is the best form of all. Exercise for legs is particularly important during pregnancy because, like constipation, the weight of the baby puts pressure on blood vessels supplying the legs.

Take supplementary vitamins C and E. If your legs ache you can wear support stockings, but you should not wear them all the time.

Wonderful water for tired legs

Water treading

Run six inches of cold water in the bath. Walk back and forth in it for forty-five seconds to five minutes, as long as you are comfortable. (You can get the same effect walking on dewy grass in the morning or in a lake or stream.) Then get out and dry your legs well and put on warm woollen socks. If you can, lie down on a slant board or a bed with your feet propped up with a pillow so they are above your head for five minutes. As you get used to the treatment you can increase the amount of cold water in the bath so it covers your calves. Make sure that during the treatment the bathroom is warm and keep the top half of you dressed while you are doing it.

Cold sitz bath

Use this a couple of times a week. Run a bath with cold water – just enough to come up to your waist. Make sure the bathroom is well heated, and wear something on the top half of you to keep you warm. Sit down in the water for thirty seconds.

Have a large towel ready. Get out but don't dry yourself. Instead, wrap the towel around you and immediately get into bed. Cover yourself warmly and rest for half an hour or simply go to sleep for the night.

To shave or not to shave

Think hard before you decide to rid your legs of all their hair. Is it necessary? Why should women be completely free of body hair? If hair is very dark, it can always be bleached by mixing half a cup of twenty-volume peroxide to a paste with ordinary fuller's earth or soap flakes, then adding a couple of teaspoons of ammonia. Mix well and spread on hair and leave the paste on for ten to fifteen minutes. Then wash it off. Repeat the treatment every two days until hairs are colourless. Then do it again each month.

Ways to remove hair

1 Shaving leaves an awful stubble and has to be done a couple of times a week to keep regrowth at bay.

2 Depilatories work better, although the chemical in them can be very hard on sensitive skin.

3 Waxing is the best method for non-permanent hair removal. It can be done in a salon or you can buy various kinds of wax strips to put on yourself.

4 Permanent hair removal has to be done by electrolysis. There are two forms: galvanism and diathermy. Galvanism is very slow and laborious but has a 100 per cent success rate. Diathermy is faster but you get a 20 per cent regrowth – all hairs are not completely destroyed the first time.

5 A new method of hair removal uses electronic tweezers that grasp the hair and then pass a current through the tweezers to the root.

Beautiful feet

Wash them every day, making a rich lather and massaging it over the soles of the feet. With a loofah, gently rub the tops and soles of the feet, not forgetting the heels, to loosen the dead skin cells,

and with a soft nail brush, gently brush the tips of the nails from side to side. Rinse them well in warm water and if there is any hard skin to remove, rub a pumice stone over it. Finally, rinse again in warm water and then splash with cold. Dry your feet thoroughly by wrapping them in a towel and gently rubbing and patting them, then rub dry carefully between and behind the toes until absolutely all the moisture is gone. This is important in order to protect them from infection. If your feet tend to sweat, give them a light rubdown with alcohol. If they ache, massage some cider vinegar into the soles to cool and refresh them, or make a hot and cold foot bath – three minutes of hot followed by thirty seconds of cold – and end with a good friction rub with a soft towel. Finally, dust each foot with dusting powder.

Feet need exercise too

One of the best things you can do for your feet is to walk barefoot. Wearing exercise sandals is the next best thing. When your feet are free of shoes and tights they relax and stretch; exercise sandals are designed to let them do this. They follow the natural contour of the foot, imitating and slightly exaggerating the effect of walking barefoot.

Foot exercises

There are several exercises you can do for your feet that will refresh the rest of you too.

Climbing the walls

Lie on the floor with legs and feet propped up against a wall. Using the toes to pull each foot up, 'walk' up the wall, one foot after the other. When you get as far as you can, come down and start again. Repeat three or four times. The last time, as you go higher, support your hips with your hands and stay there for two or three minutes with legs and feet raised high above the head.

Tiptoes

Sitting in a straight chair with good posture, place feet flat on floor about six inches apart. First raise one foot from the heel and then the other, pointing toes, so only the toes remain on the floor, and then lower. Repeat ten times.

Perfect pigeons

For two minutes daily walk barefoot with toes pointing inward. Try to pick up a marble with the toes and walk on the outside of the feet for another minute. (This is particularly good for trimming ankles.)

Ankle twists

Sitting with your legs crossed, rotate the ankles ten times one way and then the other. Change legs and repeat. (Good both for slimming ankles and strengthening them for skiing and hiking.)

Japanese Shiatsu treatment for feet

1 Press each toe hard three times with your thumb, working down from tips of toes to foot itself.

2 Now press between the tendons on the top of the foot, grasping the foot in your hand and working up between each tendon towards the ankle.

3 Move to the plantar arch (the sole of the foot), pressing hard with your thumb and on the bottom of the foot, moving up to centre.

4 Finally, apply pressure hard around sides of the ankles and on the Achilles tendon.

5 Repeat with the other foot, then put feet up on a cushion so that your legs and feet are above the level of your head and body, and relax with your eyes closed for five minutes.

Troubleshooting

When problems arise, deal with them immediately. A corn or a callous is a simple thing to treat if you act right away. If you wait it can turn into a serious problem.

Athlete's foot

This is a fungus infection that usually appears first just behind and between the toes. Try not to get it in the first place by keeping your feet clean, well ventilated, cool and dry. First there is only flaking and scaliness, then if it develops, you get cracks that can be extremely painful. Get rid of it by removing the dead skin with a pumice and then applying a fungicidal cream or powder (better both) and keeping it on the feet, which should be covered with cotton socks for the night. Expose the feet as much as you can to dry air. Always change socks, stockings and tights daily.

Bunions

A hard swelling at the base of the big toe is known as a bunion. It comes from poorly fitting shoes that push the big toe inward and sideways so that it forms a bony outgrowth at the side. A pocket of fluid called a bursa may also develop between the bone and the skin.

If you seek professional help at the first signs of a bunion it can probably be treated simply, and then corrected with exercise, but if you wait until it is fully developed, surgery may be the only answer.

Callouses

Areas where the skin is hard, callouses are really a form of protection devised by the foot that is suffering from pressure or friction. They can be removed by soaking your feet and then rubbing with a pumice stone or special foot scraper. You can also spread petroleum jelly over the callous and then wear a cotton sock over it in bed.

Chilblains

This painful tingling, itching and inflammation of the feet is connected with poor circulation. It can be helped by nutritional therapy – giving nicotinic acid (one form of niacin) regularly along with the rest of the B group of vitamins, particularly B6 and pantothenic acid. Vitamin E may also be helpful.

Preventative treatment is a must. This means plenty of exercise to improve circulation all over, warm socks and clothing, and no restrictions around the legs, like tight boots or garters. Soaking the feet regularly in hot water for three minutes and then plunging them into ice-cold water for thirty seconds and putting on wool socks afterwards can be helpful.

Corns

They are the result of ill-fitting shoes. A callous with a cone-shaped core develops, the eye of the cone being at the deepest level of the callous. If it presses against a nerve, you get severe pain. Small corns can be rubbed away by soaking your feet in hot and salty water for fifteen minutes and then taking a pumice to them. Larger corns have to be removed by a professional with a scalpel. If you try to do it yourself, you risk causing infection. A specially designed, padded ring worn over the corn in the meantime can relieve the pressure against the nerve.

Verrucas

The result of a virus infection that can be picked up much as athlete's foot is, verrucas or plantar warts sometimes appear in groups on the undersurface of the foot. Occasionally, you only get one at a time. They grow upwards into the foot and any pressure on them is painful. Eventually most clear up by themselves. If not, they need medical treatment and can be removed either with Formalin, burning, or surgery.

Hydrotherapy highs

Water is the finest solvent in the world. It dissolves dirt on the outside of the skin and carries nutrients to and wastes away from the cells inside. Many a fine-skinned grandmother claims her exquisite complexion is the result of washing with pure water and soap. And health spas have long relied on the magic of water – hot and cold – mixed with mud, herbs, the essential oils of plants, or carefully selected mineral salts, to smooth skin, relax tense muscles, refine pores, and revitalize bodies.

Hydrotherapy treatments

The treatments listed here are those that I find particularly useful.

To get rid of tension and a headache

Half fill a bath with cold water. Then, making sure you are well covered so your body doesn't get cold, walk about in it with bare feet for three

minutes. Immediately afterwards, put on warm socks and lie down for ten minutes.

To recharge yourself quickly after a hard day

Fill a bath with hot water (110° F) and soak for a couple of minutes, preferably with a towel under your head so you can lean back and close your eyes. When you have relaxed, let half the water out, turn on the cold tap, and lie back again, this time circulating the fresh water with your hands. By the time the bath is full again you will feel revitalized. And you won't be cold either. Just tingling and glowing. Now wrap yourself in a bath towel and lie down for five minutes.

Cold showers can do a lot to revive you too. First shower in hot water for three to five minutes until you are warm and relaxed. Then switch to cold and stand under the nozzle, moving about so the cold water reaches all around you – for thirty seconds to one minute, not longer. Now stop. Get out of the shower and dry yourself briskly, then dress warmly. This will protect you from a chill. The pre-shower with hot water prepares your skin for the invigorating effect of the cold. Make sure that your bathroom is well heated and that you wrap up thoroughly after any cold plunge to give your system a chance to readjust to normal temperature. This is one of the first rules of hydrotherapy.

The beauty of bathing

Bathing should be a pleasant ritual that should treat your mind as well as your body. There are a number of useful pre-bath techniques and tools.

- **A loofah:** rub this against the skin to slough off dead cells and to increase circulation.
- **A hemp glove:** rub this briskly up from the feet to the abdomen; from the hands to the shoulders and across the back and torso. Should you get broken veins under the skin from the treatment, stop it and increase your intake of vitamin C.
- **Sea salt rub:** keep a bowl of coarse sea salt by the bath. Wet your body, then rub the salt briskly all over into the skin. Now step into a bath and soak in it for ten to fifteen minutes.
- **Oil massage:** rub half a cup of vegetable oil (safflower or sunflower) well into the skin of the face and body and massage it in for a couple of minutes before taking the plunge. In the warm bath, use only a mild soap to wash with or none at all. Then when you step out, briskly rub yourself dry to distribute the remainder of the oil.

Relaxing baths (85-95° F)

- **Vinegar soother:** add 1 cup of cider vinegar to the bath.
- **Essential calmer:** add 3 drops of essential oil of basil, 3 of rosemary, and 3 of mint to the water while it is running.
- **Herbal calmer:** infuse a handful of camomile flowers and a handful of comfrey leaves in a pot of water just off the boil for half an hour. Strain and pour into the bath and then soak.

Invigorating baths (65-75° F)

- **Pine extract:** make a pine extract by simmering pine cones and needles in a large covered pan (one part needles and cones to four parts water) for half an hour. Then strain and continue to boil the liquid until it starts to get thicker. Add 4 fluid ounces of it to a bath and store the rest in the refrigerator for another time.
- **Aphrodisia:** add two drops each of oil of basil, cardamom, jasmine, patchouli, and myrrh to the bath water when it is running. This is a particularly beautiful-smelling mixture that is supposed to have aphrodisiac properties thanks to the cardamom and jasmine.

After-sports baths

Start with water at 100° F and decrease temperature to about 55° F.

- **Mineral bath:** add 1 1/2 cups of Epsom salts to the bath. Stay in for twenty minutes.
- **Vinegar bath:** add one cup of cider vinegar to the bath to relieve aching muscles. It can help to rub the vinegar right on the muscles themselves and then to step into the water.

Skin-softening baths (85-95° F)

- **Milk bath:** add two cups of instant dried non-fat milk to the water to smooth and soften skin at a fraction of the cost of buying an expensive milk bath. A few drops of oil of geranium added to the water will make it smell lovely too.
- **Herb softener:** make a muslin bag and fill it with camomile flowers, elder

flowers, comfrey, and linden blossoms. Sew it up and use it to wash your skin in the bath and let it soak in the water.

- **Bran wash:** bran is an excellent skin softener. Stuff a muslin bag with it, sew up, let it soak in warm water, and then use the bag to wash all over with. It will last through several washes.

Easy on soaps and bath foams

These are not very good for your skin. If you bathe every day, you don't need soap to get clean. If you do use it, choose a neutral soap (one that is not alkaline) or one of the pH balanced detergent bars that are mild on the skin and don't remove the natural acid mantle from it. Mix your own bath oil by combining one cup of safflower oil or sunflower oil in a blender with three tablespoons of an acid balanced shampoo. A good soap substitute can

be made by mixing half a cup of powdered orris root with half a cup of cornflour and sewing it into a bag. It can be used several times.

Underwater exercises

The bath is an excellent place for doing some isometrics to keep specific areas of your body in shape. All the following exercises are done lying in the tub.

Tummy flattener

Push out your abdomen as far as it will go and hold it for six seconds. Then let go and rest for six seconds. Now pull it in as hard as possible again. Let go and rest six seconds and repeat. Go through the whole series four times.

Arm firmers

First, with your hands against the sides of the body, press as hard as you can in towards the centre. Hold for six seconds

and then release. Repeat three times. Second, with arms and hands against the side of the bath, press out as hard as you can and hold for six seconds. Release. Repeat three times.

Back strengthener
With your toes against the end of the bath, press hard, curving your neck and bringing your chin down to your chest. Hold for three seconds. Now let your back sag in the bath, let your head fall back, and press against the end of the bath with your heels. Hold for three seconds. Repeat the two movements in succession three times.

Leg shapers
Press your legs against the side of the bath and hold for six seconds, then release. Repeat three times. Press your legs hard inward together and hold for six seconds, then release. Repeat for another three times.

Leg looseners
Taking one leg at a time, lift it high, bending the knee towards your face and pointing your toe. Then straighten your leg and curve your toes back towards you. Now, leg still straight, point toe again hard. Finally, return the leg to the bath and do the same thing with the other leg. The whole exercise is done to a slow count of four. Repeat six times with each leg.

Ankle twisters
Twirl your ankles around first one way and then the other, ten times each.

Neck looseners
Gently rock from side to side as far as you can comfortably go, ten times.

Perspiration and odour

There is a common misconception that body odour comes from perspiration. It doesn't. Perspiration or sweat consists of nothing more than almost odourless water plus a few mineral salts that are responsible for that slightly salty smell many find has an almost aphrodisiac appeal to it. The unpleasant smell often thought to be the result of perspiration or sweat is in fact caused by waste products from the bacteria on the skin.

All-over perspiration can be controlled by daily bathing. You can get extra protection against excess moisture and body odour by using an antiperspirant or deodorant. Deodorants and deodorant soaps work by restricting the action of bacteria on the skin.

If you shun chemicals and prefer do-it-yourself products, chlorophyll is the natural deodorant to try. You can use green leaves, fresh green vegetables (such as spinach or beetroot tops), and fresh herbs such as mint as natural alternatives to the chemical products. Rub them briskly under the arms a couple of times a day or make the following lavender water and use it instead:

Take six drops of lavender and shake together with a pint of distilled water. Store in a dark bottle or keep in the refrigerator. Apply with a ball of cotton-wool twice a day to parts of the body that perspire easily.

STEP NINE: LOOK GREAT

Face value

For most people the face is the focus of attention and the most immediate expression of who you are. It is certainly the area of the body women worry about most. They spend a great deal of money looking after it with creams and lotions, cleansers and toners and masks, and of course the traditional facials, special treatments, and face-lifts.

After this comes make-up, which, if skilfully applied, enhances the natural features of your face. Eyes, to be beautiful, have to be healthy and looked after carefully.

Another important aspect of looking great is hair. Shining, clean, healthy hair is a must if you want to feel and look your best.

The craft of skin care

A living, breathing thing, skin is far more than just a superficial covering for your body. It is your largest organ. It covers a surface area of about 17 square feet and weighs between six and eight pounds.

Lasting skin health is a question of lasting care, not just spending lavishly on fancy creams and treatments. But to know how to look after your skin you must first know something about it and the many things that affect it for better or worse.

From the inside

All the nutrients your body needs for optimum health, your skin needs to keep it supple and healthy, including the vitamins, minerals, protein, essential fatty acids, trace elements, and unrefined carbohydrates. So many specific problems such as brown patches or early wrinkling are mostly the result of internal neglect, and no amount of expensive stuff rubbed on the outside will stop their formation.

You need a diet high in natural fibre, or roughage, from raw vegetables and/or wholegrains. If ever you find yourself constipated, try a high-raw diet for a week or put yourself through one of the good colon cleansing programmes of herbs plus psyllium husks available from health food stores.

Drink plenty of water, an essential nutrient you may never have thought of. It helps detoxify skin, dissolving hard debris that interferes with proper circulation and removal of wastes and which can cause cellulite. You should drink at least six to eight big glasses a day for the sake of your skin.

Vital vitamins and minerals

- *Vitamin A*
- *B-complex vitamins*
- *Vitamin C and the bioflavonoids*
- *Vitamin E*
- *Fatty acids such as GLA, EPA and DHA.*

- *Silica*
- *Zinc*
- *Sulphur*

- *Selenium*
- *Calcium*
- *Magnesium*

Skin destroyers	Skin helpers
Stress	Exercise
Coffee	Sleep
Alcohol	Healthy liver
Tobacco	Plenty of water

From the outside

There are three parts to any good external skin care regimen, regardless of your age or the type of skin you have:

1 Regular, thorough cleansing.
2 Protection from moisture loss and external roughness.
3 Protection from the ultraviolet rays of the sun.

Cleansing

THE SOAP WAY

Soap is an excellent cleanser. Manufactured from caustic alkalines and fats, it removes grease and dirt from the skin's surface easily. Its disadvantage lies in its being extremely alkaline. This means that using soap reduces the natural acidity, or pH, of the skin, which helps protect it from bacterial invasion. Soap is capable of penetrating the skin's outer protective layers and leaching away the hydrolipidic film, making the skin of women who tend towards dryness even drier. Surprisingly, it can also have just the opposite effect on skin that tends to be oily.

Thanks to modern technology, there are now many pH-balanced soaps, foaming cleansers, and detergent bars that don't disturb the pH of the skin, so that if you are a soap fancier you can find one to suit you without many of the disadvantages of the conventional type.

THE CREAM OR OIL WAY

The cream and lotion cleansers, oils, and cleansing milks available now are also good. They usually cut through makeup and grime even better than soap and, provided you use enough of one and that you remove it with tonic water or water afterwards, will do an excellent job of keeping your skin clean. A cleansing milk is an oil-in-water emulsion that cleans by emulsifying water-soluble dirt in its aqueous phase and oil-soluble dirt in its oil phase. Put a lotion or cream cleanser on with your hands as you would soap and then tissue it off, repeating the application until the tissue shows no sign of dirt on it. Then follow with tonic or freshener, preferably one without alcohol in it, or simply rinse your face in cool water.

THE DOUBLE TREATMENT

If you live in a city or a highly industrialized area where air pollution is a particular problem, the oil-and-water technique is the most effective means of all. It entails using two types of cleansers, first an oil-based one, which removes makeup and oil-soluble dirt, followed by a water-based one.

Choose a pure vegetable oil, such as cold-pressed sunflower oil, corn oil, or one of the more expensive hazelnut or apricot oils. Buy it in small quantities and keep it in a cool place (preferably in the refrigerator), to protect it from oxidation. Pour a tablespoonful of the oil into the palm of your hand and spread it on your face, rubbing it in well. (This is a good opportunity to give yourself a gentle massage to stimulate circulation while the oil is leaching up the makeup and grime on your skin.) Then, using pads of damp absorbent cotton-wool wiped over your face, remove the oil and with it much of the dirt on the skin.

You are ready now for the second stage. Wash your skin in warm water and use a pH-balanced soap, detergent bar, or liquid detergent cleanser, adding plenty of water and rubbing gently with the tips of your fingers and the palms of your hands until the whole face is well covered. Now rinse thoroughly ten times in warm water and then splash with cool.

Whichever cleansing method you choose, follow it twice daily.

Keep moist
One partial answer to the problem of dry skin is humidification: the use of a humidifier or simply simmering a pan of water in a room to raise the moisture level of the air to somewhere between 75 per cent and 90 per cent humidity – the ideal range for preserving the skin's

water balance. A humidifier is a worthwhile investment for anyone who values their skin and wants to keep it from rapidly ageing. But you need surface protection against water loss too.

Some moisturizers come in lotion form and contain humectants, or lactic acid, which tend to attract water from the air and draw moisture from the skin's deeper layers.

Other moisturizing products – creams and lotions – form an occlusive film on the skin's surface. These contain substances like lanolin, collagen or water-in-oil emulsions. For very dry skin by far the most effective way of moisturizing is simply to prevent water in the skin from escaping into the air.

Most moisturizers, particularly the kind that feel so cool and delightful on your skin when you apply them, are oil-in-water emulsions whose fat content is too low to provide the coating on the skin's surface that it needs to be effective in keeping its natural moisture in. But GLA in a moisturizer in good concentration enables better overall function of the skin including enhancing its ability to hold moisture long-term. These GLA moisturizers are great for the over thirty-fives.

In the past few years, with increased awareness of how to deal with moisture-loss problems, a few new creams of the water-in-oil type or containing good quantities of GLA have appeared on the market. Find one that you like and wear it every day, applying it twice a day if you can under makeup when you are wearing it or just on its own when you don't.

Light relief
Heavy exposure to the sun's light at the age of eighteen will result in early wrinkling, between twenty-five and forty. This is an unfortunate law of nature that nothing can change – except, of course, wearing some form of adequate sunscreen on the skin.

Which sunscreen product you choose depends on how much light you are exposed to. It must offer not only a UVB screen against burning but also UVA protection against ageing. Wear it all the time, day in day out, winter and summer. It should offer at least an SPF of 4 or more for day to day care in winter or when overcast, rising to a 15 or higher when you will be in direct sunlight.

These three things – cleansing, protection from moisture loss, and a sunscreen – are all there is to basic skin care.

The art of treating skin

The vitamins and anti-oxidants
Vitamin A applied to the surface of the skin either from a capsule on its own or mixed into cream and oil preparations has been used successfully in the treatment of dry and ageing skin and acne. It appears to work particularly well in combination with vitamin D, which itself has a healing effect on the skin. (This is why vitamin D is often used in nappy-rash remedies and in burn ointments.)

Vitamin E, about which there has been such controversy, and vitamin C are certainly useful in the treatment of skin healing from a cut or burn. Both vitamins are natural anti-oxidants and as such are probably useful in preventing premature ageing of the skin (as well as the whole body) but for this purpose should be taken internally as well. In a few people, vitamin E used on the skin can cause allergic reactions. So, if you decide to use this vitamin, test it out on a small area first.

Fatty acids can be very helpful in treating skin. GLA from borage oil or evening primrose oil squeezed from a capsule enhances both the health of skin as a whole and improves the ability to hold moisture in all kinds of skin.

There are two ways of applying vitamins to the skin. You can squeeze the vitamin oils directly from the capsules (which works well with E but tends to smell very strong with vitamins A and D) or you can mix any of the vitamins into a simple carrier oil and then spread it on the face. Good times for doing this are before you take strenuous exercise (the physical exertion improves the skin's absorptive abilities) and after a facial sauna, steaming, or hot bath (when the skin is warm and moist). Leave your preparation on for twenty minutes, then either remove with cleanser or simply tissue off the excess.

The essential oils

Plant extracts, or essential oils, are some of the most useful substances for skin treatment that you will find anywhere. Make sure when choosing them that you are buying the pure essential oils of plants, not their synthetic substitutes, which are much cheaper but have no therapeutic action.

Mix your own formulas, using fifteen drops of plant essences (that is, all the various essential oils you may use should total only fifteen drops together) to each ounce of carrier oil. Almond oil, apricot oil and hazelnut oil are particularly good carriers for the face. You can add vitamin E or A, squeezed directly from the capsules (the scents of the plant essences do wonders to mask

the unpleasant odours of vitamins). Keep your mixture in a cool place (mix only small quantities each time), preferably in a brown glass bottle to protect them from the light.

- *For skin that is too oily: lavender, lemon, basil, geranium, juniper, and ylang-ylang.*
- *For skin that is dry: sandalwood, geranium, rose, lavender, jasmine, and camomile.*
- *For ageing skin: fenugreek, wheat germ oil, sandalwood, rose, myrrh, frankincense, lavender, mace, clary.*

Liposomes

They are nothing in themselves but little delivery vans for active ingredients. Filled with GLA or plant fractions or anti-oxidants they are a great way of making sure these treatment substances and complexes are carried to just the right place in the skin where they can do the most good.

Retinoic acid

Available only on prescription, this derivative of vitamin A comes in gel, lotion or cream form, and is only for sun-damaged skin. It has little to offer natural ageing skin.

The acids and enzymes

'Fruit acids', otherwise known as alpha hydroxy acids or AHAs, include such compounds as glycolic acid from sugar cane, malic acid from apples, pyruvic acid from pawpaws and lactic acid from milk. With regular use they dissolve the intercellular glue that sticks old dead cells together allowing them to slough

off and make the skin clearer. They also help plump up the skin of the epidermis, help to fade age-spots and increase the skin's supply of hyaluronic acid – a natural moisturizer.

Home treatments
On a do-it-yourself level, raw fruits and vegetables from your own kitchen are rich in acids and enzymes and will, in my opinion, give you an even better effect used regularly on the skin than most of the expensive 'fruit acid' preparations you can buy. For instance, the cosmetic effect of the juice of fresh cucumber, which contains the ascorbic acid oxidase, has long been known. It is slightly diuretic and astringent and good for all types of skin. Similarly, the juice of fresh lemons, which also contains phosphates and the enzyme esterase, is also beneficial, particularly for oily skins. It is antiseptic and refining. So are fresh carrot juice and fresh papaya, as well as

the juice and pulp of many other fruits. The enzymes contained in them help stimulate the life processes in your skin's cells, making it firmer and fresher-looking and giving it a glow of health. Here is an easy way of treating skin inside and out. Every day, whenever you prepare raw juices in a juice extractor (see Step 7), spread a couple of tablespoonfuls on your face at the same time. Masks are also particularly beneficial when made with fresh fruit and vegetable juices or pulp plus other ingredients from the kitchen – beaten egg yolk plus a tablespoon of raw, unheated honey for dry skin, or two teaspoons of natural yoghurt for oily skin. They are best used after a facial sauna, when the skin is highly receptive to whatever is put on it. The following fruits and vegetables can be juiced or puréed in a blender. Play with them until you find the ones that work best for you, for every woman's skin is unique.

FRUIT/VEGETABLE	GOOD FOR	EFFECTS
Blackberry	oily skin with enlarged pores	astringent, diuretic
Blackcurrant	delicate skin that is blemished	soothing, healing, decongesting
Cabbage	acne and pimples	disinfectant, good for promoting healing of fresh scars
Carrot	sensitive skin; dehydrated, ageing skin	stimulates cell reproduction; moisturises
Celery	all skin types	stimulates waste removal from cells, brightens complexion
Cucumber	all skin types, especially normal to oily	helps bleach freckles; soothing, diuretic, anti-wrinkle treatment
Dandelion	all skin types, especially sallow skin	tonic, soothing; stimulates cell proliferation
Grapefruit	troubled skin, oily skin, enlarged pores	astringent, mild bleach, brightener
Grapes	blackheads, acne-prone skin	diuretic; encourages cell proliferation
Lemon	oily skin, particularly skin losing its tone; skin with uneven pigment such as 'liver spots'	mild bleach, antiseptic, disinfectant
Orange	normal to oily skin, enlarged pores, uneven pigmentation	mild bleach, astringent
Peach	all skin, particularly dry	diuretic, soothing, anti-inflammatory
Pear	sensitive skin, inflamed skin	emollient; encourages elimination of wastes
Raspberry	large pores, oily skin	astringent
Spinach	dehydrated skin, ageing skin, troubled skin	soothing, stimulating circulation
Strawberry	oily skin, uneven pigmentation	astringent, diuretic, toning
Tomato	oily skin, blackheads	rebalances skin acidity; mild emollient

Air – let your skin breathe

Although most of the oxygen your skin needs comes by way of the bloodstream, the skin also helps itself to as much as 2.5 per cent of the body's total oxygen from the air by direct absorption. Skin also directly eliminates almost 3 per cent of the body's carbon dioxide waste. The ability of the skin to take in oxygen directly from the air appears to play an important part in maintaining its health and beauty.

Recently cosmetic manufacturers have begun to produce products – foundations and complex emulsion moisturizers – that do not interfere with the skin's air absorption. There are also several good treatment creams for older skin that contain ingredients designed to stimulate the skin's use of oxygen, which can be particularly helpful in ageing skin. But whatever products you use on your skin, give it time to rest some of each night by cleansing it thoroughly and then leaving it free.

For instance, there is no reason to wear a night cream all night long. With any treatment product you put on your skin, the lion's share of what the skin will pick up is taken in during the first twenty minutes after you apply it. Leaving it on longer than that is a waste of time.

Herbal saunas

Every now and then skin needs deep cleansing, and one of the most effective ways of getting it is from a facial sauna. The only skin condition that doesn't benefit from facial steams, or saunas, is that in which broken capillaries appear in the cheeks and nose.

Making a herbal sauna

Toss a couple of handfuls of mixed herbs (see below) into two quarts of water you have brought to the boil and then removed from the heat. Now cover your whole head with a towel and put it over the steaming pot so the towel forms a tent to catch the steam. Sit in front of the steaming pot (not closer than one foot from the water), and breathe in the scent of the aromatic herbs for five to ten minutes. Finish the treatment by splashing with cool water to remove wastes accumulated on the surface of the skin, and follow either with a treatment cream or mask, or your usual moisturizer.

Some of the herbs you can choose from:

- *camomile, elder blossom*
- *mint*
- *basil*
- *rosemary (particularly good for oily skin)*
- *sage*
- *slippery-elm bark (good for sensitive skin)*
- *comfrey*
- *leaf and root (also good for delicate or inflamed or troubled skin)*
- *strawberry leaf*
- *raspberry leaf*
- *acacia flower*
- *lavender*
- *rose petal*

The mask effect

Masks are one of the mysteries of the cosmetic world. The manufactured kinds come in many varieties and are designed for several purposes. Chosen carefully, I believe, a mask can be a boon to beauty.

A mask is designed to perform one of the more specific tasks: to deep-cleanse, to tone, to stimulate circulation, to moisturize the skin, or to exfoliate. The deep response to elements in a mask comes through the vascular network in the dermis, where active ingredients coupled with physical tension from the mask drying on the skin bring about increased circulation and help stimulate cellular activity.

The medium of massage

Provided it is done skilfully, massage is a wonderful treatment for the face. But it must be done gently and carefully, for the muscles of the face and neck are made up of fibres which, unlike muscles in the rest of the body, are attached not

only to bone but also to the skin itself. They are therefore delicate and must never be pulled hard, or massage can have a detrimental effect. Always following the direction of the muscle fibres themselves, massage will stimulate blood circulation, which improves the tone of muscles and skin, and promotes the use of nutrients in the cells and the elimination of wastes. Massage will also help the skin to absorb active ingredients in creams and essential oils.

Always begin a massage by covering your face with a cream or oil. Begin with effleurage, which means moving the palm of your hand and your fingers lightly over the surface of the skin. This has a soothing effect and a relaxing one which encourages blood and lymph flow. Start at the centre of the chest with your right hand, sweeping it outward towards the left shoulder and then upward over the left side of your neck. Then do the same for the other side with your left hand. (Actually these movements can be done simultaneously, using both hands at once.) Now massage from the base of the neck at the rear to the hairline. Do each stroke five times. Massage the neck, bringing first one hand and then the other around the curve of the neck from back to front also five times. Now bring each hand, one at a time, upward over the front and sides of the neck, under the chin, and outward at the jawline (five times each side). Stroke upward from corners of the mouth to temples (five times). Now, using the palms of your hands, stroke upward from the chin, over the jawline to the hairline so that the fingers cover the centre portion of the face and the cupped

palms go over first jaw and then cheekbones to end at the temples (five times). Stroke around the eyes. Begin at inner corners, at both sides of the nose, and using your middle finger, stroke outward around the eye to the outer corner. Then begin at the same inner corner and stroke upward and outward in a half circle around the top part of the eye, just underneath the bone that forms the eye socket. (Repeat upper and lower semi-circle five times each side.) Now stroke across the forehead, using the left hand to move from right to left, followed by the right hand moving from left to right – five times each side. Finally, with the tips of your fingers tap lightly several times all over the chin and jawline, then over the cheekbones, then all across the forehead.

Finish off the massage by removing the excess oil that is still left on the skin and then splashing the face with cold water several times.

Skin: troubleshooting

Theoretically, having beautiful skin is simple. Take one part clear young skin, add the forty or so known nutrients from fresh foods eaten as much as possible in their natural state and whole, and mix together with exercise for overall tone and proper breathing for good oxygenation of cells. Put in a dose of fresh air and a pinch of stimulation now and then. Stir well and you've got a recipe that will last for years. That's the theory. In practice, however, things can go wrong: an early wrinkle, brown spots to mar a perfect complexion, acne, dryness, roughness – that's when you need help from special cosmetics, vitamins, and treatments.

Too dry

THE CAUSES
- Under-active sebaceous glands.
- Drying weather conditions, central heating, or air conditioning.
- A diet too low in essential fatty acids, such as a crash diet.
- An incorrect water balance in the skin cells as a result of their being exposed to water (e.g. in swimming) for so long that they have swollen and burst, or to their having been deprived of water for so long that they gradually desiccate.
- Subclinical deficiencies of vitamin A or C or any one of several of the B-complex group or of linoleic acid.

PREVENTION AND CURE
- Use a water-in-oil emulsion or a GLA cream on your face night and day.
- Ensure that you get enough essential fatty acids in your diet by using olive oil in your salad dressings and cutting out convenience foods full of junk fats.
- Take supplements of vitamins A and D in the form of fish liver oil, fresh carrot juice a couple of times a day and EPA and DHA and GLA in supplement form.
- Use a humidifier.
- Don't wash your skin with soap.
- Don't use any skin product containing alcohol.
- Use a mask for dry skin.
- Use aromatherapy oils you mix yourself to contain the essences most useful for dry skin, such as geranium, camomile, rose, sandalwood, lavender, and ylang-ylang.
- Always choose an oil-based makeup foundation.

Too oily

THE CAUSES
- Overactive sebaceous glands.
- A diet too high in fats and fried foods or refined sugar.
- Too much stimulation of the sebaceous glands by heat, the sun, or skin-care products containing chemicals such as sulphur.
- Diets slightly deficient in some of the B group of vitamins.

PREVENTION AND CURE
- Using a mild, lotion cleanser without any drying agent (which would degrease the skin) for cleansing and removing makeup. It should be an oil itself or an oil-in-water emulsion. Rub it on gently with clean hands, then wipe it off completely with tissues before rinsing with fresh, cool water. You don't need a tonic or a freshener, but if you want one, make sure it contains no alcohol (alcohol is also a drier).
- During the day, wear a water-in-oil moisturizer.
- As soon as the moisturizer has had a chance to set, powder your face with double the amount of powder you would usually use, dust off the excess, then spray the face with a fine mist of water, blot with a tissue and then powder again.
- Stay out of the sun.
- Don't eat fatty foods or fried foods.
- Eat plenty of raw green vegetables and B-complex vitamins from wholegrain breads and cereals, and liver.

Too sensitive

THE CAUSES

- A tendency to allergies, allergic reactions and sensitivities to particular substances can be inherited. If, for instance, both your mother and your father suffered from allergies, you have a 57 per cent chance of them too.
- If you are allergic to something your body reacts to it with hostility. This seldom happens the first time you meet the substance (called an allergen), but if for some reason your body takes a dislike to it, it will create an antibody that is a chemical specifically made to repel any future invasion by the same substance. Then, when sufficient antibodies are available, they combine with the allergen, and this combination triggers the release of histamines and histamine-like substances, which by a series of reactions finally results in raised, red, itchy splotches on the skin. This is known as an acute reaction.
- Delayed reactions, which come about only after a few hours or even days after coming into contact with the allergen, have no histamine formation, but during contact with the allergen the body's white blood cells come to recognize it as foreign and mobilize themselves to attack. Then the capillaries in the area become clogged with waste, and the skin flakes and scales, becoming red and itchy or even very sore.

PREVENTION AND CURE

- Antihistamines will alleviate the first sort of allergic reaction.
- Special injections will build up tolerance to the allergen.

- Antihistamines will do nothing for the delayed-reaction type allergy.
- Cortisone and cortisone-like medications are useful in quelling both types of allergic skin reaction, but should be used only in very serious cases and then only for short periods of time.
- Be careful about what you put on your face.
- Locate the allergen – the substance or product causing trouble – and then remove it from your life (see chart overleaf).
- Cleanse your skin thoroughly with two cleansers: a cream or lotion first, to dissolve makeup and grime, then a specially formulated hypoallergenic soap or detergent cleanser that is pH-balanced. Always dry your skin thoroughly.
- When you apply creams or oils, use the fleshy parts of your middle or ring fingers, never your index finger, and make sure your hands are scrupulously clean. For applying eye shadow, use cotton-tipped sticks, which can then be tossed away after use. Throw away your powder puff and instead always use a fresh piece of sterilized cotton-wool. Always wear a water-in-oil moisturizer during the day.
- Get to know the hypoallergenic cosmetics – skin-care and makeup products made without known irritants.
- Take vitamin B6, PABA and B2 supplements and vitamin C.
- Skin inflammations usually respond well to calamine lotion, simple witch hazel, and some poultices made with herbs such as calendula. One of the best to use is comfrey, whose very name denotes healing in Latin.

213

ALLERGEN	COMMON COSMETICS AND HOUSEHOLD PRODUCTS CONTAINING IT
Aluminium salts	Deodorants, antiperspirants, astringents
Ammonia	Bleaches, household chemicals
Ammoniated mercury	Freckle creams, antiseptic ointments
Aniline dyes	Hair colorants, eyebrow pencil
Barium salts	Depilatories
Beta-naphthol	Freckle creams
Boric acid	Lipsticks, baby skin creams and lotions
Cresylic compounds	Household antiseptics
Essential oils	Perfumes, deodorants
Formaldehyde	Plastics, preservatives, air fresheners, disinfectants, nail hardeners
Lanolin	Face creams and lotions, hair preparations, skin softeners
Lauryl alcohol sulphates	Water-soluble preparations, cleansing creams, shampoos, body, hand and skin lotions
Mercuric bichloride	Freckle creams, antiseptic lotions
Para-aminobenzoic acid	Sunscreen lotions and creams
Phenylenediamine compounds	Eye shadow, eyelash and eyebrow colouring, other cosmetics, hair colours
Phenyl salicylates	Suntan lotions, creams, sprays
Phthalates	Insect repellents
Propylene glycol	Water-soluble creams, hand creams
Resins	Plastics, hair spray, nail varnish
Salicylic acid	Face-peeling compounds, dandruff shampoos, acne lotions and soaps, corn removers
Soaps	Cleansing creams and shampoos
Sulphur	Dandruff shampoos, acne preparations
Thioglycolate	Cream rinses, body builders for hair, perm solutions, shampoos
Zinc salts	Astringents, deodorants

When acne strikes

THE CAUSES
- An infection of the sebaceous glands.
- High levels of testosterone and progesterone. Testosterone, known as the male hormone (although women have it in small quantities too), spurs the sebaceous glands to increase their production of sebum.
- A food sensitivity or allergy – the most common allergens being wheat, milk, or preservatives and colourings.
- When the elimination of wastes via the alimentary canal is inadequate, often they are eliminated through the skin.
- A diet high in fat and sugar.
- Iodides and bromides – iodized salt, saltwater fish and shellfish.
- Drugs including cough syrups, sedatives and cold medications.
- Stress and emotional upset.

PREVENTION AND CURE
- Eliminate sweets, sugared soft drinks, and fatty foods such as nuts and fried foods.
- Vitamin A or the carotenoids, taken internally in a daily dose of 10,000 to 25,000 international units in the case of vitamin A and/or the equivalent potency of beta-carotene or mixed carotenoids.
- Riboflavin and pyridoxine (B6).
- Vitamin C in large doses – from 6 to 8 grams a day
- Vitamin E both taken internally and used on the surface of the skin.
- Zinc taken as chelated zinc or zinc gluconate, 15mg twice a day.
- Niacin (B3) taken in doses of 50 to 100mg a day (any B vitamin should never be taken alone but be accompanied by the full B group).

- Keep the skin clean with gentle, pH-balanced soaps or detergent cleansers that do not contain sulphur or bactericidals.
- Topical agents such as Retinoic acid (available only by prescription) applied to the skin.

TREATMENT OF SCARS
The treatment of acne scars is a different matter altogether. It should only be attempted after the acne has completely cleared up. There are three methods: dermabrasion, chemical peels, and plastic surgery.

Avoid stretch marks

THE CAUSE
- A sudden increase in weight or volume of an area of the body or the swelling of breasts and abdomen in pregnancy.

PREVENTION AND CURE
- Take adequate zinc, silica and vitamin B6 in your diet – if necessary by supplementing it. Oral contraceptives have a marked effect on the body's need for and use of zinc and B6.
- Rub on an aromatherapy oil for your skin type twice a day, or use cocoa butter.

Once stretch marks are formed, however, there is, as yet, supposed to be no cure for them.

Your eyes: the windows of your soul

Not only are your eyes the truest of all physical reflections of who you are, they are also an ageless expression of beauty. For there can be something breathtaking about the eyes of an old woman, as there is about the eyes of a child. Like any other part of your body, to be beautiful your eyes have to be healthy, and to be healthy they need care.

But the care they need is quite different from what we are usually led to believe. For eyes are not the delicate, poor, vulnerable things we have been taught they are – overworked, constantly struggling against inadequate light and overstrain, and longing for some well-deserved tinted glasses to rest them. Far from it. Your eyes are tough. They were made for use and the more you use them, to read and to see with – both far away and up close – and the more you exercise the muscles around them, and the more they are exposed to the full spectrum of natural sunlight, the healthier and more beautiful they can become. And not only will your eyes benefit, so will the rest of your body.

How do you see?
Sight is a highly complex phenomenon. In fact, it is not your eyes that do the seeing but your brain.

The part of the eye that allows you to focus (and which is usually at fault when there is a vision problem such as near-sightedness or farsightedness) is the crystalline lens in the front of the eyeball, which changes from an elliptical shape when you are looking at distant things to a shape more like a sphere when you are examining something close up. This variation takes place thanks to a group of muscles that hold the lens. They are highly elastic when your body is young but become much less so as you get older. This, along with the thickening and hardening of the lens itself, is responsible for presbyopia, the inability to focus on things close to you, which is experienced by the majority of people over the age of forty-five.

A window to the body
The eye appears to be a window not only to the soul but also to the internal state of the body. A doctor looking into the eye with the use of a light is able to see if the patient is suffering from many more things than just those ailments affecting the eye itself. Eighty per cent of all brain tumours can be detected from an examination of the shape and colour of the optic nerve and the fundus, at the back of the eye.

The light entering your eyes appears to do a great deal more than simply transform electromagnetic wave patterns into nerve impulses for your brain to interpret as images. There is considerable evidence that, acting directly on the pigment granules in the epithelial cells of the retina, it also stimulates the pineal gland, the hypothalamus, and the pituitary gland through neurochemical channels, thereby influencing the health of the whole body.

Let there be light

Like plants and animals, we need light to stay in optimum health. Not only the light available through the tinted windows of the cars we drive and behind our fashionable sunglasses, but the full spectrum of ultraviolet rays one gets only when naked eyes are exposed to the sun in the open air.

Photobiologists are becoming increasingly concerned with three things in modern life which, they say, could prove strongly detrimental to human health in the long run: increasing environmental pollution, which is changing the variety of electromagnetic waves and the intensity of light that now reaches the earth; the increasing use of artificial light, which does not offer the full spectrum of natural sunlight that the body appears to thrive on; and the increasing use of coloured glasses as a fashion accessory.

We live increasingly, at home and at work, under artificial lighting, which almost eliminates the important ultraviolet wavelengths. Researchers claim that as a result we are experiencing a kind of 'light pollution', which may seriously affect our health and well-being over time.

The fashion-conscious woman who wears sunglasses day in and day out may be seriously undermining her health and vitality in the long run.

Most women who wear tinted lenses do so because they believe they make them look better, because their eyes feel particularly sensitive to bright light. But much of the sensitivity comes from the practice of wearing the tinted lenses in the first place.

For the sake of your health and vitality, it is important to spend at least an hour a day out in the open with your eyes exposed to the sunlight. Wear sunglasses when you need them, by all means, but don't wear them incessantly as a fashion accessory.

Good glasses

This is not to say that sunglasses don't serve a purpose. They do. Wear them when your eyes are exposed to excessive quantities of light to which they are not accustomed – when you are near the sea, for instance, or when you go skiing. If you are in very intense heat and sunlight, protect your eyes with a pair of glasses that block out not only some of the ultraviolet rays but also much of the infrared band too.

Sunglasses can be useful in another way too: worn in moderation, for example, they can help discourage frowning and scowling – two practices that slowly and imperceptibly etch permanent lines around eyes.

When choosing a pair of sunglasses for yourself, look for some that state what percentage of the ultraviolet spectrum they absorb. For wearing in bright sunlight, they need to be dark enough to eliminate 70-85 per cent. Also check that the lenses have a scratch-resistant surface.

Photochromic lenses (check that they conform to British Standard 2724 (1987)) are pale in subdued light and then darken, increasing their filtering capacity when you are exposed to strong ultraviolet rays, and they are excellent too. But neither polarized nor photochromic lenses are good for driving. The windscreen of a car absorbs ultraviolet rays, so the photochromics don't darken as they should and polarized lenses show up the toughening marks in windscreens, which can be distracting. Simple glass or plastic lenses are better.

From the inside

Many eye problems, from poor vision and eye watering or itching to premature wrinkles and crow's feet, can be eliminated and often prevented by improving general nutrition. Japanese expert on eye nutrition, Jin Otsuka, Professor of Ophthalmology at Tokyo University, believes that eating refined sugar is one of the worst things you can do if you want to preserve your vision. He has shown in animal experiments that giving sugar in large quantities will make an animal myopic. This is probably because sugar tends to rob the body of other nutrients essential for the health of the eye and the nerves which supply it.

Your need for various nutrients increases if you are under stress, drink alcohol, smoke, or take drugs. If you have an eye problem or if you find the skin around your eyes sagging or wrinkling rapidly, you might well be someone who needs

more of the vitamins particularly important for eyes, which are:

- Vitamin A
- Vitamin B Complex
- Vitamin C
- Vitamin E.

Just how much of these nutrients you need for eye health depends on your own, inherited metabolism. But they play such an important part in eye health and beauty that it seems strange that they are so often ignored.

From the outside

How, physically, you handle your eyes has a lot to do with how long the skin around them looks young and how clear and bright they are themselves. Eyes don't need to be favoured to stay beautiful and healthy, but they don't need abuse, either. Yet they are faced with it most of the time, in the form of air pollution, smoke, misapplied makeup, and mismanaged makeup removal. The skin surrounding your eyes is thinner and finer than anywhere else on your face. It is also only sparsely supplied with oil glands and therefore highly prone to expression lines. This is where a good eye cream can help. If you don't want to spend money on eye cream, a rich oil such as avocado, hazelnut, or apricot dabbed on, in the barest traces, around the eye area will do just as good a job, used mornings before applying makeup and evenings before bed. It is important never to use too much of it or you can end up with swollen, irritated eyes, particularly if you are using the plumping-up variety of cream. Apply it gently with your third finger tapping lightly all around the eye. Never rub or pull the skin. How you apply mascara and how you remove it matters too. The best way is to hold your mirror at chin level and look down into it; then you don't etch wrinkles into your forehead.

Think twice before you opt for waterproof mascara. It is difficult to remove, so you need a special strong remover to do it and you can end up rubbing and irritating the eye area every time you take off your makeup. Unless you go walking in the rain or swimming with your makeup on, it is better to choose a conventional variety. To take it off, use a non-oily eye-makeup remover if your eyes are sensitive (most are), and saturate a pad of absorbent cotton with it. Then put the pad over the closed eye and hold it there for ten seconds to dissolve the makeup so you can easily stroke it away.

Eyes work

Like the rest of you, your eyes need exercise. So do the muscles around them, in order for the skin that covers them to remain firm and wrinkle-free. Here are a few useful toners and refreshers:

Eye toner

This not only strengthens eyes and helps to keep them healthy, it also improves the musculature that supports the skin and helps prevents sags and bags that belie your age. Hold a pencil in front of your eyes about twelve inches away from them. Focus on it for a couple of seconds, then focus far beyond it. Repeat this fifteen times.

A Victorian trick

With the thumb and forefinger of one hand, press firmly for thirty seconds on the sides of your nose at the inside corner of your eyes. It hurts a bit. But it is a wonderful way of eliminating tired eyes and getting rid of tension in the face, which usually goes unnoticed and can result in scowl lines. This is something the Victorians used quite successfully to treat hysteria. It does calm emotional pressure a lot.

Quick freshener

Close your eyes tightly, then more tightly, pressing the lids together as hard as you can. Now open them slowly. This is good for when you are stuck in traffic and your eyes are tired from driving, or if you have been reading for a long while, or when you wake up and find your vision is not clear.

Put your elbows on the table in front of you and close your eyes. Then cover them with the palms of your hands. Press gently against the whole eye area for a minute or so. This refreshes the eyes and, provided you breathe deeply and calmly while you are doing it, also revitalizes the rest of you.

Light matters

Lie for five minutes with your eyes closed in the morning or afternoon sun. When closed eyelids get used to the light filtering through them, raise the top lid of one eye at a time, looking downwards while the sun's rays shine on the sclera – the membrane that covers the eyeball. Whenever you want to blink, do so. This treatment is one recommended in the Bates method of restoring sight without glasses. It helps relax tense muscles so the circulation of blood to the area is improved.

Troubleshooting

Here are some useful treatments for such common troubles as red and irritated eyes, black circles, and puffy lids:

Swollen eyes

Do the palming exercise and then cover your eyes with cold compresses made from absorbent cotton dipped in ice-cold eyebright tea (1 tablespoon of the dried herb to a cup of water). Or lie down for ten minutes with grated raw potatoes between two pieces of gauze on your lids.

Red and irritated eyes

Dip your hands into ice-cold water and then press them against your eyelids, dipping and pressing several

times. Put a slice of cucumber on each closed lid while resting for five minutes.

Black circles

Are you anaemic? Retaining wastes? Are your kidneys not working optimally? Do you have a low-grade infection? All of these things can cause dark-rimmed eyes. But one of the most common causes is poor elimination or the retention of toxic wastes in the system. A vitamin B12 deficiency should also be suspected.

Hair health

The cut is the thing

A good cut is more important than any other single factor when it comes to the way a head of hair looks. Leave enough time to get acquainted with your hairdresser and for her or him to get to know your hair, how it grows, the way it swings (or doesn't) and all the other little things that make your particular head of hair unique. Everyone is an individual, and hairstyling that doesn't take this into account is worse than second-rate. Changing your cut or style every year or two prevents you from getting stuck in an unsightly time warp and can lift your spirits like nothing else can short of falling in love.

If your hair is very straight and shiny, a blunt cut often looks great, since it is easy to care for and shows off straight, healthy hair as well. If your hair tends to be thin or lack body, a layered cut can give it shape.

Hair nutrition

The type, the length of growth, thickness, thinness, straightness, and curl of your hair depend on your inheritance, but the condition of your hair depends on the internal state of your body. For hair to be beautiful, the cuticle and the cortex have to be strong.

What occurs in each hair follicle depends on the current nutritional state of your bloodstream and on adequate oxygen reaching the cells. So true is this that when you put someone on a poor diet, you will detect detrimental changes in the hair bulb even on the second day of the regimen.

The worst thing you can do for your hair is to go on a crash diet for weight loss or live on typical Western fare, high in refined carbohydrates, processed foods, and white sugar. Both upset the vitamin and mineral balance in your body, and adequate vitamins and minerals are vital to good hair nutrition.

Vitamins and minerals vital for healthy hair

Silica – Make sure the kind you buy has been processed without chemicals and is highly bio-available – which means in a form your body can easily use (see Resources, pages 253-4).
Sea Plants – All seaweeds – from kelp to dulse, to the Japanese foods like nori and kombu.
Iron
Sulphur – Eggs are particularly rich in the sulphur-containing amino acids: other natural sources include cabbage, dried beans, legumes, fish, nuts, and meat.
Zinc
The B Vitamins
Vitamin C.

How fast your hair can grow depends on adequate – but not too much – protein, since more than adequate amounts can deplete your body of the minerals it needs. The condition of your hair is greatly affected by medicines that you take – and I don't just mean antibiotics and sulphur-drugs, although these two are common culprits for causing trouble. Aspirin, the Pill, diet pills, tranquillizers, thyroid pills, cortisone, anticancer drugs, and even cold remedies are a common cause of brittleness, dullness, breakage, and loss – although you should of course be careful not to come off any medication suddenly or without your doctor's supervision.

The craft of hair care

The shampoo for you

There are certain kinds of shampoo that are particularly good for certain kinds of hair.

- *Lemon these shampoos are especially good for oily hair, because they help remove the oil without leaving the hair lacklustre and lank.*
- *Balsam this is a good ingredient to choose if your hair is very fine or lacks body.*
- *Camomile this is an excellent ingredient for blonde or light brown hair, since this flower has mild bleaching properties.*
- *Herbs 'herbs' added to a shampoo doesn't mean a great deal, for many herb formulas (unlike camomile) have no real action on the hair.*

- *Protein these shampoos come in two types. The first contains a simple protein made from eggs, milk, soya, gelatin, beef (or an exotic vegetable called tong bean), which helps to coat the outer layers of the hair, making it look thicker. Most protein shampoos are of this type. The second type is called substantive protein and is particularly good for use on treated, damaged, or fine hair.*

When buying a shampoo, don't worry if it does not give much lather, since this is more a measure of the sequestering agent it contains than of its cleaning ability. It should have a good conditioning action, to leave your hair soft and gleaming, and your hair should be easy to comb out afterwards. It should also rinse out easily.

How often you shampoo depends on you and on the type of hair you have. If it is dry, not more than a couple of times a week is best. If it is normal or oily you can shampoo every day if you like, provided you use a pH-balanced shampoo. However often you do, you need only lather once, unless your hair is really grimy. More than once strips away too much of the hair's natural oils from the cuticle.

Getting condition
All cream rinses, conditioners, and treatments are on the acidic end of the pH scale. In addition, a cream rinse should contain ingredients such as quaternary ammonium salts to separate the individual hairs and make them really easy to comb out and to protect against

static electricity. Finally, they coat hairs with an ingredient such as protein or balsam, which is supposed to give some more body and protect the cuticle from moisture loss.

Some conditioners contain a large quantity of oil. They are fine for dry hair but will make normal and oily hair into a lank mop that needs to be washed again in the next day or so. If you ever have this trouble with a conditioner or cream rinse, then try one of the oil-free ones. They do a better job in adding body and protecting hair, without causing lankness. Protein packs or concentrated treatments should be left on the hair for from five to twenty minutes.

Brushing and combing

Brushing is good for hair, provided you have a good brush and you do not overdo it. It stimulates circulation of the scalp, removes loose scales from the skin on the head, and distributes your hair's natural oils well, which means it helps protect the cuticles and create shine. The brush you choose should have evenly spaced bristles with rounded ends. The best brushes for your hair are still made from animal bristles.

About thirty to fifty strokes a day is good – more than that is too much, and with less you are not really doing anything. When you brush, you need to bend at the waist and brush your hair from underneath as well as back from the crown. The more positions you can brush from (leaning to the side, with head hanging down, etc.) the better job you will do. Lowering your head while you brush back the side does something else, too. It brings circulation to the scalp in the way that the yoga headstand does. If your hair is long, don't pull the brush through the full length of it. Instead, brush to the shoulder and then, taking hold of the rest of the hair with your other hand, pull the brush down the rest of the way to the ends. You should always brush firmly, but never drag.

When choosing a comb, pick one with the largest teeth you can find that are blunt at the ends so they don't scratch the scalp. Hard rubber, nylon, or bone are the best. Always ensure that you comb your hair gently, never yanking or pulling at a tangle.

Wonderful massage

Anything that increases circulation to the scalp and activates the papillae and follicles tends to make for sturdier hair shafts and to improve hair growth. Besides daily brushing, the best thing you can do for the hair is to massage the scalp (see overleaf).

Here's how to massage

Using your finger tips and the palms of your hands just below the thumb, push them firmly into your scalp at the sides and, keeping them in the same place, rotate them in small circles. You will be moving the scalp, not your fingers. It is important that fingers stay in the same place to stimulate circulation well and so that you never pull your hair. After you have worked in one position for about thirty seconds, remove both hands from your head and take up a new position, rotating fingertips again firmly for thirty seconds there and so on until you have done your whole scalp. The massage really shouldn't take you more than three minutes, and it will leave you feeling fresher as well as doing something good for your hair.

If you suffer from tension in your neck and shoulders, this too, can interfere with proper circulation to your scalp and create hair problems. Use the relaxation exercises to correct this. An electric vibrator is also a good investment for hair. Use it both on your scalp and on your neck and shoulders.

The treatments

Perms
There are two types of perms: acid-based which are soft and used to give a subtle lift at the roots to create an illusion of fullness; and the conventional alkaline perms. Acid or 'body' perms don't last as long as the rest and need to be redone every three or four months. They are more natural and soft-looking, adding fullness and swing to hair without heavy curls. Acid waves use heat lamps instead of compounds of ammonia to open the shaft of hair and are less damaging since they don't break so many sulphur bonds.

Caring for processed hair
Once your hair is waved, it is more vulnerable to damage than ever before, so there are a few special precautions you need to take in order to preserve its health and sheen. For instance, instead of brushing 50 strokes a day, cut it down to only 20. Use scalp massage or an electric vibrator instead, to give scalp circulation the stimulation it needs. Also, only use acid-balanced shampoos when you wash your hair, and always apply an acid rinse such as lemon juice in water. Substantive protein treatments are particularly good for permed and coloured hair.

Provided your hair is healthy and you look after it well after the perm, there is no reason to worry about its condition being spoiled by the waving. A perm will add a lot of body to lank hair and often improves an over-oily condition as well.

Straightening hair
Besides the thioglycolate straighteners, which are put on hair still damp from having been washed, left on for about fifteen minutes, and then combed through for another fifteen minutes before neutralizing, there are two other types of chemical straighteners commercially available. The first are the ammonium bisulphate or sodium bisulphate straighteners, which are not

as effective on very curly hair as the thioglycolates but are much safer. You put them on wet hair, tuck it under a plastic covering for fifteen minutes, and then comb it out for twenty minutes. They are ideal for hair that is not excessively curly.

The other type, the sodium hydroxide straighteners, are highly alkaline and have to be carefully applied or they may irritate the skin. They can also be very dangerous if you get any in your eyes. They are the fastest-acting of all the straighteners and demand only about half the combing time to do their work before you apply the neutralizer. But they are not good for hair that is in less than perfect condition.

There are also some short-term but simple ways to straighten hair. It can be done by blow-drying with a brush to smooth it out or by washing your hair and then wrapping it wet around your head in a circle, like a cap, fastening it with clips and letting it dry. Then, when it is dry, you simply comb it out straighter. Finally, the old-fashioned and very efficient method for long, curly hair is simply ironing it with an electric iron. Spread the hair out on a board, keep the iron on the lowest setting, and go over it gently from roots to ends. Be careful not to put too much heat on it. Burnt hair is irretrievably lost.

The temporary colorants

These are the easiest to use. They coat the cuticle of the hair with colour that washes away with the next shampoo. They will darken the hair – say from blonde to red or to black, but are really designed for minor colour changes only.

The semipermanents

Like the temporaries, these contain no peroxide. Some are 'oxidisers' or 'colour baths' which penetrate the hair so that they last up to a dozen shampoos. If you use one, be sure to use a pH-balanced shampoo and a lemon and water rinse afterwards.

The permanents

THE VEGETABLE DYES

- Henna is the best-known, since its use dates back thousands of years. The standard way of using henna is to add hot water to make a creamy paste and then put this on the hair and leave it for up to one hour.

  It will give brunette and black hair a lovely reddish glow, lighter hair goes Titian. Henna does not do well on mousy hair, as the resulting tone is usually an unattractive orange. It should never be used over a tint, is no good on grey hair, and can be very drying to any hair. The only colour of henna you should use is red which in its natural, powder form, is a pale green.

- Camomile has a gentle lightening effect on hair and is wonderful for 'sun-streaking' blonde and light brown hair. But you must be patient,, for it takes several applications and plenty of time to work. Camomile-bleached hair looks exactly like natural hair with sun streaks. It is not useful for brown hair or dark hair, but it will gently lighten red and works especially beautifully on all shades of natural blonde hair.

Camomile rinses

1 Take 2 tablespoons of dried camomile flowers and toss them into a pint of boiling water. Simmer for fifteen minutes, strain, cool and use as a final rinse (you can make more at once and refrigerate it for up to ten days).

2 Add one cup of dried camomile flowers to half a pint of boiling water for fifteen minutes. Cool. Simmer and strain. Add the juice of a fresh lemon to the infusion plus two tablespoons of a rich cream conditioner. Put it on dry hair, comb through, and then go and sit in the sun (with a sunscreen on your face, of course) until it dries. Finally, shampoo and condition as usual.

BLEACHING

Hair bleaching is done with hydrogen peroxide, which affects the hair shaft physically and chemically. There are products on the market that are simple bleachers, called lighteners, and they consist of peroxide together with ammonia.

THE ANILINE OR OXIDATION COLORANTS

• The most permanent (and the most successful), these dyes are included in a number of products for colouring hair such as tinting shampoos, highlighting shampoos, and the single-step and double-step permanent colorants you can buy in packs at the chemist.

• Aniline dyes are potential allergens, since about one woman in ten cannot tolerate them without reacting adversely. This is why it is important, whenever using a permanent colourant on your hair either at home or at the hairdresser, that a patch test be done first.

• You put the products on as you would an ordinary shampoo and then leave them in the hair for a few minutes while the peroxide and dye does its work, and then rinse off. They are simple to use.

• The single and double-step tints also fall into this category. They are the dyes most frequently used by hairdressers. If you want to change the colour of your hair dramatically, you should have it done professionally.

• The single-step tints are a mixture of aniline dyes, peroxide, and ammonia in an oil base. They are applied carefully to sectioned hair, starting an inch or so away from the roots and moving to the end. The hair is left to sit for a few minutes and then the root area is done. The hair is rested for another half hour or so. These dyes can change the colour of your hair to almost any other colour, but they are not successful in changing very dark shades to blonde. For that, you need a two-step tint, which bleaches out the existing pigment in the hair shafts in the first step and then adds dye separately in the second.

HIGHLIGHTS

• One of the best and most easily manageable ways of changing your hair colour is to have it highlighted or lowlighted. This involves the same procedures as the single- and double-step tinting, but instead of being done all over your head, they are added only on some strands or areas of your hair. Highlighting and lowlighting are particularly useful for older hair that has darkened or faded.

Special care

The golden rule for processed hair is to stay out of the sun. The sun does harm in two ways: it dries out the hair, and it alters the colour. You can use one of the sunscreen products especially made for hair or simply rub in some high-protection suntan lotion you use on your body, shampooing it out at the end of the day.

Troubleshooting

Too dry

Naturally, dry hair needs an occasional oil treatment to coat the cuticle and help protect it from further moisture loss.

An oil treatment

Place 2 ounces of olive oil in a blender and add to it the same amount of boiling water. Turn on high for a few seconds, until all the oil has been broken up into little droplets, and then immediately put it on your dry hair, massaging it in well all over. Wrap a hot towel around your head and leave it for twenty minutes, changing the towel for another hot one whenever it cools. Then remove the towel, and shampoo with your

regular shampoo, finishing off with a cream rinse that contains a hair-softening chemical such as quaternary ammonium salts.

Silicone and balsam can be useful ingredients in shampoos and rinses for dry hair, since, like the oil, they coat the cuticle and help protect it from excess water loss. But don't over-use them or you will end up with lank, dull-looking hair.

You should stay out of the sun, be careful about blow-drying your hair, and use heated rollers only when absolutely necessary. Make sure you get enough B-complex vitamins – dry hair is often a symptom of insufficiency. Try eating organic liver a couple of times a week.

Too oily

Wash and brush it often and well to distribute the oil evenly throughout the hair shaft and make it shine. Massage your scalp daily.

Lemon shampoos and a fresh lemon (the juice of a lemon in a pint of warm water) as the final rinse after washing is good for controlling too much oil in the hair. Buy three different shampoos for oily hair and alternate them each time you wash your hair. You can also leave the shampoo in your hair for five minutes before rinsing it away, which helps dry out the hair shafts. When choosing a conditioner, look for an oil-free one. Don't be afraid of washing your hair every day if you want to. It won't do any harm to you or your hair.

Too dull

Usually dull hair is dry hair, so much of the problem and advice for dryness goes for you, too. If the dullness is a colour problem, it is best to seek professional advice, since correcting it is usually easy, provided you know how. The hot oil treatment can help dull hair, as can an intense protein treatment that is applied every two weeks.

Are split ends inevitable?

Yes, everybody has them to some extent although on a normal head of hair they are few and far between. Split ends in large numbers are almost always the result of poor hair care such as blow-drying with too hot a setting, sun damage, washing with a highly alkaline shampoo, too much brushing with a sharp-bristled brush, or over-processing. Don't wash your hair more than once or twice a week, keep it away from heat and sunlight, don't tease it or brush it with nylon bristles, and avoid chlorinated swimming pools. Have the ends cut.

When hair turns grey

When hair turns grey, there are several things you can do for it:

1 Use a semipermanent rinse or highlighting shampoo, provided no more than 30 per cent of your hair is affected.

2 Have your hair tinted with an aniline dye, in a colour two or three shades lighter than your original colour.

3 Use one of the new quick emollient-based one-step colours which condition where they tint.

4 Have highlights and lowlights done.

5 Leave it grey, and should you have any yellowing, simply treat it with a gentle rinse to tone it down and turn it silvery.

Two kinds of dandruff

Simple dandruff, which affects 60 per cent of the population, is nothing more than a dry flaking of the scalp. In most cases, the presence of dandruff indicates too little brushing (which will remove the offending flakes before they fall, unwanted, on their own); poor circulation of the scalp, which can be improved by daily massage; or the use of too many alkaline products, which have irritated the scalp and encouraged it to scale. If your scalp is dry, use a mild dandruff shampoo once a week to keep it under control – one containing zinc pyrithione or selenium sulphide. Brush your hair well every day with a natural bristle brush, and use pH-balanced products to condition hair and for 'in between' washes.

If your dandruff is the other variety, which is far rarer, it will look like thick, rather greasy or crusty scales on your scalp. Shampoos containing coal tars or selenium sulphide are usually better for this. Regular brushing and massage are important here, too. If self-treatment doesn't clear up the condition, it is a good idea to see your doctor about it. Use three different shampoos and alternate them, using a regular shampoo after each application of dandruff shampoo.

What is the cause of hair loss?
Ask yourself the following questions:

- *Are you taking any medication? The Pill and hormone-replacement therapy are a common cause of thinning hair – thinning that is usually corrected a few weeks after the treatment is stopped.*
- *Have you had any major traumas in your life or illnesses recently? Shock, illness, and emotional worry are among the most common causes of heavy shedding of telogen hairs – called telogen effluvium.*
- *Is your scalp tight? Poor circulation, particularly in a scalp that tends to be oily, can result in hair loss. Give yourself a daily scalp massage. Brush fifty strokes a day.*
- *Are you anaemic? Women, who suffer from anaemia far more often than men do, frequently find their hair has thinned greatly.*
- *Is your hair breaking off near the roots from over-processing, sun bleaching, or too much heat on it? Consider cutting your hair short until the damaged hair has grown out.*
- *Have you recently been pregnant? Women commonly lose hair during pregnancy. Happily this condition usually disappears a few weeks after the baby is born, provided the diet is adequate and you are generally well.*
- *Do you wear your hair pulled back too tightly, or have you been putting rollers in too tightly?*

Another common cause of hair loss is simple traction caused by a tightly wrapped rubber band around a ponytail, or curlers that are too tight. Change your hairstyle, stop rolling curlers tightly, and give yourself daily massage or treatment with an electric vibrator. If you are using a nylon-bristled brush or rollers with brushes in them or too fine-toothed a comb, you should replace them.

- *Is the hair coming out in patches? Then you might be suffering from alopecia areata, which looks like bald patches the size of a 2p coin sprinkled here and there in a normal head of hair. In most cases the condition cures itself and the hair grows back into the bald patches. You can seek medical help, although there is no standard treatment.*

What is male-pattern baldness?
It is a hair-loss condition that occurs as a result of the follicles' sensitivity to a high level of certain hormones in the system, primarily the androgenic, or male hormones. It is more common in men than women, hair loss from hormonal causes is particularly likely to occur around the time of menopause, when oestrogen levels fall dramatically in the body. The tendency to this kind of hair loss is genetically determined, although there appear to be dietary factors which influence its onset – particularly insufficiencies of some of the B-complex vitamins. It occurs in a specific pattern, thinning at the crown and at the hairline.

The magic of makeup

When you use makeup, you are practising the age-old art of illusion for enhancement. But the illusions makeup offers you are subtle ones, not complete changes of character, age, and colouring. So the first rule of good makeup is simple: never try to change your face with it.

After that has been said and after you have come to terms with the fact that whether or not you like it, your jaw is square or your eyes small or your skin a different colour from what you ideally would like, then there is a lot you can do with colour to make you feel better. Whether you are after a freshly scrubbed, natural look (which incidentally takes a lot more artifice to achieve than you might imagine) or a more elaborate-looking, sophisticated face, the makeup you choose and the way you apply it should make you look more attractive, more interesting, healthier, and simply more yourself.

The naked face

What about going without makeup? Great – provided you are healthy and your skin is good and provided you wear a moisturizer and sunscreen day in, day out for protection. Half of my life is spent without even the faintest touch of makeup. There is something I like about the 'honesty' of an un-made-up face. When you blush, it shows. When you are tired, it shows. When you are really well and vital, there is no mask to cover up the translucence of your skin. A naked face can be beautiful. Indeed, why should any woman feel she has to wear makeup simply because most do?

No excuse for neglected skin

If your skin is less than perfect, spend your time and money on getting it into shape before indulging in makeup products and colours (see Skincare on pages 202-15).

The tool box

2 large brushes for powder
3 slightly smaller brushes for blusher, highlighter, and shader
1 blunt ended brush for blending concealers
4 small brushes for eye shadows and for highlighting small areas
1 stiff toothbrush-like or circular brush for brows
1 circular hard tiny brush for clearing excess mascara from lashes
1 fine-line lip brush
sponges for applying foundation and liquid blushers, either natural sponges (the tiny ones used for cosmetics) or white rubber
Cotton-wool balls or pads
Cotton-tipped sticks (the kind used for cleaning babies' ears)
Facial tissues
A spray bottle, used for misting plants, filled with pure spring water. The spray should be very fine.
Good light – either natural light, which is best, or ordinary incandescent lighting, which is second best
A scarf to tie back your hair

It is important to keep your tools and brushes for makeup immaculate. Wash them at least once a week and keep them well aired and ready for use.

The colours

There are two basic possibilities: warm colour schemes and cool ones. The effect of a warm colour scheme on the face which includes the earth colours such as browns, greens, beiges, golds, yellows, apricots, coppers, oranges, and peaches – is to enliven it, making your face look healthier and stronger and more glowing. Warm colours look wonderful on older women, too, because they accentuate youth. This is why some of the best foundations and powders now contain yellow pigments. A little peach or apricot blusher can make almost any face look younger, whereas bluish-pink blusher applied to a face over forty can age it drastically.

The cool colours – the blues, purples, pale ivories, silvers, fuchsias, berries, magentas, blue-pinks, and whites give a look of delicate vulnerability to a face, especially when they are applied, as they should be, over a very pale foundation.

They can be exciting because they are almost electric in their boldness. But to wear them you have to have perfect skin and you have to be young; otherwise they can make you look tired, older, and even unwell.

Putting it into practice

Every good makeup begins with a fine moisturizer complete with sunscreen lavishly applied over clean skin and then given a chance to settle in. It is rather like making a mayonnaise. You can't rush things. You need to wait for your skin to take to the moisturizer before you put on your foundation, otherwise you will end up with a flawed finish and your makeup will not last. 'Taking' time is usually between two to five minutes. In addition to the ordinary moisturizers, there are also tinted ones on the market. Some of them also contain sunscreens. When choosing a tinted moisturizer, look for one that is not too far away from your own skin tone, or you will find it doesn't blend in and cover well.

Among the tinted moisturizers are the 'colour correctives' – products tinted a specific hue in order to change the look of your own, natural colouring. They are worn under your ordinary foundation. When you use a corrective, put it on with a sponge that has been dampened and then had all the excess water removed from it by wiping it against a towel.

The foundation

Once your moisturizer has set, you are ready for the foundation. But why all over? Instead you can wear it only on parts of your face such as around the eyes, on your chin, and on your cheeks which gives the wonderful, delicate shading of natural skin. Or you can wear two shades of foundation: a lighter one in the centre of your face and the slightly darker one of the same tone around the outside (near the hairline and along the jawline). This has the effect of preserving a natural-looking gradation of colour.

Or go without foundation altogether, applying your colours directly to well-moisturized skin that has been lightly covered with a translucent powder.

The kind of foundation you choose depends on what kind of skin you have as well as on personal preference. Dry skin does best with a cream or oil-based liquid foundation. Ageing skin needs the finest of liquid foundation. Anything heavily oily collects in the lines and makes you look haggard. Oily skin demands a water-based liquid or cream, or a cake or block-type makeup.

TO APPLY
Put a little foundation in the palm of your left hand (if you are right-handed), and then dip the sponge into it and apply it to your face, brushing it lightly over your skin again and again until everything is well blended into your skin. If you want a heavier cover and very matt look – important for television work for instance – instead of applying a thick coat of foundation, apply two thin coats, allowing a couple of minutes for the first one to dry before applying the second.

Covering the blemishes
Now is the time to deal with any problems you want to conceal, such as black circles under your eyes or discolourations here and there. Concealer creams and sticks are good

here, although some of them are greasy and, particularly under the eyes, tend to sink into tiny lines and make matters worse. If you use a concealer, buy one that is not too light-coloured.

Put your concealer on with a flat wedge-shaped brush and smooth into the skin until it blends perfectly with the surrounding areas.

Magical shading

- *To minimize a jaw that is too large or too square, apply darker shade along the jawline, blending it under the jaw and fading into nothing at the sides of the face.*
- *To shorten a pointed chin, apply shader to chin only, blending underneath into the neck and fading to nothing at the sides.*
- *To fade a double chin, put shader on the double chin and blend it skilfully.*
- *To give more interesting shape to a square face, apply shader in the temple area and all around the jawline, carefully blending.*
- *To minimize a nose that is too large, apply shader (preferably liquid or cream) in a single stripe down the centre of the nose, carefully blending into the colour at the sides so that no definite line appears.*
- *To slim a broad nose, apply a shader – preferably a slightly darker foundation or cream – in a stripe down each side of the nose and blend it carefully into the skin to make the nose look narrower.*

Here are some of the things you can do with highlighter. But don't do more than two of them at any one time, or the effect will be counterproductive:

- *Add a thin edge of matt lightener just under the brows to make the eyes look wider.*
- *Brush highlighter down the two ridges between the centre of the bottom of the nose and the bow of the upper lip, to draw interest there.*
- *Brush highlighter on the bow of the upper lip at the centre before applying lipstick.*
- *Brush a touch of highlight in the centre of the upper eyelid to add brightness to the eyes and more shape to the eyelids.*
- *Stroke a little highlighter across the cheekbone, just under the outer corner of the eye, to exaggerate the bone's prominence.*
- *A carefully blended line of light down the centre of a beautiful nose will draw attention to it.*
- *A little, very light foundation used in the hollows that run from the edge of the nose to the corners of the mouth will minimize the age hollows there.*
- *Put a little highlighter on collarbones when you are wearing a décolleté dress.*

The eyes have it

There are lots of ways to use eye makeup to improve eyes but all of them begin with the same principles. Use neutral tones such as slabby browns (without red tones in them), flat greys, and greyed greens, or even terracotta, for establishing the shape of the eyes (the darker shades to define the sockets and the lighter beiges or yellow, peach or apricot, or pink, on the lids and under the brows).

All eye shadows are best applied with a brush, whether they are liquid, cream, or powder and are best applied to skin that has a foundation on it. Powder shadows hold best over a light skimming of translucent powder too.

When using eye shadows, the same rules apply as on the rest of the face: alight colour will make the part of the eye it's on look more prominent, and a dark colour will make it recede. Beware of frosted shadows if you are over twenty-five or have crepey eyelids.

THE EYEBROWS

The natural shape of an eyebrow usually goes best with the face it is on. If you have heavy brows, then pluck them just enough to keep them tame, and let them be.

Before you begin, brush them first one way and then the other to remove any loose hairs or makeup, and clean the skin around the eyes thoroughly. Now put moisturizer in the area, before you reach for the tweezers. Brush your brows into shape and take a good look at them. Start by removing stray hairs between the brows and the stragglers that have nothing to do with the main body of the eyebrow. But never pluck from above the eyebrow. And always remove only one hair at a time, pulling it

in the direction in which it grows. Work carefully, from the lowest hairs upward, clearing away only the unnecessary ones. When you have finished with one brow, apply antiseptic or a simple toner to it before going on to the next one. This will help soothe the irritated skin. Don't try to apply makeup for an hour after plucking.

The shape of a brow then can be accentuated or the density gently filled in through using a sharp eye pencil in a light shade.

EYELINERS
A good way of emphasizing eye shape without looking too obviously made-up is to use a pencil in the same tone you are using for your eye shadow, dotting it all along the upper lashes and then just under the lower ones so the two lines meet at the outer corners and form a little triangle. This kind of liner looks good when it is gently smeared with a brush or fingertip to blend it into the surrounding area and keep it from looking hard.

MASCARA
Mascara makes eyes look more glamorous. Unless you are planning to walk in the rain or to go swimming with your makeup on, you are better off using a mascara that is not waterproof. Waterproof mascara is very hard to remove, and you often have to do a lot of rubbing in the process, which can stretch the delicate skin around the eyes and slacken it.

Some mascaras contain talc/kaolin and nylon/rayon fibres to lengthen the lashes and make them look even thicker. They are fine so long as you don't have particularly sensitive eyes otherwise you are better off with a simple, fibreless one.

Apply your mascara by looking down into a mirror held next to your chin and you will not etch lines into your forehead, the way most women do, by crinkling it up. You will also get better application this way, since the brush or wand strokes the lashes easily from their origins to tips from underneath and slightly curls them to make them look even longer.

Cheeks
The best colours for everyday wear for most women are terracotta, apricot-brown or dusky peach, because they make the skin look particularly healthy. Where you apply blusher depends on the shape of your face and the effect you want from it. Use it high on the cheekbones and it accentuates a well-sculptured face. Use it across the cheeks and it gives a simple warm glow.

Lips
Balance your eyes and lips, making one or the other more prominent. If both are strong or in very light colours, it tends to make a face plastic-looking, and there is little in the way of contrasts to create interest.

When applying lipstick, use a pencil or a lipbrush to outline your mouth first, so you get a good, sharply defined edge. Then apply your lipstick and blot it and apply again if you want it to stay.

Alternatively use a pencil all over the mouth as well as for outline and then apply a clear gloss.

Fashions for lip gloss come and go. If you want to wear it, it's usually best to apply it only on the bottom lip or in the centre of both lips, so it catches the light, and not to carry it all the way to the edge of the mouth, or it tends to blur the lips' outline.

Powder
The best way to apply powder is either with clean cotton-wool, dabbing it lavishly all over and then brushing off the excess with a new piece of cotton-wool, or with a brush. I prefer the brush method, because it always seems to stay better that way. Always use a powder that gives no colour, just a matt, smooth finish, and always brush away every speck of excess once you have applied it.

The finishing touches
Last of all, after you have applied your makeup completely, you need to set it with water. Spray your face with spring water in a fine mist from a plant-misting bottle. Then blot gently once with a tissue.

The whole process of making up may sound complicated, but with practice it should take very little time – no more than ten minutes from start to finish. Play with it. It is a wonderful expression of who you are.

STEP TEN:
BEAT THE CLOCK

Don't let age get under your skin

Nothing betrays age like the state of your skin. When you are young, it is thick, glowing, soft and elastic. As the years go by, a number of changes take place. The thickness of the skin diminishes by half. It loses its firmness. First, expression lines and minor discolorations form, then these tiny imperfections gradually become wrinkles and blotched skin, which is no longer able to retain water as it once could; skin that has lost its elasticity turns crepey and old-looking. How fast all this happens depends not only on your genetic inheritance but also on the internal state of your body, your stress levels, and the care and protection you provide for your skin from the outside.

When ageing begins

The ageing process in your skin is really no different from anywhere else in the body, except that it can be faster. This is because, first, the skin's cells tend to divide more often than most other kinds of cells, so genetic mutations are passed on more rapidly, and second, because your skin has to put up with so many external insults from what it is exposed to environmentally.

At the centre of the ageing process in the skin is a disruption of the genetic material in the cells – the DNA and RNA. This leads to corresponding degenerative changes in the collagen and elastin fibres of the dermis. These changes are brought on by many factors.

Free radicals
Free radicals are highly reactive chemical groups that wreak havoc with

the cells and cause damage both to the cell membranes and to the genetic material. Ultraviolet radiation from the sun also produces free radicals. Both these factors cause the proteins in the

dermis to harden and thicken so that collagen fibres twist and bind together in a process called cross-linking. Because the firm, wrinkle-free look of skin is dependent on the collagen in it remaining flexible and orderly, when this process takes place the skin begins to sag and wrinkle from habitual expression patterns being etched into skin tissue no longer resilient enough to resist them.

Environment and nutrition

Inadequate nutrition, which leaves the cell membranes particularly vulnerable to free radical attack – particularly a diet high in fat – also plays an important part in ageing, as does a diminished blood supply from poor circulation to the tissues as a result of physical inactivity. Finally, some cell loss and damage associated with ageing are probably results of environmental factors such as air pollution, smoking, and drugs and alcohol in the body. All of these degenerative changes on a cellular level contribute to your skin's losing its elasticity – as well as its ability to hold water.

Sluggish skin

It is firm, healthy collagen and the skin's water-holding ability that give a face its youthful contours and cushiony feel. Eventually the loss of tone and firmness from these internal alterations and a diminishing hydration results in sagging, lines, and wrinkles. Meanwhile metabolism slows down the cells so that it is increasingly difficult for them to get adequate essential nutrients, while the elimination of cellular wastes also gets less efficient. The rate at which old cells die and new ones are born is also much slower. Gradually the skin becomes sluggish and loses its vital glow, and the epidermis becomes uneven in thickness, discoloured, rough, and lined.

To slow down this process and to keep a young, healthy skin for as long as possible, you have first to retain a young, healthy body. This is a total, ongoing process depending on good nutrition, stress control, exercise, and protection from the environment. There aren't any shortcuts that you can take. But the good news is this: these skin ageing changes appear to be not so dependent on the passage of time as they were once believed to be. There is much therefore that you can do to help retard them.

Stay out of the sun

To preserve your skin from premature ageing, in addition to the constant use of a sunscreen on your face as part of your everyday skin care, you should understand the art of sunbathing – that is, if you want to tan at all. Ideally, of course, you would be far better off to remain pale.

As we've already said, the sun is your skin's worst 'ager'. It has been proved that exposure to ultraviolet light brings about permanent fundamental alterations in the genetic material of skin cells and encourages the process of cross-linking. These changes are cumulative and irreversible. Even when sun-exposed skin from an arm is grafted onto a protected area such as the abdomen and left there for years, it still remains older-looking and darker than the skin surrounding it.

Beware the ultraviolet rays

Thanks to an increasing awareness of this ultraviolet damage, sun worship is becoming a highly sophisticated occupation. These days no woman in her right mind would spend hour after hour lying in the sun, developing the deep brown tan which for three generations was considered a sign that one was rich enough and idle enough to spend time lounging around resorts. The fashion in tanning now is to have a lighter skin, just touched with golden light, rather than the previously sought-after, baked look. And for the sake of your skin's future, this change has come none too soon.

Some sun is good for you

Of course in moderate doses, provided your skin is well protected, sunlight can actually be good for you. It stimulates circulation in the skin, makes you feel well, and is deeply relaxing. Also sunlight stimulates the formation of ergosterol, which when drawn into the skin becomes vitamin D. But this happens only if your skin isn't washed for at least twenty-four hours after exposure. Bathing will remove the ergosterol before it can be made use of.

UVA and UV-B rays

Some suntan products claim to screen out the harmful burning, UV-B rays while they let through the tanning UV-A ones. By now technology in tanning preparations has become very sophisticated and there are indeed products on the market that will do just that. The only catch is this: these short, UV-B rays, which are mainly responsible for burning and which these products screen out, penetrate the skin only superficially anyway – mostly to the level

of the epidermis. But, according to dermatological research, the longer, so-called beneficial UV-A tanning rays, which these products allow through, penetrate all the way into the deep layers of the dermis and the underlying tissues. These UV-A rays are most responsible for the degenerative changes in the skin's structure associated with ageing. So, whatever product you decide to use on your body, choose a high-protection product for your face that blocks out most of both the UV-A and UV-B wave bands. For the sad truth is that there is no way in which you can get yourself a deep tan and still protect your skin from premature ageing.

The tan accelerators

There are also products on the market that offer not just protection factors but also tanning factors in them. They usually contain a derivative of the essential oil of bergamot, which has a natural tendency to oxidize certain amino acids in the skin's cells, in particular tyrosine, which accelerates the darkening of the skin when it is exposed to ultraviolet rays even in greyish weather. These products can be useful if you want to begin tanning before the strong, midsummer sun appears. The advantage of tanning this way is that the melanin which is formed and built up gradually is your skin's own protection against burning. But it still won't protect you from ageing. Too much ultraviolet is simply too much. Another disadvantage of this kind of product is that begamot is one of the substances most often responsible for hypersensitive reactions in women with reaction-prone skin.

What about sun lamps?

Artificial tanning equipment is made to block out most or all of the UV-B rays. Because of this manufacturers make claims for tanning without burning and without doing damage to the skin. The first claim is valid. The second is absurd. For the UV-A ray, on which these machines rely to do their tanning, will still be at work, ageing skin at deeper levels. There is no truly safe way to tan and still preserve young skin. If you are going to tan using this kind of equipment or with a conventional sun lamp that has both UV-A and UV-B wavelengths, you can only hope to minimize the damage. If you really value your skin stay out of the sun and away from sun beds altogether.

Beware fat facts

Women are constantly being encouraged to include lots of processed polyunsaturated fats in their diet for the sake of their skin. Ironically it is probably large amounts of polyunsaturates in the system without sufficient natural anti-oxidants such as vitamin E to accompany them that is the second-biggest contributor to early-ageing skin. A large dietary survey carried out at the University of California at Irvine showed that people who frequently included polyunsaturates in the diet showed marked clinical signs of premature ageing compared with people who did not. Such factors as the degree of wrinkling, crow's-feet, frown lines, loss of elasticity, and discolouration were all evident.

Essential fatty acids
Of course essential fatty acids are a necessary part of good nutrition – in small quantities. It is only when fats and oils are taken in excess and when they are highly processed as in the production of golden oils, margarines and convenience foods, that they may be dangerous. According to age researchers Irwin Fridovitch and Richard Passwater one of the most important things you can do to protect yourself from the possible ageing effects of polyunsaturated fats is to increase your intake of vitamin E. This vitamin helps minimize damage done by the free radical chain reactions triggered by these fats. The collagen fibres in skin are prime targets for free radical attacks, which cause them to bind together and become disorganized, so neutralizing these free radicals by increasing one's intake of vitamin E and helping to

encourage the production of healthy collagen by taking more vitamin C may be able to slow down the ageing of one's skin. As yet there is no scientific proof of this, for no one has done human experiments; however, animal experiments give a strong indication that this can help.

How many vitamins to take?
Just how much of these vitamins in supplementary form one should take for this kind of protection depends on your individual metabolism and age and state of health.

A dermatologist friend who takes a total-body approach to skin care (an unusual approach among dermatologists I have met) recommends daily supplements to all his patients over twenty. Here is his basic list, which he varies to suit each person's individual condition:

- 15,000 to 20,000 IU vitamin A or the carotenoids
- A good, full B-complex vitamin taken at meals, three times a day
- 100mg of additional PABA taken once a day
- 100mg additional pantothenic acid taken once daily
- 2,000mg vitamin C taken twice a day
- 400 IU vitamin D taken once a day
- 400-1,600 IU vitamin E taken once a day.

Expert on vitamin C, Irvin Stone, believes that a person may need more C – up to 10 grams daily spread in doses throughout the day – to protect against early ageing. Passwater believes that we need extra vitamin C, E, and B complex, and the sulphur amino acids, which occur in eggs, cabbage, muscle meats, and onions, as well as selenium, to help protect the body against free radical and peroxidation damage.

Pollution

The fact that our air and water are polluted and becoming more so all the time is no news to anyone. But the important questions now are:

- How exactly does pollution affect health and the ageing process in the long run?
- What, if anything, can we do to help protect ourselves from it?

That's where extra vitamins and minerals may come in.

Researchers studying the effects of various pollutants on animals and humans believe that they contribute to the development of some diseases, particularly respiratory ailments (such as asthma, bronchitis, and even chest colds), cardiovascular diseases, and eye troubles. Pollution from gasoline fumes alone has a significantly detrimental effect on health. For three months during the fuel shortage several years ago, researchers in the United States counted the number of deaths from heart and lung diseases and compared them with figures for the same three months the preceding year. When only 10 per cent less gasoline had been available for cars during the period, deaths from cardiovascular disease had fallen by 17 per cent.

Ozone

Another pollutant that is causing concern is ozone. Nowadays, in many areas, ozone levels are even used as a measure of general pollution in the atmosphere. Relatively new to public attention, ozone is a kind of oxygen with three atoms to a molecule instead of the usual two. It is a strange substance which in terms of animal life seems to be both hero and villain. In its helpful aspect it forms an invisible protective layer fifteen to twenty miles above the earth which shields us from the otherwise lethal amounts of ultraviolet radiation from the sun, and which environmentalists are therefore anxious to preserve and protect, and which we are not doing a very good job of looking after. As witness the enlarging holes in the ozone layer, particularly in the Southern hemisphere.

The villainous face of ozone, which is probably the most toxic constituent of city smog, is that of an unstable gas which poisons the air, hinders the activity of some important enzymes in the body, and can produce chest pains, headaches, coughing, and eye and heart problems. It also causes harm to plant life, damages tyres and buildings, makes fabrics disintegrate and, like most of the other pollutants, damages skin by altering its electrical charge, interfering with its respiration, and changing the qualities of its protective acid mantle, thereby making it more susceptible to external aggression.

Some researchers, such as Dr Daniel Menzel at Duke University, also believe that ozone, like many other and better-known pollutants, encourages ageing, since it is an oxidizing agent that promotes breakdown on a cellular level. Like soot, coal dust, cigarette smoke, and noxious chemicals, it is probably high on the list of causes of premature wrinkles and loss of skin tone, quite apart from its known detrimental effects on the lungs and the body as a whole.

Forget the cigarettes

Smoking also makes skin age rapidly. This is probably because of a substance called benzopyrene, which is found in cigarette smoke and which uses up the body's supply of vitamin C rapidly, making it unavailable for the support of healthy collagen. So the skin wrinkles earlier. Dr Harry Darnell investigated the relationship between wrinkling and cigarette smoking for almost twenty years, looking at eleven hundred patients between the ages of thirty and seventy. He found that the skin of smokers wrinkles and ages up to twenty years sooner than that of non-smokers. But the problem with cigarette smoke doesn't end there. For it is not only the smoker whose skin can suffer from it. So can the non-smoker's. She may take in considerable quantities of benzopyrene, tar, carbon monoxide, and other irritating substances just by being in a room with others who are smoking. In a recent study it was shown that in a room of smokers the carbon monoxide level from the leftover cigarette smoke in the air can be as high as twenty to eighty parts per million. The supposedly acceptable level of this poisonous gas in industrial air is only fifty parts per million.

Dangers of smoking

Carbon monoxide in the air is bad for skin in another way, too. It binds together with the red blood cells' haemoglobin, tying up its oxygen-carrying capacity for up to twelve hours. This can lead to oxygen starvation in the skin's cells, much as a high-fat diet can. There are other smoking dangers too of course which, although not directly related to skin ageing, probably contribute to all-over lowered health – such as the fact that smoking is known to be a contributor to lung cancer, osteoporosis, heart disease, strokes, bronchial diseases, and emphysema. Some dermatologists concerned about the dangerous effects of cigarette smoke on skin recommend that every smoker supplement her diet with additional vitamin C at a rate of 25mg for each cigarette she smokes. But if you are

serious about preventing ageing, give up smoking altogether – no matter how difficult it seems and no matter how many excuses you can make for yourself about why you think you can't just now.

Watch the alcohol

Alcohol is bad for skin too. Each gram of it, by the way, contains 7 calories – more than any other kind of food except fat. And the calories it gives you are empty of nutrition, as they convey no vitamins or minerals or other essential nutrients to the cells of your body. What they do do, however, is stimulate the appetite so that in addition to their calorie-supplying abilities they also tend to make you consume more food. And overeating is one of the worst things you can do to age your skin rapidly. Alcohol also robs the body of the supply of vitamins needed for skin health, and depletes resources of vitamin C. As well as all this, alcohol acts directly on the cells of the skin to cause damage.

Sludge in the capillaries

Freely soluble in water, it attacks the living cell by forcing it to lose its water and to coagulate its protein. This can result not only in cellular damage but also cellular death. And the detrimental effects of alcohol don't stop there. Dr. Melvin Linsely has shown that alcohol also brings about sludging in the capillaries. Instead of the millions of red blood cells circulating freely, they tend to pile up and clog these tiny blood vessels, interfering with circulation so that the cells don't get enough oxygen. As a result of this oxygen starvation, cellular deterioration occurs, and small

haemorrhages, or leakages of blood from the capillaries, take place. This sludging phenomenon interferes with skin cell metabolism, as it does with that of cells elsewhere in the body. The tiny ruptures that take place in small blood vessels as a result of the sludging are also a major factor behind the appearance of broken veins on the face. While it is true that the occasional glass of good wine may do nothing but good in relaxing you and improving digestion, more than this is bad for the long-term youth and health of your skin.

Slough off the dead cells

Men's skin ages less rapidly than women's. One of the reasons for this may be that a man shaves every day and the act of shaving itself removes several

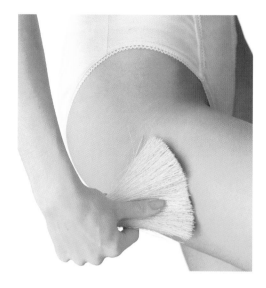

layers of the stratum corneum. A slowing down of cell reproduction is one of the things that happens when your skin ages. Many dermatologists believe that exfoliation – the deliberate removal of the old dead cells on the skin's surface – will help keep skin younger-looking. It stimulates cell reproduction in the basal layer and refines the skin's surface, making it look more translucent and smoother, getting rid of the mottled surface that comes with age. That is where fresh fruit and vegetable treatments can be a great help.

Banishing brown spots

The cause
• These so-called liver spots are changes in pigmentation in the skin as a result of the ageing process coupled with exposure to the sun's rays. Their proper name is lentigines. They usually mar hands and faces most, and in truth they have little to do with the liver, from which they have borrowed their name.

• Women deficient in B vitamins – particularly folic acid and niacin – or women who have a particularly high personal requirement for them, thanks to their genetic inheritance or their taking of oral contraceptives, are particularly prone to developing liver spots in areas of the body that are regularly exposed to the sun's light or artificial ultraviolet rays from a sun lamp.

Prevention and cure
• Many dermatologists claim there is nothing internal that one can do either to prevent or to eliminate liver spots. However, some nutritionists – and I have seen evidence of this – say that a B-complex vitamin supplement which is particularly rich in folic acid and niacin (400mg folic acid and 100mg of nicotinamides taken with each meal) can help clear them up – provided, of course, that the rest of your diet is sufficiently adequate.

• There are also bleaching creams, which, used regularly three times a day, will gradually fade them. But if your skin is particularly sensitive or you are concerned about allergic reactions, you should do a patch test (as one does to test for allergens) before trying any of them, as they contain strong chemicals which may cause irritation.

• Liver spots can be removed professionally by using liquid nitrogen, frozen carbon dioxide, or electrocoagulation, or more simply by skin-peeling with the help of small fraises to sand down the epidermis. One thing is certain: at the first sign of any kind of irregular pigmentation like this, you need to shield yourself from the sun at all times on the area where it is developing, using a high-protection sun product. If you are prone to brown spots, stay away from sun products that contain oil of bergamot or any of its derivatives, and never put scent on before going out into the sun.

Extra care for older skin

Not only does older skin need extra protection from the sun in order to avoid the formation of brown age spots, it needs protection in other ways, too. From excessive stress, for instance, which takes a heavy toll of a woman's face when she is over forty. To help remedy this, it is important to get enough sleep.

Both sebum production and the water content of the skin decrease with age, which makes it doubly important to guard your skin from excessive dehydration. Many creams for older skin contain a sebum-like substance to make up for the gradual decline in the natural ability to hold water.

Hormone creams

Creams containing oestrogen and oestrogen-like substances can be useful in combating ageing too. They help to plump up skin that is losing much of its padding and form, thanks to their ability to increase the skin's water-holding tendencies. Hormone creams also soften the surface texture. However, bear in mind that they are only really of use to menopausal or post-menopausal women with dryish skin.

The maximum benefits from a hormone cream come about a month after you begin to use it, but they are only truly significant in skin that is genuinely aged. Hormones will do nothing for younger skin, and the benefits from using a hormone cream will only remain so long as you continue to use it. When it is stopped, your skin will gradually return to its previous state. But hormones are powerful substances, which affect the whole endocrine balance of a body. They have to be used with great care and are only available on prescription in the concentration necessary to be effective (10,000 IU of an oestrogen-like hormone per ounce of cream). The best I have ever come across is made in France and contains estrone, estradial, testosterone and progesterone (see Resources, pages 253-4).

The professionals

Chemosurgery

Chemosurgery is sometimes recommended for the removal of fine lines on older skin. It involves the destruction of the top layer of the skin with a caustic solution – a 10 per cent solution of resorcinol for instance – spread on and left for a specific length of time. In a week or so the crust formed falls off, revealing firmer, pink skin underneath. This is superficial chemical face peeling. Alternatively, the use of a combination of phenol – a derivative of carbolic acid – and other chemicals, which is applied to the face to burn away not only the epidermis but part of the dermis as well, is known as deep peeling. Phenol penetrates and coagulates at a certain level of the skin.

Ideally the surgeon or dermatologist will use a solution of about 80 per cent which keeps the coagulation from taking place too deeply in the skin (the lighter the concentration the deeper the penetration). They are both supposed to stimulate the formation of fresher, younger-looking skin and also to eliminate many wrinkles.

Both superficial and deep peeling are painful, and the good results they bring in terms of younger-looking skin are short-lived. They usually last no more than a few months. Gradually the new skin loses its plumped-up look and returns to looking much as it did before.

Dermabrasion

Another so-called cure for ageing skin is dermabrasion – the planing operation that is supposed to minimize wrinkles much the same way except that it uses a motor-driven brush, rather than chemicals. In my experience, it is less effective. The one thing both operations will do, though, is eliminate liver spots, freckles, and superficial scars such as some of the scars from acne. Neither can change the condition of the collagen fibres in the dermis, on which depends the long-term look of your skin. But beware – all of these things must be used in the hands of an expert if they are not to do serious damage. And just because somebody has a medical degree doesn't mean he or she is an expert.

Face-lifts

Face-lift surgery can be useful, too, particularly if you are lean. Face-lifts work far better on under-fat women. But again, you must find yourself a good surgeon, for there is a real art to it. It is not just a mechanical job; and you must take good care of your face and the rest of your body both before and afterwards. But it is not the cure-all that many women believe it to be. Your diet, level of physical activity, and general lifestyle have to be good in order to maintain the benefit you'll get from it.

Line filling

Since the mid 1970s animal collagen has been injected directly into lines on the face to fill out furrows and wrinkles. It can work well on vertical lines around the mouth and cheeks, but the collagen eventually (in a few months) becomes metabolized by the body and the effect is quickly lost. This is particularly true on the face, which is highly mobile and has a good blood supply. Injections of minute quantities of silicone are now frequently done instead, mostly in continental Europe, because, unlike collagen, when added to the skin silicone is permanent.

Silicone injections

This can be a great advantage. In the hands of a master silicone can be used in minute quantities on any vertical line – around the mouth and forehead – and to fill in tiny areas of scar. In the hands of a mediocre doctor silicone's permanence can be a great disadvantage, leaving you disfigured for life. Done properly, minute quantities of silicone are injected and then between two and four weeks are allowed to go by during which the body's tissues form a honeycomb-like area around the silicone, plumping it up. Then another silicone injection is done, and so forth, until the desired effect is achieved. Silicone injections are now outlawed in the United States as part of the silicone implant scare in relation to breast surgery. Most top cosmetic surgeons worldwide, however, insist that there is almost no danger whatsoever of silicone migration to other parts of the body as the quantities used are so minute.

Toxic helper

Dev Basra, one of Britain's – and Europe's – finest cosmetic surgeons (and an accomplished sculptor to boot) is an expert on the treatment of ageing skin. In 1987 Basra pioneered a technique used before only by ophthalmic surgeons and neurologists for the treatment of involuntary facial movements or tics. This has now revolutionized the treatment of frown lines. He began to inject minuscule quantities of a toxin called botulinum into the frontalis muscle of the forehead to paralyse the muscle and stop the person from frowning and cutting a deeper groove into the face. He has had considerable success with the technique which has now been taken up by fellow surgeons in Europe and America.

No more frown lines

The injections need to be done a few times over a period of months for full effect, until gradually the muscle stops contracting and the habit of frowning can be broken. It is about the only thing that really works on frown-lines since cutting the muscle (which is the other alternative) tends to create a mask-like, expressionless face.

Go for prevention

All of these techniques, helpful though one or two may be, are only actions taken after the fact. Prevention is far more important. Basra finds, as do other leading skin care experts, that many women in their thirties whose skins are ageing rapidly are living on poor diets, often deficient in protein, vitamins and minerals. Calories-restricted slimming diets are a killer when it comes to ageing skin. Basra uses free form amino acid supplements as well as vitamins and minerals on these women and encourages them to alter their diet. He is also very much an advocate of face-exercise.

Move into youth

Premature ageing is one of the worst threats to your good looks, and one of the best ways of avoiding it is by getting plenty of exercise. This is not only because exercise stops your body from losing its youthful shape, firms muscles that could go flabby, and helps keep you slim. Physical activity is also essential in maintaining the strength and form of your whole muscle-skeletal system. When bones are not used they lose calcium, become weak and brittle, break easily, are slow to repair, and shrink in mass – the condition known as osteoporosis. What is worse, physical decay is progressive; a lack of physical activity results in an almost inevitable further lack of activity and further shrinkage.

Keep the hormones flowing

When muscle mass shrinks, so does the production of steroid hormones from the adrenal and sex glands – in direct proportion to the loss of muscle tissue. (This occurs as a natural process in the passing of years as well, but more slowly.) These hormones are essential for the maintenance of young-looking, wrinkle-free skin and healthy hair. They also fulfil numerous other roles in the maintenance of internal health. Your level of physical activity is an important factor in the maintenance of optimal functioning in your endocrine system, helping to make possible the continued flow of sufficient hormones for youth and vitality.

Move your face

One of the most useful things you can do yourself to prevent your face from ageing and to correct sags and bags even after they have occurred is to practice face exercises every day.

The bones you were born with give your face its individual shape and structure. Short of plastic surgery or adjustments to your skull through cranial osteopathy, there is nothing you can do to change them. But your muscles are constantly changing either for better or for worse. They are made up of bundles of fibres, each of which works independently to shorten muscle and draw a part of the face into a particular expression. Just like the muscles in the rest of your body, each of these groups of fibres has an antagonistic group. This means that for each muscle that pulls an area of your face into one expression, there is an opposite muscle to pull it the other way.

Work your muscles

For instance, one muscle lifts the eyebrow and another lowers it. So as one muscle lengthens, the other shortens, and vice versa, in a team effort. At least that is how it is supposed to work. What often happens, however, is that because of habitual expressions (the polite mask a woman shows to the

world, the continual worry that draws the eyebrows together, and so forth) and because of the constant pull of gravity on the face, particular muscles tend to be usually contracted, or shortened, while their partners are just as usually flaccid, or stretched, so that neither get the workout and movement they need to remain firm, full, strong, and in good tone. Then you get muscle tightness and muscle shrinkage, which interferes with proper circulation in that area of the skin and gradually results in distortions of facial contours, such as hollows around the eyes, the valleys that run between the edges of the nose and the outer corners of the mouth, and the sag of the typical double chin.

Keep your contours youthful

The only way to maintain the health and firmness of muscles that will preserve youthful contours in a face is exercise. The more you are able to make use of all your muscles in all movements, the stronger they will become. And with it the firmer and more contoured your skin will look. Also your circulation will improve with exercise and you will have a better colour. No matter what condition your face is in, whether it is young and smooth, just beginning to lose its firmness, or sagging heavily, exercise will help it. And the worse its condition, the greater the improvement you will see. It is never too late to start and you will find that before long, beginning to work each muscle restores more youthful contours to an ageing face.

Face exercises

After thirty, if lines have begun to form, you have to be more specific about the kind of exercises you do. In effect you have to locate a problem area, say a developing hollow under the cheek, or loose flesh under the jaw and chin, and then work on the specific muscles that will counterbalance it.

This can be done through some simple but specific isotonic-type exercises in front of your mirror, or you can use faradic exercise equipment such as the Minitone by Slendertone to do contractions for you. There are facial electrode attachments, which you can get to go with most passive exercise machines of this type, which when placed at specific points on the face will automatically contract the muscles in that area. There is also a battery-operated face exerciser, which works on the same principles but is small enough to put into a handbag for travel. (Faradic exercises are also recommended by many plastic surgeons for use before and after surgery to restore muscle strength and tone.)

The exercises given opposite and overleaf are designed to treat the four problem areas of the face:

- Eyes
- Chin and throat
- Cheeks (where little smile lines form)
- Forehead.

The exercises should be done with a well-creamed skin. Moving the face about without this lubrication may only have the effect of deepening any lines that are already there. The cream you use should be rich – one of the old-fashioned, rather greasy night creams will do nicely, or you can use olive oil or coconut oil.

Regular workouts

Either isotonic movement or passive exercise will work, provided you are conscientious about exercising every day. It is the regular workout you give your face muscles that brings results, and although results can be slow to show themselves – in some cases demanding several weeks' work before you detect significant changes for the better – they can also be astoundingly good. For regular face exercising can transform your face completely, not only making it look ten years younger by eliminating excess and softening expression lines and filling in hollows, but also by enlivening the whole look of the skin.

All exercises have to be done slowly and steadily. The muscles of your face, unlike those of the rest of your body, are attached to the skin itself. When you move them, you naturally move your skin, too. You need never be afraid of the movements, but you should never overtire muscles. Slow and steady is the pace to adopt.

EYES

This exercise is excellent for the eye area, which usually goes slack faster than any other part of the face. It is particularly designed to prevent or eliminate crow's-feet. It is in two parts.

- **Part one:** looking into a mirror, lower your chin to your chest and open your eyes looking straight ahead. Then, slowly and in eight definite steps, close your eyes by bringing the lower lids up to the upper, all the while looking into the mirror until the very last moment. Hold this position with your eyes tightly shut for four counts, then release in the same eight definite steps. Repeat four times. Once you can control these movements in definite steps, you are ready to go on to the toughy that really does the work.

- **Part two:** place both elbows firmly on your dressing table and, using two small folded pieces of cotton fabric or tissue, place your index fingers over them on the crow's-feet areas and press firmly. Lower your chin to your chest and, looking straight ahead into the mirror, do the same exercise as before but this time working against the pressure of your fingers, which hold the skin in place, as you move lower lids up to eight counts, hold for four, down for eight, rest for four. Do this three times. You will be surprised what it does to tone the eye area and to brighten the eyes themselves.

CHIN AND NECK
- **Exercise one:** this exercise strengthens and firms the platysma which covers the neck from jaw to chest and when firm keeps the skin on the neck smooth and helps prevent it turning crepey.

Tilt your head slightly backward, placing your hand gently on your throat. Now make your mouth into a hard 'O' shape, then pull the muscles around your mouth downwards and outward into a turned-down 'smile' – a smile in which the corners of the mouth turn down as though you were making the sound 'ee'. Now push your mouth back to 'O' again, then back to 'ee', repeating the change a dozen times.

- **Exercise two:** this movement helps tighten the muscles in the neck and lower jaw while bringing circulation to the skin of the face.

Lying on your back on a firm bed, or better still on a table, let your head and neck hang over the side, bend your knees and place your feet flat on the surface you are lying on. Now you are ready to begin. Slowly, to the count of five, lift your head up so your chin is on your chest. Then, opening your mouth, jut out your lower jaw as far as it will go. Hold for five counts. Finally, keeping your lower jaw thrust forward, let your head flop back over the edge of the table and hold for another five counts. Return your lower jaw to its normal position and repeat. Do this exercise six times.

- **Exercise three:** this exercise strengthens the pterygoids at the side of the jaw. With your lips together, smile to the sides gently, then push your lower jaw as far forward as possible. Now, maintaining the tension, move your jaw from side to side four times and then return to the starting position. Repeat the full movement twelve times.

CHEEKS
- **Exercise one:** this exercise helps eliminate nose-to-lip creases by strengthening a tiny muscle, just above the side of the mouth, called the canius, as well as the muscles in the cheeks themselves. This will lift the

area between nose and mouth corners upward.

With your lips together, smile upward at the corners of your mouth as hard as you can. At the same time, try to make your lips into an 'O' shape so that the muscles are pulling against each other and the whole area is tightened. Hold for five seconds. Repeat twice.

- **Exercise two:** this exercise is designed to remove tell-tale hollows in the lower cheek area, soften lines, and lift mouth corners. It needs to be done in two parts. The first will train the muscles to your conscious control. It should be followed for a week before beginning the second part. The second part works on the principle of isometric resistance, but it will be effective only after you have trained your muscles in that area to work.

Facing a mirror, smile to the sides – smile so that there is no movement in the muscles of the eye area – in a series of small, definite movements to the count of eight, all the while making sure there is no movement whatever in your eye area; if there is, then you are not using the right muscles. Hold the smile for a count of four. Then, to a count of eight in definite steps, release the smile, returning to the starting position. Rest for a count of four. Do the exercise five times. When you can do this smoothly and with control, leave it behind and go on to the second part.

Using a piece of cotton cloth or a folded tissue, left elbow firmly placed on your dressing table, with thumb and middle finger grasp the left cheek area, ensuring that the cloth is centred under the thumb to prevent slipping. Then, holding your cheek firm, smile to the sides, just as you did in the first exercise but this time on the left side of the face only, so that your muscles are working against your grasped cheek – again to a count of eight, hold for four, release in eight, and rest for four. Then, using the right hand, do the exercise on the right cheek. Do each side three times.

FOREHEAD

- **Exercise one:** this movement strengthens the frontalis muscle, on the forehead, which is the antagonist to the corrugator, which pulls the eyebrows together in a frown. It will help soften lines between the brows.

Looking into a mirror, as slowly and gradually as you can, put your brows down, closing your eyes tighter and tighter into a frown. Now open your eyes wider and wider, lifting your forehead as you do. Repeat six times.

- **Exercise two:** this is for smoothing out a lined forehead. It also has two parts. Once you have mastered the first, forget about it and go on to the second.

Facing a mirror, raise muscles of your forehead in tiny controlled steps to the count of eight, all the while opening your eyes wider (good for you if you tend to be a squinter) and getting the feel of your muscles in this area. Hold for a count of four, then release in eight steps. Do this five times twice a day.

When you have mastered this completely, do the second part, but before you do any of the other exercises, because it needs to be done with a cream-free forehead.

Ensure that your forehead is clean and dry and, taking three pieces of cellophane tape cut to the breadth of your forehead, place them on the brow area, using a small piece to fit between the eyebrows. The tape will act as resistance the way your finger did in the cheek exercise. You work against it for really effective muscle toning. Move your brow up in tiny definite movements, this time to the count of six. Hold for four, opening your eyes wide and looking straight ahead. Release in six. Repeat five times.

Take control

It is my belief that each one of us is here on this planet to live out most fully the unique nature of our being. Each person, like each flower in a garden, brings a form of beauty and energy, values and love to the world that only they can bring.

Real beauty is authentic. It has little to do with age or culture and nothing whatsoever to do with the superficial copying of somebody else's style. It is about being who you are in a way that celebrates the role you have to play in life – a unique flower.

Transformation – the process by which we become more fully on the outside what we are in our inner nature – takes place in fits and starts. It also goes on throughout the whole of our lives. It is the nature of life itself to destroy that which is decaying or no longer useful in order to give birth to something more vital, fresh, beautiful and joyous.

RESOURCES

Aloe vera: Available from Xynergy Products, Lower Elstead, Midhurst, West Sussex, GU29 0JT. Tel 01730 813 642. Fax 01730 815 109.

Broda Barnes: *Hypothyroidism: The Unsuspected Illness*, Broda Barnes, Harper & Row, New York, 1975.

Digestive enzymes: Good digestive enzymes from plant sources are available from BioCare, The Lakeside Centre, 180 Liffard Lane, Kings Norton, Birmingham, West Midlands, B30 3NT. Tel 0121 433 3727. Fax 0121 433 3879. **Polyzyme Forte** is a very strong, broad spectrum digestive enzyme, **Digestaid** is excellent for more general consumption, and **Biocidin Forte**, taken by those with low blood-sugar problems, is traditionally used to help maintain the balance of intestinal flora.

Essential oils: Top quality aromatherapy products are available from The Fragrant Earth Co Ltd, PO Box 182, Taunton, Somerset TA1 1YR. Tel 01823 335734. Fax 01823 322566. I also like the essential oils supplied by Purple Flame, Clinton Lane, Kenilworth, Warwickshire CV8 1AS. Tel 01926 855980. Fax 01926 512001. Essentially Oils Ltd also do good quality oils. Essentially Oils Ltd, 8,9,10 Mount Farm, Junction Road, Churchill, Chipping Norton, Oxfordshire OX7 6NP. Tel 01608 659544. Fax 01608 659522.

GABA: Available from The Nutri Centre, 7 Park Crescent, London W1N 3HE. Tel 0171 436 5122. Fax 0171 436 5171.

Green foods:

Lifestream Spirulina, Pure Synergy and other good green products are available mail order from Xynergy Products as above, Lower Elstead, Midhurst, West Sussex, GU29 0JT. Tel 01730 813 642. Fax 01730 815 109.
Chlorella is available in capsule form from Solgar Vitamins Ltd, who also do an excellent powdered green supplement, Green & More. For your local stockist contact: Solgar Vitamins, Aldbury, Tring, Herts HP23 5PT. Tel 01442 890 355 Fax 01442 890 366.
Wheat-grass juice in powdered form is available from Malcolm Simmonds Herbal Supplies, Freepost, Hove, East Sussex BN3 6BR. Tel 01273 202 401. Fax 01273 705 120.
Green magna, the dried juice of young barley leaves, is available from good healthfood stores.

Ginseng: A good ginseng comes in the form of Jinlin Ginseng Tea, Jinlin *Panax ginseng* dried slices, ampoules and Jinlin whole root, available from health food stores. If you have difficulty finding it contact Alice Chiu, 4 Tring Close, Barkingside, Essex IG2 7LQ. Tel 0181 550 9900. Fax 0181 554 3883.

Herbs: An excellent supplier of tinctures, fluid extracts, tablets and loose dried herbs is Phyto Pharmaceuticals Ltd, Park Works, Park Road, Mansfield, Woodhouse, Notts NG19 8EF. Tel 01623 644 334. Fax 01623 657 232. Minimum order £10.

Another good source is Malcolm Simmonds Herbal Supplies, Freepost, Hove, East Sussex BN3 6BR. Tel 01273 202401. Fax 01273 705120.

Herbs are also available from Solgar Vitamins Ltd, Aldbury, Tring, Herts HP23 5PT. Tel 01442 890 355. Fax 01442 890 366.

Herb teas: Some of my favourite blends include Cinnamon Rose, Orange Zinger, and Emperor's Choice, by Celestial Seasonings; Warm and Spicy by Symmingtons; and Creamy Carob French Vanilla. Yogi Tea, by Golden Temple Products, is a strong spicy blend perfect as a coffee replacement.

Honey: The Garvin Honey Company have a good selection of set and clear honeys from all over the world. These can be ordered from The Garvin Honey Company Ltd, Garvin House, 158 Twickenham Road, Isleworth, Middlesex, TW7 7DL. Tel 0181 560 7171. Fax 0181 569 8036.

The New Zealand Natural Food Company have a fine range of honey, including organic honey, in particular Manuka honey, known for its anti-bacterial effects. The New Zealand Natural Food Company Ltd, Unit 3, 55-57 Park Royal Road, London NW10 7LP. Tel 0181 961 4410. Fax 0181 961 9420.

Hormone creams: Most are available by prescription only. The best of these is a French cream called **Fadimone Creme Senescence Cutanee**. There is also an excellent cream (called **Progest**) derived from the wild Mexican yam containing natural progesterone which is wonderful for menopausal and postmenopausal women. Progest is available from Higher Nature Ltd, The Nutrition Centre, Burwash Common, East Sussex TN19 7LX. Tel 01435 882 880. Fax 01435 883720.

Iron supplements: A highly absorbable organic iron compound suitable for people sensitive to iron supplementation, **Iron EAP2** is available from BioCare, The Lakeside Centre, 180 Liffard Lane, Kings Norton, Birmingham, B30 3NT. Tel 0121 433 3727. Fax 0121 433 3879.

Desiccated liver tablets and a wide range of other iron supplements are available from the Nutri Centre, 7 Park Crescent, London W1N 3HE. Tel 0171 436 5122. Fax 0171 436 5171.

A good plant-based iron supplement for vegetarians is **Floradix** available from good healthfood stores.

Juicers:

The Champion Masticating Juicer – Veteran juicers wax lyrical about the virtues of the Champion, an indestructible, American juicer that some people claim makes better juice than any centrifugal extractor can because its masticating action is more effective at the process of splitting open the fibres of the plant matter and liberating its nutrients in the form of juice. Expensive, the Champion is guaranteed for five years and can well last a lifetime, easily repaying the investment in the long run. Available from The Nutri Centre, 7 Park Crescent London, W1N 3HE. Tel 0171 436 5122. Fax 0171 436 5171.
The Vita-Mix Total Nutrition Centre, a turbo charged, super-efficient blender with indestructible stainless steel blades and an extremely powerful motor, the TNC is dynamite! It's the only machine that is properly able to make fibre-rich juices – a

molecular or *total* juicing. It is also effective for making cereal grass juices (which should be strained before drinking to remove indigestible cellulose fibres). The TNC not only makes juice, but can also be used to make soups and ice cream. These American machines are expensive, but owning one could change your life. Contact Vita-Mix Corporation, 8615 Usher Road, Cleveland, OH 44138, USA. Tel 001 216 235 4840. At the other end of the scale, **Moulinex** do an inexpensive centrifugal juicer which is good.

Kava kava (*Piper Methysticum*): Available from Phyto Pharmaceuticals, Park Works, Park Road, Mansfield, Woodhouse, Notts NG19 8EF. Tel: 01623 644 334. Fax 01623 657232.

Organic foods: The Soil Association publishes a regularly updated National Directory of Farm Shops and Box Schemes which costs £3, including postage from The Organic Food & Farming Centre, 86 Colston Street, Bristol BS1 5BB.

Organic meat: For excellent beef, lamb, pork, bacon, ham, chicken, sausages, low in fat and full of taste – Longwood Farm Organic Meats, Tudenham St Mary, Bury St Edmunds, Suffolk IP28 6TB. Tel 01638 717 120.

Qualified nutritionists: List obtainable from The Institute of Optimum Nutrition, Blades Court, Deodar Road, London SW15 2NU. Tel 0181 877 9993. Fax 0181 877 9980.

Silica: Available from The Nutri Centre, 7 Park Crescent, London W1N 3HE. Tel 0171 436 5122. Fax 0171 436 5171.

Skin brushes: Available from good chemists – they must have bristles of vegetable origin, not nylon.

Spectra-light: Office lighting systems and light boxes for personal use are available from Spectra Lighting, York House, Lower Harlestone, Northampton NN7 4EW. Tel/fax 01604 821 902. Email 100722,1511@compuserve.com.

Vegetable bouillon powder: Marigold Swiss Vegetable Bouillon Powder is an instant broth based on vegetables and sea salt and is available from health food stores or direct from Marigold Foods, Unit 10, St Pancras Commercial Centre, 63 Pratt Street, London NW1 0BY. Tel 0171 267 7368. It comes in regular, low-salt, vegan and organic forms. I prefer the organic variety.

Supplements/products I use:
Each of the following are available by post from The Nutri Centre, 7 Park Crescent, London W1N 3HE. Tel 0171 436 5122. Fax 0171 436 5171.

Pro Green – ingredients are green organic gluten-free grasses, blue-green algae and sea algae, probiotic cultures, natural fibres, adaptogenic and support herbs, standardised bioflavonoid extracts.
Pure Synergy – (Xynergy) Klamath Lake Algae, Spirulina, Chlorella, Dunaliella Salina, Red Dumontiaceae, Longicrusis, Digitat Kelp, Dulse, Bladderwrack, Irish Moss, Alaria, the Chinese Herbal, Green Grass Juices, unique formulation of Western Herbs, the five Taoist mushrooms, enzymes, lecithin powder, royal jelly.

Missing Link – provides enzymes, mineral and vitamin saving cofactors, naturally occurring omega-3 and omega-6 essential fatty acids, soluble and insoluble dietary fibre, bowel bacteria, bioactive neutraceutical phytochemicals.
Udo's Choice – organic flax, sunflower and sesame oils mechanically pressed in a low heat, light and oxygen free environment – excellent source of essential fatty acids.

Water: As you know, getting pure water can be difficult. One in ten of us drink water which is contaminated with poisons above international standards. I have finally found a water purifier which I think is good, it is the **Fresh Water 1000** water filter system. It removes more than 90% of heavy metals, pesticides, hydrocarbons such as benzyne, trihalmethanes, chlorine, oestrogen, and bacteria without removing essential minerals like calcium. Available from The Fresh Water Filter Company, Carlton House, Aylmer Road, Leytonstone, London E11 3AD. Tel 0181 558 7495. Fax 0181 556 9270.

The Green People Company: Some of my favourite natural cosmetics. A superb company which does an excellent herbal elixir, a product called **X-Tra** for energy as well as cosmetics, toiletries, toothpaste and housecare products. I cannot recommend them highly enough. Mail order from The Haven, Billinghurst, West Sussex RH14 9BS. Tel 01403 823 456. Fax 01403 822 866.

Suppliers of quality nutritional supplements

BioCare
The Lakeside Centre
180 Liffard Lane
Kings Norton
Birmingham
West Midlands
B30 3NT.
Tel 0121 433 3727
Fax 0121 433 3879

Higher Nature Ltd
The Nutrition Centre
Burwash Common
East Sussex
N19 7LX
Tel 01435 882 880
Fax 01435 883720

If you wish to keep informed of Leslie Kenton's forthcoming books, videos, health and Shamanic workshops, and other activities, please write to her personally at: Ebury Press, Random House, 20 Vauxhall Bridge Road, London SW1V 2SA, enclosing a stamped, self-addressed A4 envelope.

INDEX

acidity 26, 29, 153, 168, 173
acne 152-3, 174, 205, 215
adaptogens 57
aerobic exercise 84-5, 87, 116
ageing 49, 206, 209, 236-52
alcohol 52, 107-8, 169, 180, 243
alfalfa 38, 42, 153
allergy 153-4, 213-14
almonds 32, 67
aloe vera 181
aluminium 130, 133
anaemia 147, 154-5, 229
anaerobic exercise 85
anger 134-5, 137
anti-depressants 135-6
anti-oxidants 159, 166, 205
anxiety 7, 79, 134, 138
apple 30, 133
  juices 153, 161, 162, 171, 180
  recipes 63, 64
apricot 35, 160
aromatherapy 184-7
arthritis 155-7
asthma 157-8
athlete's foot 196
avocado 32
  recipes 43, 66

back exercises 101, 201
baldness 229
banana 35, 63, 158, 162, 165
barefoot walking 194
barley 40, 45
barley grass 167
bathing 198-200
bath preparations 186, 200
beans 39, 40, 45, 59
beetroot 170
  borscht 46
  juices 154, 155, 160, 162, 180
  tops 154, 156, 158, 157, 170
berries 154
  juices 156, 168
beta-carotene 165, 166, 172
biofeedback 171-2
bioflavonoids 71, 153, 159, 165,
  166, 203
bleaching hair 193, 226
blood-sugar 50, 76
  low, see hypoglycaemia
blusher 235
body care 178-201
body odour 201
bran wash 200
breakfast 31-5, 62-4
breathing 30, 90, 98, 109, 111-12,
  115-20, 180
brittle nails 190
bromelin 30, 156, 163, 172
buckwheat 45, 170
bulgar wheat 45
bunions 196

cabbage 163-5, 208
caffeine 50, 169, 172
calcium 163, 166, 169, 203
callouses 196
camomile 222, 225-6
candida 136, 142-4
capillaries 159, 165, 243

carbohydrates 28, 51, 162
carob powder 60
carrot 166, 169, 206, 208
  juices 153, 160, 162, 170, 171,
  180
celery 153, 170, 175, 208
  juices 154, 162, 166, 180
cells 77-8
cellulite 27, 77, 158-9, 178-84,
  191, 202
cereal grasses 55, 167
charisma 80-1
cheese 59, 60
chemosurgery 245-6
chickpeas 39, 45
chilblains 196
chlorophyll 55, 159, 167, 201
  juice 153
chocolate 60, 157, 163, 172
chromium 140, 170
citrus fruit 156, 159, 165, 168
  juice 167
cleansers 203-4
clothing, sports 91, 92
coffee 50, 60, 180, 203
colds 159-60
collagen 237, 240, 246
colon cleansing 161, 202
colorants, hair 225-7
  colour corrective 231
concealer 232
conditioner 222-3
constipation 161-2, 192, 202
convenience foods 54, 59, 130,
  135, 139, 148
cooking methods 60-1
cool-down 96
corn soup 66
corns 196
cosmetics 214, 230-5
cosmetic surgery 245-7
cranberry cocktail 174
cravings 26, 143, 144, 145
cucumber 172, 175, 207, 208
  juices 173, 180
cycling 90

dairy products 49, 59, 60
dandelion 56, 156, 172, 208
  juices 155, 167, 171, 172, 175
dandruff 228
decanter exercise 117
depression 7, 79, 134, 135-8,
  162-3
dermabrasion 246
detox 6, 12, 25-47, 132, 136, 147,
  171, 173, 175, 180
diet 6, 12, 48-71, 134, 138
  & ageing 237
  anti-candida 142-4
  anti-cellulite 180
  detox 25-33
  for eyes 218
  for hair 221-2
  for low blood sugar 140
  for nails 188
  skin care 202, 247
dieting 25-6, 139, 221, 247
digestion 76, 163-5
dinner 32, 33, 66-7
diuretics 175

dressings 32, 42-3, 64, 66
drinks 31, 32, 35-7, 50, 59
drugs 107-8, 130-2, 135-6, 143,
  152, 169, 222, 229
dry hair 227
dry skin 204, 205, 206, 212
dull hair 228

ECG stress test 82-3
eczema 165-6
eggs 58, 60, 170, 175
electromagnetic pollution 133
elimination diet 145, 165
emotions 10, 78-9, 115-16, 134-8
energy, low, see fatigue
environment 130-1, 188, 237
enzymes 145, 163, 207
essential oils 184-7, 206
exercise 12, 72-103, 132, 134,
  169, 180, 192, 203, 247-8
  eye 219
  face 248-52
  foot 194-5
  hand 190
  underwater 200-1
exfoliation 244
eyebrows 233-4
eyes 166, 216-20, 233-5, 249-50

face 202-35
  exercises 248-52
face-lift 246
face mask 207-8, 210
face powder 235
fast, fruit 28-31
fat 49, 59, 62, 237, 239
fatigue 7, 130-51, 167-8, 191
fatty acids (EFAs) 49, 71, 156,
  163, 203, 206, 239
fear 135, 137
feet 191-2, 194-7
fibre 25, 26, 44, 152, 202
fillings, dental 131, 132
fish 33, 51, 59, 60, 156
fitness 20, 82-3
flour 60, 172
folic acid 154, 163, 169
food additives 54, 59
food allergy 26, 134, 136, 137,
  143-5, 153-4, 156-8, 165, 171,
  175
foundation 231-2
fragrant waters 185
frappé 31, 64
free radicals 166, 236-7, 239
fresh air 30
frown lines 247
fruit 25, 26, 33, 59
  breakfast 31, 32, 33, 62-4
  drinks 31, 32, 35
  fast 28-31
  recipes 32, 34, 35, 63
  skin care 207-8
  see also juices
fruit acids (AHAs) 206-7
fried foods 60-1, 62

GABA 138
game 33, 51, 59
garlic 58, 153, 175
gastric ulcers 163

ginger 172, 173
  juices 153, 156, 159, 165
ginseng 57, 138
GLA 205, 206
glucose 139-40, 170
goals 21-2
grains 25, 26, 32, 33, 37, 40-1,
  44-5, 51, 157
grapefruit 153, 156, 208
  juices 158, 160
  seeds 143
grapes 30, 169, 172, 208
  shake 35
grasses, see cereal grasses
green foods 55-6, 59, 64, 173, 188
  juices 153-7, 169-72, 180
  recipes 67
  supplements 55, 133, 147
  vegetables 159, 163, 167, 170,
  175
grey hair 228
groats 61

hair 220-9
  on legs 193-4
hairbrush & comb 223
hair loss 229
hand cream 188-9
hands and nails 187-91
hangover 168
headache 197
heart 74-5
heart disease 74, 83
heavy metals 26, 130-1, 133
henna 225
herbicides 131, 154
herbs 32, 61, 137, 138, 222
  baths 198-200
  dressing 43
  sauna 209
  teas 31, 32, 36, 60, 180
Hi NRG 158
Hi Mag 158
highlighter 233
highlights 226-7
hip exercises 100, 102
honey 60, 172
hormone creams 245
hormones 175, 179, 247-8
horsetail 188
household products 130, 131, 214
humidifier 204
hummus 66
hydrotherapy 149-50, 182-3, 197-
  201
hypoglycaemia 139-40, 169, 170-1
hypothyroidism 140

immune system 130, 131, 137, 159
insomnia 169-70
insulin 140, 170
ionizer 133
iron 147, 154, 163, 167, 221
isometrics 85, 200
isotonics 85-6

juices 32, 33, 37, 152-75, 180
  fruit 30-2, 37
  vegetable 32-3, 37, 64, 170
juicing 30, 31

kale 165
kava 138
kelp 58, 68, 188

lamb's quarter 56
lavender water 201
lead 130, 133
leaky gut syndrome 144
lecithin 58
legs 192-5, 201
legumes 61, 167
lemon 158, 207, 208, 222
　juice 171
lentils 39, 45
lettuce juice 170
lifestyle 139
light 132-3, 205, 217, 220, 238
line filling 246
linseeds 163
Linusit Perfect 163
liposomes 206
lipstick 235
liver 131-2, 171, 175, 203
liver (food) 58, 147, 170, 175
liver spots 244, 246
lower-body stretches 103
lunch 31, 32, 33, 66-7

magnesium 158, 163, 167, 169, 172, 173, 203
makeup, see cosmetics
manganese 170
mangetout 67
mango 30, 32
manicure 189-90
mascara 218-19, 234-5
massage 182-4, 198, 210-11, 223-4
massage oils 181, 186
maté tea 180
meat 49, 51, 59, 60, 180
meditation 81, 106, 107-9, 111-12, 173, 180
melatonin 132
melon 153, 172
　juice 168
menopause 173, 245
mercury 131, 133
metabolism 76, 141
microwave 132, 133
migraine 171-2
milk 26, 60
milk bath 198
millet 33, 40, 45
mineral bath 198
minerals 68-9, 148, 203, 221
mint 157, 163, 170
moisturizer 204-5, 231, 245
molasses 58, 158, 175, 188
mood 78-9
mucus 157
muesli 33-5
muscle 75, 76, 85, 97, 98, 248

nails 188-91
neck exercises 101, 201, 250
negative emotions 134-8
nettle 56, 175, 180
niacin 169
noise 130
nut-milk shake 35
nutrition, see diet
nuts 25, 68, 167

oedema, see water retention
office pollution 133
oil 26, 49-50, 59
oily hair 227
oily skin 206, 212
olive oil 59, 62, 152
onions 58, 158
orange 153, 156, 208
　juices 160, 166, 180
osteoporosis 247
overeating 139, 243
overweight 192
oxygen 84, 209, 243
ozone 241

pantothenic acid 173, 240
papain 30, 163
papaya 30, 163, 207
parsley 153, 166, 173
　juice 154
pasta 60
pau darco tea 143
peach 208
pear 160, 161, 208
　& apple juice 161
　supreme 65
pectin 26, 30, 133
peppers 153, 156, 159
perms 224
perspiration 201
pesticides 131, 154
phosphorus 166
pineapple 30, 156, 163, 169
　juices 157, 160, 165
pine extract 198
polenta 67
pollution 12, 130-3, 158, 179, 217, 240-1
pomades 185
potassium 26, 29, 52, 173, 175
　juices 158, 159
potato soup 47
poultry 33, 59, 60, 61
prana power exercise 118
pre-menstrual syndrome 172-3
processed food, see convenience food
protein 51, 188, 221-2
prunes 161, 175
　tropical 162
psychic essences 187
pulse 83, 88
Pure Synergy 64, 147

radish 38, 160
raspberry & apple frappé 64
raw foods 25-33, 51, 153, 159, 162-3, 167, 173
rebounding 87-8
recipes 61, 34-47, 62-7
refined foods 139-40, 172, 180
relationships 137
relaxation 6, 108-29, 173, 190
resentment 134-5, 137
restaurants 32, 61
retinoic acid 206
revitalizer exercise 118
rhubarb 161, 162
rice 33, 45, 61, 175
rolfing 183
room scenter 185
root salad 64
running 92-5

SAD 132-3
St John's wort 138
salad 28, 31-3, 41-2, 64-6
　juices 160, 166
salmon stir-fry 67
salt 52-3, 175
sauna 183, 209
scalp massage 223-4
scars 215, 246
sea salt rub 198
sea vegetables 68
seaweed 56, 58, 68, 133, 169, 188, 221
　juice 168
sedentary lifestyle 139
seeds 25-6, 31, 37-41, 58, 68
selenium 203, 240
self-esteem, low 7, 134, 137
sensitive skin 213
serotonin 51, 162, 169-70
sesame seeds 38, 58
shader 232
shakes 32, 35
shampoo 222
Shiatsu 195
shoes 65, 191-2
side stretches 102-3
sight 216
silica 188, 203, 221
silicone injections 246-7
sitz bath 193
skin 186, 202-15, 230
　ageing 236-52
skin brushing 27, 159
skin-softening bath 198-200
sleep 79, 106, 162, 203, 245
smoking 107-8, 130, 131, 180, 203, 241-3
snacks 62
soap 200, 203
solidago tea 180
soup 33, 44, 46-7, 66
soya beans 39, 45
soya milk 60
spices 170
spinach 161, 167, 208
　& apple juice 162
　salad 42
spine 119
spirituality 10, 12, 81
spirulina 56-7, 154, 188
split ends 228
split nails 190-1
spreads 60
sprouter 37
sprouts 28, 31-2, 37-41, 58, 68
　juices 154, 157
　salad 42
stir-frying 32, 47, 67
store cupboard 60
straightening hair 224-5
strawberry 208
　juices 168, 174
stress 57, 79, 107, 117, 130, 173-4, 179, 203
stretch exercises 86, 98-103
stretch marks 215
sugar 50, 139-40, 159, 172, 175, 218
sulphur 203, 221, 240
sunbathing 237-9
sunflower seeds 39, 58
sunglasses 217-18

sun lamps 239
sunscreen 189, 205, 227, 231, 237
superfoods 58-9, 64
supplements 55, 58-9, 145, 147
　vitamin/mineral 68, 147
sweeteners 60
swimming 88-90, 192

tanning 237-9
tea 28, 50, 157, 159, 169, 172
tension 117-18, 197, 224
thickeners 60
thyroid gland 140-1, 174
time, allocating 151
tofu dressing 66
tomato 156, 159, 160, 165, 208
　& avocado soup 66
　juices 162, 168
tranquillisers 169
tummy flattener 200

underwater exercises 200-1
urinary infections 174-5

varicose veins 191, 192-3
vegetables 25, 26, 51, 59, 188, 207-8
　breakfast 64
　cooking 32, 33, 47, 62
　kebabs 67
　snacks 62
　soup 46
　see also juices
vegetarian diet 156
verrucas 197
vinegar bath 198
visualization 113-14
vitamins 68-71, 148
　anti-ageing 239-40, 243-4
　eye care 166, 218, 220
　hair care 221
　skin care 203, 205-6

wake-up drink 31
walking 83, 87, 90-1, 132
warm-up 95-6
wastes 12, 148, 160, 178
　see also detoxification
water 37, 53-4, 133, 148-9, 180, 202, 203
watercress salad 65
watermelon 30, 172
　juices 161, 168
water retention 29, 53, 172, 175
water treading 193
weather 130, 133
weeds 55-6
weight loss 25-7, 31, 75
weight training 85-6
wheat 26, 40, 144, 152
wheat germ 58
wheat grass 167
wholegrains 59, 61, 188
wrinkles 205, 236, 245-7

yeast 142-4
yoga 119-29
yoghurt 36, 59, 60

zazen 111-12
zinc 159, 165, 166, 173, 203, 221